T0311682

Organizational Psychology of Mergers and Acquisitions

Organizational Psychology of Mergers and Acquisitions provides a comprehensive perspective that helps you understand, empathise, and protect the well-being of employees who experience mergers and acquisitions. This book gives a state-of-the-art review that crosses different subjects within psychology including psychobiology, neuroscience, social psychology, interpersonal relationships, and organizational psychology.

This book discusses why many employees think of mergers or acquisitions as scary or threatening events, why negative emotions are prevalent, their psychobiological impact, and how to assess employees' emotional responses using a new toolkit. It helps readers learn what counts as good leadership, considering the role of charisma, personality, context, and information processing abilities. This book includes the issue of organizational learning, and the relevance of occupational health and safety to due diligence about mergers and acquisitions through case studies about organizations sued for cancer or cancer-related mortality after a merger or acquisition.

This book is mandatory reading for students, academics, and practitioners working with organizations experiencing a merger or an acquisition such as consultants, human resource professionals, psychologists, occupational health professionals, and employees involved in strategy, management, or people development.

Camelia Oancea is a machine learning engineer at Airbus Defence and Space. She currently combines her career in artificial intelligence at Airbus with doctoral research at Birkbeck University of London, UK.

Caroline Kamau is a Senior Lecturer in Organisational Psychology at Birkbeck, University of London, UK.

Routledge Studies in Leadership, Work and Organizational Psychology

Organizational Psychology of Mergers and Acquisitions

Camelia Oancea and
Caroline Kamau

Routledge
Taylor & Francis Group

LONDON AND NEW YORK

First published 2021
by Routledge
2 Park Square, Milton Park, Abingdon, Oxon OX14 4RN

and by Routledge
52 Vanderbilt Avenue, New York, NY 10017

Routledge is an imprint of the Taylor & Francis Group, an informa business

British Library Cataloguing-in-Publication Data
A catalogue record for this book is available from the British Library

Library of Congress Cataloging-in-Publication Data
A catalog record for this book has been requested

ISBN: 978-1-138-81488-2 (hbk)
ISBN: 978-0-367-52342-8 (pbk)
ISBN: 978-1-315-74715-6 (ebk)

Typeset in ITC Galliard Pro
by Apex CoVantage, LLC

Contents

Figures

Tables

Preface

This book was jointly written by Camelia Oancea and Dr. Caroline Kamau, with roughly 50% of contributions by each author in writing and developing each chapter. Camelia is a machine learning engineer at Airbus Defence and Space, and she has been working on a part-time doctoral degree in organizational psychology with Caroline as her supervisor. Caroline is a senior lecturer at Birkbeck, University of London, and she has been an academic for nearly 20 years. Caroline's specialism is research about occupational health. She has published in prestigious journals such as *Nature*, and she is a fellow of the Royal Society of Medicine. Caroline's research about burnout and other aspects of occupational health has been featured in national newspapers such as *The Guardian* and *The Times*.

Camelia felt inspired to study for a PhD in mergers and acquisitions while she was working in marketing and strategy development at Repower, an energy company that experienced two cross-border acquisitions. At the time, she was working on marketing new products and services, and was involved in various projects relating to the acquisition. This included analysing market data, such as by examining the volatility of prices and consumer markets. She started working on a part-time PhD with Caroline's supervision and, together, they worked on this book about the psychology of mergers and acquisitions.

Both Camelia and Caroline are interdisciplinary scientists with a knack for synthesising vast amounts of information and making it accessible to readers from any field. Camelia's work at Airbus involves using artificial intelligence and machine learning. Before that, Camelia was a senior data scientist at E.ON, an energy company, and a data scientist at A&D Pharma, where her work included using machine learning and natural language processing. Caroline's work includes systematic reviews, meta-analyses, experiments, and randomised-controlled trials. Together, they have applied their detailed, methodological approach to write this book.

This book offers a fresh perspective on how employees who experience mergers or acquisitions tend to feel, think, and act by giving you a state-of-the-art review of the field. This book is written in a way that avoids jargon and crosses different subject fields in psychology including psychobiology, neuroscience, social psychology, interpersonal relationships, and organizational psychology. This book is accessible to you whether you are a student, academic, practitioner, or an employee researching or learning about mergers and acquisitions. This book is mandatory reading for any type of practitioner or employee who is working with an organization that is experiencing a merger or acquisition such as consultants, human resource professionals, psychologists, occupational health professionals, and employees involved in strategy, management, or people development. For those of you who are students or academics, this book is for you whether or not your primary field is psychology – your field might be business, management, organizational behaviour, or any other field concerned with the perspectives of employees who are experiencing a merger or acquisition.

The ultimate purpose of this book is to help you understand, empathise, and work on protecting the wellbeing of employees who experience mergers and acquisitions.

1 Understanding and classifying different types of mergers and acquisitions

This chapter will introduce you to different types of mergers and acquisitions, helping you understand the reasons that inspire organizations to engage in them. A merger or acquisition is a legal transaction in which one organization transfers or combines some or all of its operations to or with another organization. In an acquisition, one organization transfers operations "upwards" to another organization that becomes its legal "parent." In a merger, two organizations transfer "sideways" to a new organization that is the sum of its two parts and they often rebrand the name of the organization with a new name, a hyphenated name, or one of the two organizations' names. By "operations" we mean an organization's stock (e.g. products to sell to customers), assets (e.g. buildings, equipment, vehicles, or staff), liabilities (e.g. debts), and equity (e.g. net profit). This chapter will start by discussing commonly used words in mergers or acquisitions to extrapolate what different words really mean and whether they are useful or superfluous (not necessary). We will discuss ways in which the media and public sometimes confuse mergers with acquisitions, and how organizations sometimes misrepresent acquisitions as mergers because acquisitions are stereotyped as "hostile" whereas mergers are stereotyped as "friendly." We will then discuss five types of mergers, with examples from real organizations that have combined their brands and operations in such deals. We will discuss horizontal mergers, market extension mergers, vertical mergers, product extension mergers, and conglomerate mergers, and we will briefly discuss the psychological implications for employees as an introduction to this book. After this, we will present a new taxonomy defining different types of acquisitions in 15 ways, with examples from organizations that have embarked on such deals. We will also draw some conclusions about the psychological implications of acquisitions for employees as an introduction to this book. Finally, we will summarise the conclusions you can draw from this chapter. Let us start by understanding what mergers and acquisitions are and how they differ.

Understanding how mergers differ from acquisitions

When you read press releases and news reports about mergers or acquisitions, you will probably come across organizations describing something that is an acquisition as a merger. Even more confusing is the conflation in media reports between the word merger and words that allude to acquisitions, such as takeovers. Organizations that describe acquisitions as mergers might do this for public relations reasons, because mergers sound like "friendlier" events than acquisitions, which are often stereotyped as "hostile" or "takeovers." You might also come across words such as "consolidation," which can literally mean two different organizations becoming legally recognised as a new organization, or it can be used as a metaphor by organizations to describe their new partnership while leaving researchers unsure about whether the deal is a merger or an acquisition. You may also read words like "synergy," which is the idea that the two organizations combining will reduce their average costs while increasing profits. The word synergy is sometimes used in a way that leaves you uncertain about whether an acquisition or a merger has taken place. It is therefore important for you to probe a lot deeper than press releases and news reports by looking at government or court websites showing the details of a merger or acquisition, and company registration information, in order to understand whether indeed a merger has taken place or whether it is an acquisition. A key difference between a merger and acquisition is in the legal aspects of the transaction, and this depends on the laws set by the relevant country or countries. In some countries, a proposed merger or acquisition may need to be approved by the government because of competition laws that are designed to prevent some organizations from becoming too large in terms of their share of a specific product or service market.

Typically, an acquired organization becomes a legal entity that is subsumed within the parent organization, which means that the acquired organization becomes a subsidiary. Sometimes, acquired organizations cease to be known by their previous names but, often, acquired organizations continue trading with their previous name because it is commercially useful to keep the brand identity that customers are familiar with, even if the organization is actually owned by the acquiring organization. For example, after Apple acquired Shazam in 2018 for $400 million, Shazam continued to trade as Shazam, but legally, Shazam is actually registered as an Apple subsidiary. Likewise, Pixar continued to be known as Pixar even after being acquired by Disney in 2006 for $7.4 billion dollars. You can see why people in the public can remain unaware that an organization has been acquired, and why some people in the public might assume that the deal was a merger. An example is the 2017 acquisition by Amazon of Whole Foods for an estimated $13.7 billion. Whole Foods is a supermarket chain with stores in the US, UK, and Canada, and the acquisition gave Amazon (an internet-based retailer) important diversification into "bricks and mortar" retail, which means that Amazon can now sell products online *and* on shop floors. "Diversification" is when an organization broadens its operations from X to X+Y, where Y refers to additional stock, assets, or equity gained from the organization to be acquired and that are different from X in type, source, or size. In this example, X was comprised of Amazon's operations before the acquisition as a largely online retailer, and Y was comprised of Whole Food's operations before the acquisition as a supermarket chain. Therefore, we see that an acquisition enhances an organization's existing operations by giving it a new type of revenue, helping it cushion itself against risks within its existing revenue streams, such as problems with retaining consumers that make profits unpredictable. That said, consumers might remain unaware about most acquisitions because their experiences as consumers in terms of the branding of a product or service often stay the same.

Whereas in an acquisition, one organization takes over and legally incorporates another organization within itself, in a merger, the two organizations become one new legal entity. Typically, after a merger, the two organizations choose a new name or bridge their previous names to form a new name. An example is the 2000 merger between Glaxo Wellcome and SmithKline Beecham that resulted in a new organization name, GlaxoSmithKline or GSK. Another example is the 1999 merger of Exxon and Mobil to become ExxonMobil, now the second-most successful US organization in terms of revenue (Fortune, 2018). Mergers are thus typically better defined than acquisitions from the point of view of consumers. That said, in order to understand whether a certain deal is really a merger or an acquisition, you need to examine the legal procedures that the organizations went through and their subsequent registration(s) as legal entities. This book will start by introducing you to different types of mergers and acquisitions to help you understand the differences among them and the psychological implications of mergers versus acquisitions from the point of view of employees. For example, employees might think of acquisitions as events that threaten more jobs than mergers, and thus they might feel less shocked, angry, and stressed by a merger compared to an acquisition. However, just as stereotypes of acquisitions as "hostile" events are not always true, stereotypes about mergers as "friendly" events between equal organizations are also not strictly true because mergers can be unequal in terms of the proportion of jobs that are cut or the operations that are scaled down in each organization. Let us now examine what mergers are in more detail by looking at five types of mergers and understanding the differences among them.

Understanding the five types of mergers

The Federal Trade Commission provided a five-fold system for classifying mergers and acquisitions (United States Federal Trade Commission, 1984; Brealey & Meyers, 2006) and it is a classification system that is commonly used in the empirical literature (Walsh, 1988; Buono & Bowditch, 1989). Figure 1.1, which follows, shows the five ways of classifying mergers.

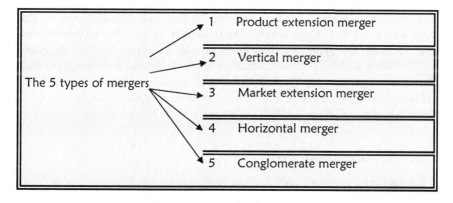

Figure 1.1 Five common ways of classifying mergers

1. Product extension mergers

When two organizations produce similar products that can complement each other in a way that increases profits, they engage in a type of merger called a product extension merger. An example is the merger of an organization A that supplies gas and electricity to domestic customers with an organization B that fits "smart" technology to customers so that they can control the heating of their homes remotely, thus creating an organization C. The new organization C has more products than either A or B alone (gas, electricity, and smart technology), and it can sell the smart technology to the gas and electricity customers who are already registered with organization A. Therefore, organizations A and B merge because they have products that complement each other. An example is the merger between DuPont and Dow Chemicals, both of which manufacture chemicals for agriculture and other uses (Reuters, 2015). The merger led to the formation of DowDuPont, although there was a subsequent sub-packaging of the merged company and a break-off that was ostensibly pre-planned at the merger stage, according to the news reported by Reuters. A sub-packaging is a portioning out of an organization's operations, assets, or other entities in the formation of a new organization or subsidiary, and a break-off means that the new organization or subsidiary becomes independent of the original organization(s) involved in the merger.

2. Vertical mergers

When two organizations produce different products within the same industry, and one organization is "lower" on the supply chain whereas the other organization produces the end product, they engage in a type of merger called a vertical merger. An example is a house building company A that merges with a bricks manufacturing company B, creating organization C that builds houses with cheaper bricks. In this example, organization B is lower on the supply chain than organization A because B manufactures products (bricks) that are needed by A to create the finished products (houses). An example of a vertical merger is that between Heinz and Kraft Foods. Heinz is known for manufacturing condiments such as mayonnaise and ketchup, whereas Kraft Foods manufactures a wider range of groceries. If Kraft Foods were to launch its own line of condiments, that might be less profitable than merging with a popular condiments brand such as Heinz with an established brand and existing manufacturing operations. The well-known investor Warren Buffett and a private equity company called 3G bought both Kraft Foods and Heinz and then, after that, they merged Kraft Foods with Heinz (Treanor, 2015) to form the Kraft Heinz company.

3. Market extension mergers

When two organizations produce similar products but each have access to different consumer markets, they engage in a type of merger called a market extension merger. An example is organization A, a retailer that sells electronics to consumers in Africa, merging with organization B, a retailer that sells electronics to consumers in Asia. This creates organization C, which accesses both consumer markets. A potential example of a market extension merger is the proposed deal between the UK's Just Eat and the Netherland's Takeaway, both of which specialise in delivering food to consumers who order online (Kollewe, 2019). The merger would result in the combined company having a large share of the online food delivery market in the UK, the Netherlands, and other countries, although at present, the merger is still under discussion and there might be counter-bids from other organizations. Market extension mergers sometimes get blocked by government bodies when they are concerned that the merged organization will unfairly dominate a certain consumer or service market because this could result in price fixing and less choice for consumers. For example, the UK supermarket chains Sainsbury's and ASDA wanted to merge as a way of reaching consumers in different markets, but the government's Competition and Markets Authority blocked it (Wood, 2019).

4. Horizontal mergers

When two organizations produce similar products reaching the same consumer market and they have equivalent market shares, they engage in a type of merger called a horizontal merger. An example is organization A, a hamburger chain, merging with organization B, also a hamburger chain. This creates organization C, a hamburger chain without the competition between A and B. An example is the £5 billion merger between two online gambling companies, Betfair and Paddy Power, to create a new company called Paddy Power Betfair (Press Association, 2015). This can be classed as a horizontal merger rather than a market extension merger because of the similarity between the two organizations in their geographical reach and type of consumers.

5. Conglomerate mergers

When two organizations produce unrelated products and work in unrelated markets, they engage in a type of merger called a conglomerate merger. In a pure conglomerate merger, the two organizations are entirely different. For example, organization A is a restaurant chain merging with organization B, a fashion chain, to create organization C that operates in both catering and clothing. In a mixed conglomerate merger, the two organizations have the opportunity to extend their products or markets. An example is a restaurant chain merging with an organization that sells baked goods to supermarkets, creating an organization that can sell the baked goods within the restaurants and also advertise the restaurants to consumers who are buying the baked goods from supermarkets. An example of a conglomerate merger is that between Carphone Warehouse, which specialised in selling mobile phone products and services, with Dixons, which specialised in selling home electrical products, to create Dixons Carphone, a chain of stores that sell both sets of products and services (Garside & Farrell, 2014).

Understanding different types of acquisitions

Whereas mergers can be neatly categorised into one of five types, acquisitions are often far more complex, and best categorised in terms of the extent to which a subsidiary organization is subsumed within its new parent organization. To help you broadly understand what this means, we have created a new method of classifying acquisitions in three ways in Figure 1.2. We have applied the five common ways of defining mergers, which we discussed in the previous section, to acquisitions while creating a framework that can help you broadly define the *extent* of an acquisition. For example, when organization A acquires organization B, it is not necessarily the case the organization A is buying everything within B. In some cases, B can break-off parts of its operations, products, services, or assets, thus selling to A only part of what was originally a whole B. In other words, acquisitions can be partial, or they can be full acquisitions. Although there is much more complexity to partial acquisitions in the financial and legal sense in terms of company assets, liabilities, shares, and registration, as an organizational psychology reader, what is important is for you to appreciate the broad rules of thumb in the first instance. We have created a way of broadly defining acquisitions that help you define an organization A that fully buys out organization B's operations (a full acquisition), organization A that buys out part of organization B's operations but B terminates the unbought operations (a type 1 partial acquisition), and cases where B repackages the remainder as a new entity that continues to operate or that is sold elsewhere (a type 2 partial acquisition).

Figure 1.2 shows the difference between a full acquisition, a type 1 partial acquisition, and a type 2 partial acquisition. You will notice that, in the full acquisition, organization A buys out all of organization B's operations (and you may define operations as considering not just products, equipment, or physical space but also staff, stock, assets, and debts). In the type 1 partial acquisition,

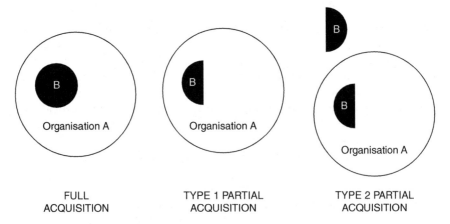

| FULL ACQUISITION | TYPE 1 PARTIAL ACQUISITION | TYPE 2 PARTIAL ACQUISITION |

Figure 1.2 A new method of classifying acquisitions

organization A buys out only some of organization B's operations. The figure illustrates a scenario in which A buys out precisely 50% of B's operations, but note that the proportion bought can be anywhere from more than 0% but less than 100% of B's operations. In a type 1 partial acquisition, the remainder of B's operations (that is, those not bought by A) cease to exist in the sense that they are closed or dissolved. A type 2 partial acquisition is defined exactly the same as a type 1 acquisition except that the remainder of B's operations continue to exist as an independent organization or they are sold to other organizations in full or in part. To understand exactly what operations have been acquired and/or sub-packaged during the transaction, you need to define the staff, stock, assets, debts, equity, and anything else involved within B before and after the acquisition. From a psychological point of view, the important point to note is not so much the specifics of a type 1 or type 2 partial acquisition, but the fact that employees can be confused about what the future holds for their jobs. You also need to critically consider whether published studies about employees experiencing an acquisition have appropriately classified the type of acquisition that took place because many studies fail to appropriately define the type of acquisition involved, and they also fail to acknowledge the complexity of partial acquisitions from the point of view of employees who may feel confused and not sufficiently informed about what is happening to the organization. We thus recommend that researchers exploring topics relating to the organizational psychology of mergers and acquisitions start defining acquisitions (and mergers) properly within their methodology, and start investigating the effects of different types of mergers and acquisitions on employees, because that is lacking within the published empirical literature.

We will now combine our new method of defining three types of acquisitions with the five common ways of classifying mergers or acquisitions (United States Federal Trade Commission, 1984; Brealey & Meyers, 2006). The reasons why organizations engage in acquisitions are similar to the reasons why organizations engage in mergers; therefore, these are the same types of deals captured in Figure 1.1. We now cross the three types of acquisitions that we described previously (see Figure 1.2) against the five common ways of classifying acquisitions, and you can now see that there are 15 broad ways of understanding different types of acquisitions. Table 1.1 shows some useful examples illustrating the differences between the various types of acquisitions. As a psychology reader, you may not need to know the precise financial details about an acquisition that you are studying or evaluating, but you do need to appreciate the complexity involved in many acquisitions. It can confuse employees, leaving them unsure about what is happening and what is going to change. Table 1.1 shows what we call the 15-point taxonomy, and it will help you understand the general ways in which different types of acquisitions differ from each other.

Determining what kind of acquisition has taken place requires an understanding of the details of the deal, what operations, assets, liabilities, or products were transferred or disposed of during the deal, and the market in which each organization operates. A recent example of a product extension acquisition is Google's proposed buyout of Fitbit, the company that manufactures gadgets that track

Table 1.1 Kamau and Oancea (2020a) 15-point taxonomy of classifying acquisitions

	Full acquisition	Type 1 partial acquisition	Type 2 partial acquisition
Product extension acquisition	**1. Full product extension acquisition** Organization A manufactures and sells women's clothing. A buys organization B, which manufactures and sells men's clothing. A buys B's factory, stock, and staff.	**2. Type 1 partial product extension acquisition** Organization A only buys organization B's men's fashion design staff and the stock. Organization B then closes its factory and makes remaining staff redundant.	**3. Type 2 partial product extension acquisition** Organization A only buys organization B's men's fashion design staff and the stock. Organization B keeps their factory operations, changes its name, and starts manufacturing children's clothing.
Vertical acquisition	**4. Full vertical acquisition** Organization A is a fast-food company selling sausages and chips to consumers. It usually buys these frozen. Organization A buys organization B, which manufactures frozen sausages, chips, vegetables, and herbs, and packs them for retail and wholesale.	**5. Type 1 partial vertical acquisition** Organization A only buys the operations within organization B that produce frozen sausages and chips for wholesale. Organization B closes its operations producing the other types of frozen food, makes some staff redundant, and closes its operations for supply to retail.	**6. Type 2 partial vertical acquisition** Organization A only buys the operations within organization B that produce frozen sausages and chips for wholesale. Organization B moves its remaining staff and operations for retail, and involving other frozen foods, to new premises under a new name.
Market extension acquisition	**7. Full market extension acquisition** Organization A sells used cars to the luxury consumer market. A buys organization B, which sells used cars to consumers on tight budgets.	**8. Type 1 partial market extension acquisition** Organization A buys B's premises, sales staff, and stock, but not B's website, website staff, or computer servers. B closes its online operations and makes non-sales staff redundant.	**9. Type 2 partial market extension acquisition** Organization A buys B's premises and stock, but not its website operations. B sells its online operations to a different used car company that wants to purchase the ready-made website infrastructure as well as retaining some staff.

	Full acquisition	*Type 1 partial acquisition*	*Type 2 partial acquisition*
Horizontal acquisition	**10. Full horizontal acquisition** Consultancy company A provides psychometric staff assessment services to government organizations. Company B supplies the same services to government organizations.	**11. Type 1 partial horizontal acquisition** Company A buys company B's client accounts (contracts with clients to supply services) and 25% of B's staff, but not B's financial assets or 75% of their staff. Company B closes some operations and makes the staff not hired by A redundant.	**12. Type 2 horizontal acquisition** Company A buys company B's client accounts (contracts with clients to supply services) and 25% of B's staff, but not B's financial assets or 75% of their staff. Company B renames itself as a new company providing psychometric assessment services to private-sector clients and retains some staff.
Conglomerate acquisition	**13. Full conglomerate acquisition** Organization A is a pharmaceutical company. A buys organization B, an electric parts company, with the plan of launching new electric products.	**14. Type 1 partial conglomerate acquisition** Organization A buys B's building assets (a factory and equipment), staff, and client accounts, but not B's stock. B sells the stock through an auction house and closes its operations.	**15. Type 2 partial conglomerate acquisition** Organization A buys B's building assets (factory and equipment), staff, and, client accounts, but not B's stock. B sets up an online retail company selling its remaining stock (electric parts) to electricians and electrical companies.

people's exercise activity, for $2.1 billion as part of Google's expansion into consumer products, just as Google's acquisition of the company Nest was an expansion into home products (Guardian, 2019a). Another example is the acquisition of the satirical website the Daily Mash by digital media company Digitalbox for £1.2 million, as part of the company's expansion of its portfolio of digital technologies to include entertainment websites (Waterson, 2019). An example of a vertical acquisition is the acquisition by Spotify by the company The Echo Nest. Spotify streams music to consumers and it benefited from The Echo Nest's technology of analysing the properties of a song, and the acquisition helped Spotify have the technology to recommend new songs to consumers based on their previous song choices (Hern, 2014). The acquisition most likely helped Spotify access this technology at a cheaper cost than had it used The Echo Nest as a supplier of the technology. Another example of a vertical acquisition is private equity company Bain (with the investment of Apple and other organizations) acquiring the microchip-making company owned by Toshiba (Gibbs, 2017) as a way of cutting the costs of microchips needed to manufacture iPhones and other Apple products. It should be noted, however, that the deal had a complex structure and this was therefore not a direct acquisition by Apple itself. An example of a market extension acquisition is the acquisition of Versace by the fashion company Michael Kors for $2.1 billion (Conlon, 2018). The two fashion brands can be said to attract different types of consumers, in terms of their budget or brand expectations, therefore the acquisition will allow Michael Kors to gain profits from new types of consumers within the fashion market. An example of a horizontal acquisition is Ladbrokes' acquisition of Gala Coral, with both companies comprised of betting shops (Farrell, 2016, who erroneously calls the deal a merger rather than an acquisition). An example of a conglomerate acquisition is Google buying various companies involved with home products, radio communications, and cameras (Arthur, 2014). When you study published evidence about mergers or acquisitions, or when you are working on research or consultancy, try and evaluate how a particular acquisition fits within the 15 new ways defined in Table 1.1. You will notice that many published studies do not clarify what type of acquisition happened. Therefore, we encourage researchers who are planning new studies to start defining the acquisitions involved more clearly. If you use the Kamau and Oancea's (2020a) 15-point taxonomy in Table 1.1 you can cite it as follows:

Kamau, C. and Oancea, C. (2020a). 15-point taxonomy of classifying acquisitions. In C. Oancea and C. Kamau, *Organizational Psychology of Mergers and Acquisitions*. Routledge.

How this book helps you understand what mergers and acquisitions do to employees

This book will help you explore the implications of mergers and acquisitions from a psychological perspective. First, we will examine why some employees view mergers and acquisitions as scary, threatening, or distressing events by discussing their history in Chapter 2. We will discuss how mergers and acquisitions emerged and became common just over a century ago, and how trends in society have tended to correspond with their success or failure. In Chapter 2, we discuss the fact that the quantifiable reality about mergers and acquisitions (e.g. how many succeed or fail) is often less important from a psychological point of view than the *perceptions* that employees have about them based on their expectations, news reports, anecdotes, or personal experiences. This book does not assume that mergers or acquisitions are bad, but rather, this book reviews published evidence and theories about their psychological implications for employees. Chapter 2 will thus set the foundation for understanding why evidence shows that employees often experience negative emotions and expectations about mergers and acquisitions, which we will discuss in Chapter 3. That chapter will give you comprehensive insight into the state of the evidence about employees' emotions through our systematic review and our application of theories from psychobiology which is, to our knowledge, the first literature of its kind. Chapter 3 will then present a new method of measuring, scoring, and calculating employees' emotional responses to a merger or acquisition. The new measurement tool that you will see in Chapter 3 will be useful if you are a researcher planning a new study, a manager or human resource professional interested in surveying your employees, or a consultant working with an organization.

Uncertainty and fear are some of the negative emotions that employees experience (see Chapter 3), and these influence their behaviour, such as by making them want to switch jobs. Chapter 4 will give you a comprehensive review of the published evidence about how employees behave in response to a merger or acquisition, based on our systematic review. That chapter will discuss evidence showing that employees can be supportive of mergers or acquisitions under certain circumstances, while resistant under other circumstances, such as in cases where they feel that their employer has breached a psychological or unspoken contract to honour certain promises. Chapter 4 will then discuss evidence showing that mergers and acquisitions are associated with a notable quantity of employees and managers planning to quit the organization. Although some previous literature exists about the issue of intentions to quit, Chapter 4 is the first within the literature to give you an overview of the evidence and an understanding of the factors that increase the likelihood that employees will want to quit. To our knowledge, Chapter 4 is also the first to critically evaluate evidence about how employees versus managers differ in their behavioural responses. Among the factors that we will discuss in Chapter 4 will be the issue of how the two organizations involved in a merger or acquisition are compatible or a good fit, versus being different in their working culture or status. The issue of status is one which we will explore further in Chapter 5, which will discuss how attempting to bring together two organizations can promote thoughts, feelings, and behaviours inspired by group processes. The term group processes refers to the psychological and social dynamics that exist within and among people when a category (or group) exists and is psychologically relevant. Chapter 5 will discuss evidence about how some employees hold biased attitudes against the status or competence of partner organizations involved in a merger or acquisition, and how feelings of loyalty to their old organization can hinder their psychological attachment to the new one. Chapter 5 is the first piece of literature within the field, to our knowledge, that reviews evidence about group processes in a way that is accessible to readers who are not familiar with theories in the field.

Chapter 5 focuses on the impact of employees perceiving category differences of "us versus them" in and of themselves, as well as category differences relating to the status of the two organizations involved in a merger or acquisition. This will lead to Chapter 6, which will explore the issue of category differences in more detail by focusing on ways that the problem of "us versus them" dynamics among employees from different organizations can be made worse by cultural differences between organizations in the way that employees interact with each other. Chapter 6 will provide a new perspective on the notion of cultural differences between organizations in mergers and acquisitions by examining an aspect of cultural differences that has received little attention within previous published literature in the field of mergers and acquisitions. This concerns cultural differences in nonverbal communication between employees, a previously unexplored topic within literature about mergers and acquisitions, and it draws on wider evidence about how nonverbal language helps employees achieve success in goals at work, such as successful communication with other employees, promotion, and other self-enhancing goals. Cultural differences can lead to unmet goals or even negative outcomes for employees who break cultural norms.

We will then turn to the topic of leadership because managers, executives, and other types of leaders within organizations have an important role to play in preventing many of the negative psychological outcomes of mergers and acquisitions through good leadership that helps employees feel less uncertain or fearful about what is going to happen and more enthused about supporting an impending merger or acquisition, as is evidenced by published literature (see Chapters 2, 3, 4, 5, and 6). Chapter 7 will discuss theories about leadership that help you understand what constitutes good leadership from a psychological perspective. We will discuss theories about how leaders can inspire employees to feel motivated and inspired to use their work in support of a merger or acquisition. To our knowledge, this is the first chapter of its kind because it helps you explore not just the "good" side of leadership, but also the advantages and disadvantages of different types of "good leadership" in the context of mergers and acquisitions, as well as helping you become familiar with relatively new perspectives on leadership, such as those concerning "bad" personality traits like narcissism. One of the issues that relates to leaders being able to inspire employees is the issue of encouraging them to participate and cooperate with the goals of a merger or acquisition, such as goals connected with exchanging knowledge or expertise between organizations. The next chapter, Chapter 8, will then discuss the issue of organizational learning as a common reason why organizations embark on a merger or acquisition, but something that evidence shows can be hindered by problems discussed in Chapters 2, 3, 4, 5, 6, and 7. Chapter 8 will discuss this evidence after helping you understand what organizational learning is, how organizations approach learning differently, and evidence about why mergers or acquisitions achieve or fail to achieve optimal organizational learning. For example, Chapter 8 discusses evidence showing that employees often enact negative emotions such as mistrust or an attitude of "us versus them" by refusing to cooperate with organizational learning.

Having helped you discover what mergers and acquisitions are (Chapter 1), and what psychological impact they have on how employees feel, think, and behave (Chapters 2 to 8), we will then help you understand the implications of mergers and acquisitions for the occupational health and safety of employees. There is a lack of published evidence about this, therefore Chapter 9 takes on the cutting-edge approach of focussing on one common occupational health and safety concern – the cancer risk facing employees who are exposed to certain substances within the workplace. In Chapter 9, we discuss case studies showing how a merger or acquisition can make an organization legally responsible for employees who were ill or died because of being exposed to carcinogens (substances that raise cancer risk). This chapter thus completes the book by highlighting a topic within the organizational psychology of mergers and acquisitions that requires urgent attention with the due diligence taken by organizations considering a merger or acquisition. We hope that Chapter 9 will be helpful to consultants and other practitioners when advising organizations during the due diligence stage, and that they will appropriately generalise the examples in the chapter to help them identify and evaluate the risks and liabilities from other types of workplace hazards. Occupational health and safety is a core component of organizational psychology, therefore, we hope that Chapter 9, the first of its kind within the literature, will inspire new research and publications about the topic among academic researchers.

We intend that Chapters 1 to 9 will inspire organizations, researchers, managers, consultants, human resource professionals, and other practitioners working with organizations experiencing a merger or acquisition to place the psychological welfare of employees higher on the agenda.

Conclusions

In conclusion, this chapter has helped you discover what mergers and acquisitions are and what this book is about. We have explored the five types of mergers and a new 15-point taxonomy that helps you understand different types of acquisitions. As a reader, researcher, or consultant within organizational psychology or many other fields, you might not need to know the intricate financial or legal details about a merger or acquisition, in terms of the complex structure of the way that operations, shares, stock, liabilities, or assets are transferred or sold. However, you do need to be aware that mergers and acquisitions are very complex organizational events and they are highly important to employees in the way that they feel, act, relate to each other, and so on. This chapter has also helped you understand how this book is structured and what you will broadly discover in each chapter, starting with the history of mergers and acquisitions, and the social, political, or economic trends that inspire them in Chapter 2, which is next. We aim for this book to be accessible to readers of all levels, from undergraduate or postgraduate students to university researchers, from psychologists to non-psychologists, from people working in consultancy to in-house human resource professionals or organizational development specialists, and from people highly familiar with mergers and acquisitions to readers with no prior experience in the field. This book is for any reader who is interested in learning more about the organizational psychology of mergers and acquisitions. We avoid using jargon or unnecessarily convoluted writing, and we hope that you will enjoy reading this book.

2 Historical trends in mergers and acquisitions, and why employees think of them as scary events involving job losses and other negative outcomes

Chapter 1 examined what mergers and acquisitions are, how they differ, and what different types of mergers and acquisitions there are as a way of appreciating their complexity. Chapter 1 set the foundation for understanding why employees perceive them as major organizational events, and Chapter 2 will now help you discover why many employees think of mergers and acquisitions as scary or threatening events because of their history. Historical trends in mergers and acquisitions can shape employees' negative perceptions, feelings, and expectations about the organization they work for. This chapter will start by looking at the history of mergers and acquisitions by introducing you to the seven historical waves as a way of helping you discover the reasons why employees can think of them as risky, scary, or threatening organizational events that tend to result in job losses, management changes, relocation, and site closures. This chapter will then extrapolate from the historical trends what sorts of factors tend to inspire organizations to enter into a merger or acquisition (we can call these "entry factors") which, from the perspective of employees, suggests that organizations tend to focus on organizational goals, such as increasing revenue or taking advantage of the opportunity to cut costs, rather than concerns about what is best for employees. The idea that businesses are motivated by profits is, of course, unsurprising, but the history of other mergers and acquisitions can make employees fear that job cuts and other cost-cutting measures such as site closures are very likely to happen. This can explain why employees often fear for their job security and why many plan to quit after hearing of an impending merger or acquisition. The history of mergers and acquisitions can also suggest to employees that they are risky or volatile organizational events that could end in failure. We will discuss factors that tend to inspire organizations to quit a merger or acquisition (we can call these "exit factors") such as stock market crashes, economic recessions, and burst product "bubbles." Stereotyping mergers and acquisitions as organizational events that tend to fail or that are historically volatile can explain why employees often feel a range of negative emotions about them, including a sense of uncertainty and cynicism, which we will explore further in Chapter 3. After discussing the historical trends, this chapter will then summarise the entry and exit factors, as well as what we can call common psychological casualties of mergers and acquisitions, such as job losses, site closures, and management changes. Chapter 2 thus helps you discover why mergers and acquisitions can evoke the psychological processes or outcomes that we discuss further on in this book.

A history of mergers and acquisitions

This chapter will start by looking at the history of mergers and acquisitions by introducing you to the seven historical waves since the 1890s, helping you understand the social, economic, and political conditions that tend to tally with organizations entering or exiting a merger or acquisition (Martynova & Renneboog, 2008). This section will set the foundation for helping you learn the reasons why employees can think of mergers and acquisitions as scary, risky, or threatening organizational events that tend to result in job losses, management changes, relocation, and site closures.

The 1st wave

When there are many sellers of a product in any given market there is competition between sellers and this forces them to reduce the price of the product to consumers. If, however, there are fewer sellers in a market, sellers are able to keep the price of the product higher. This basic principle in business inspired the first wave of mergers and acquisitions. In the "Great Merger Wave" within the United States (US), starting in the late 1890s, companies could join together as sellers of certain products or services, monopolise a market because of the lack of competition, and fix the prices paid by consumers. There were few laws or public policies preventing companies from doing this, and that inspired the wave of mergers and acquisitions (Bittlingmayer, 1985). Organizations were also inspired by booms in industrialisation, such as in manufacturing, railways, and the steel industries, giving companies the opportunity to expand (Gaughan, 2007). The organizations that joined together were often called "trusts," such as the Standard Oil Trust of 1881 that led to a monopoly of over 90% of the global market in oil refining, and that inspired other companies to embark on similar ventures (Lamoreaux, 1985). These ventures succeeded in helping some organizations to monopolise certain markets. For example, JP Morgan founded US Steel by merging Carnegie Steel with Federal Steel and then acquiring a number of companies, giving US Steel a monopoly of nearly 70% of the US market (Hessen, 1975). Although the United States government had established a law prohibiting trusts that monopolised a market such as by keeping prices high (the 1890 Sherman Act, which was something called an "antitrust" law), the problem was that the law was reactive in the sense that the onus was on the government to investigate suspected monopolies, which could take years (Molodovsky, 1968; Wilson, 2003). Some authors argue that these sorts of ventures had high failure rates because of "diseconomies of scale" arising from their uncontrollable size (Livermore, 1935; Stigler, 1950; O'Brien, 1988), but they remained quite popular until, ironically, an attempted monopoly of the railway market contributed to the New York stock market crash in May 1901 (Block, 1970; Hidy, Hidy, Scott, & Hofsommer, 1988). President

Theodore Roosevelt had taken office earlier that year in March 1901 and made a determined effort to apply the Sherman Act and develop policies against monopolies, instigating prosecutions and earning him a reputation for "trust busting" (Bittlingmayer, 2001; Harbeson, 1958). This had the effect of breaking up some trusts and dissuading the formation of some new trusts, therefore, the Sherman Act and Roosevelt's efforts demonstrate the importance of competition laws in regulating mergers and acquisitions that monopolise a market. Gradually, at least in the United States, the idea of monopolising a market as a reason for a merger or acquisition became less popular and less feasible because of regulations. This first wave shows that entry factors that inspire organizations to enter to a merger or acquisition include industrialisation and the desire to monopolise a market in order to keep prices high, whereas exit factors include antitrust or competition laws that regulate such behaviour. From an employee's point of view, this can suggest that organizations are primarily motivated to enter into a merger or acquisition because of the desire to increase their market share and revenue, but the downsides for employees are losing their jobs when economies of scale make it possible for organizations to save costs by reducing expenditure on staffing. The first wave of mergers and acquisitions slowed down and is said to have ended around 1914 when World War I started (Lamoreaux, 1985).

The 2nd wave

After World War I ended in 1919, the second wave of mergers and acquisitions began, with some authors suggesting that the second wave included not just the US but also Europe and the UK, albeit at a much smaller pace and size than in the US (Cartwright & Cooper, 1996; Vancea, 2013). It is estimated that, by the end of the second wave around 1929, organizations engaged in the transfer of ownership with assets of about $13 billion (Gaughan, 2007). The US regulations against monopolies (such as the Sherman Act and the later Clayton Acts of 1914) steered organizations away from trying to monopolise markets (Martynova & Renneboog, 2008; Stigler, 1950) because it was no longer legally possible to do so. Some authors suggest that whereas the first wave tended to involve horizontal mergers or acquisitions, the second wave involved more vertical and conglomerate mergers or acquisitions (Gaughan, 2007); see Chapter 1. It is estimated that during the first wave, about 3,000 organizations "disappeared" and in the second wave the number was 12,000 (United States; Fligstein, 1990), suggesting that the number of mergers or acquisitions increased. The second wave lost momentum in 1929 when the stock market crashed and the Great Depression of the 1930s started, followed by World War II from 1939 to 1945 (Gaughan, 2007). Employees who are aware of the impact of stock market crashes on organizations could feel fearful that organizations inspired to expand during "good times" within the national or global economy could likewise be inspired to contract when there are negative events within the national or global economy. In other words, it is plausible that employees could fear that their jobs will become insecure after a merger or acquisition if the national or global economy suffers a setback such as a stock market crash.

The 3rd wave

The third wave started in 1950 at a time when there was even stricter government legislation about mergers and acquisitions and curtailing of monopolies in the US and other countries. In the US, the 1950 Congress Celler-Kefauver Act was an amendment to the Clayton Antitrust Act of 1914 which made it even more difficult for organizations to embark on mergers or acquisitions as a way of reducing market competition (Gaughan, 2007). Some organizations had used loopholes within the Clayton Antitrust Act to embark on mergers and acquisitions that eliminated competition and the Celler-Kefauver Act helped to close these loopholes. Following the Great Depression, Roosevelt's administration adopted a series of policies, reforms, and public works meant to restore the economy between 1933 and 1939. This comprehensive legislative program is also known as the New Deal (Hawley, 2015). Under this program, there were some initiatives meant to impose tighter control on antitrust pricing practices, which led the U.S. Congress to pass the Robinson-Patman Act in 1936 (Kovacic & Shapiro, 2000). Other countries imposed tighter antitrust regulations, such as or France (Derenberg, 1955) and Canada's Combines Investigation Act (King, 1912; Stanbury, 1976). From 1963 to 1970, about 26,000 mergers or acquisitions took place in the United States (Gaughan, 2007). The intense activity is often known as the "conglomerate wave" because these types of deals became more popular than horizontal deals (Kaplan, 1955; Melnik & Pollatschek, 1973; Michel & Shaked, 1984; see Chapter 1 about different types of mergers or acquisitions). One inspiration for this was that announcements of a conglomerate mergers or acquisitions tended to create more market excitement and increases in the value of shares than horizontal deals (Matsusaka, 1993). The third wave started ending during the oil crisis of 1973 or 1974 when some Middle Eastern countries placed an embargo on the US, UK, and other countries for supporting Israel in the Yom Kippur War (Issawi, 1978). The price of oil quadrupled, and later on in 1979, there was a second oil crisis after the Iraq-Iran war started, halting oil production there. There were lasting economic consequences spanning until the early 1980s (Sachs, 1982). Employees whose organizations sell products or services whose profitability can change because of international events (e.g. oil crises, wars, or a breakdown in international relations) could fear that a merger or acquisition that is followed by a major international event will be short-lived and therefore that their jobs could be at risk.

The 4th wave

The fourth wave began in 1984 after economies started to improve and investors developed more optimism; about 2,543 mergers or acquisitions were concluded in the first year, involving up to $122,000 million in assets (United States; Gaughan, 2007). During the fourth wave, which peaked in 1988, aggressive takeovers (or "hostile" acquisitions) became common because it became fashionable to view companies as a bundle of liquid assets that could be bought (Gaughan, 2007). Some authors suggest that organizations started to focus on scaling down operations for better efficiency, de-conglomeration, and correcting managerial flaws by replacing non-performing executive teams (Manne, 1965; Fama, 1980; Fama & Jensen, 1986). It is possible that "hostile" takeovers played the role of inspiring confidence in shareholders by changing or disciplining the team responsible for leading or managing an organization earmarked for a merger or acquisition (Walsh & Kosnik, 1993). The trend among investors of conglomerate mergers or acquisitions became less popular during the fourth wave (Gaughan, 2007) because the financial performance of conglomerates tended to be worse than that of non-conglomerates, particularly when a conglomerate had too much of a mixture of operations (Lee & Cooperman, 1989; Mason & Goudzwaard, 1976). Acquisitions were often portrayed in the media as ruthless, aggressive, and unethical, with significant consequences for the companies and employees involved (Hirsch, 1986) because many workers lost their jobs, factories closed, and wages were cut (Jung & Dobbin, 2012). What some authors call "predatory capitalism" was common during the fourth wave (Freeman, Gilbert, & Jacobson, 1987; Newton, 1988; di Norcia, 1988). Investors tended to think that there was nothing immoral or unethical about acquisitions or mergers that improved efficiency or profit, viewing their strategies as "necessary evils" (Newton, 1988; Almeder & Carey, 1991; Fama, 1980; Jensen, 1986; Fama & Jensen, 1983) or a way of "separating the wheat from the chaff" in an organization (Bhide, 1989). Evidence is nonetheless mixed as to whether "hostile" acquisitions were genuinely motivated by a desire for growth or whether a bigger motive was the desire by organizations to build an empire (Eddey, 1991; Walsh & Kosnik, 1993). Around 4,000 mergers and acquisitions were concluded in Europe in 1988, almost half of which were carried in UK and involved almost £1 trillion (Martynova & Renneboog, 2008). The fourth wave started to slow down after the 1987 stock market crash, and ended in 1989 when the stock market crashed again, leading to the economic recession of the early 1990s (Gaughan, 2007). For example, the total global deal value decreased from around $600 billion US dollars in 1988 to merely $200 billion in 1991 (M&A Statistics Database – Institute of Mergers and Acquisitions). This wave can be said to have built a narrative among employees, through anecdotes or stereotypes, that mergers and acquisitions are "predatory capitalist" strategies for organizations to cut costs by axing jobs, changing management teams, and embarking upon measures that improve profits irrespective of the human impact for employees' job security and the enjoyment of their previous working conditions.

The 5th wave

The fifth wave began in the early 1990s, and some authors suggest that there was a trend of consolidating organizations involved in highly fragmented markets through large-scale mergers or acquisitions that allowed expansion from regional markets to national markets (Gaughan, 2005). This period was marked by deregulation in several industries, including financial services (DeYoung, Evanoff, & Molyneux, 2009), and cable television and telephone services (Chan-Olmsted, 1998), which created a more fertile legal ground for the pursuit of mergers and acquisitions in these sectors. Just as organizational expansion from regional to national markets became popular, so did expansion from national to international markets, which is said to have been a characteristic of the fifth wave (Martynova & Renneboog, 2008; Geroski & Vlassopoulos, 1990). As well as in the US, there were more mergers and acquisitions in Asia and Europe, where deregulation and privatisation allowed investors to enter new markets (Gaughan, 2007). For instance, there were many British mergers and acquisitions involving organizations inside and outside the European Community (Geroski & Vlassopoulos, 1990; Uddin & Boateng, 2014). In 1990 the number of transactions initiated by European companies on US companies exceeded those initiated by US on European targets (Geroski & Vlassopoulos, 1990). In 1991 the UK became the second-largest acquiring nation and second-largest target nation, partly due to its relatively lenient laws about mergers and acquisitions, relatively lower tax rates, and economic stability (Uddin & Boateng, 2014). However, organizations still faced the challenge of merging with or acquiring organizations in more protectionist countries. For instance, the acquisition of Germany's Mannesman AG by UK Vodafone PLC was fiercely opposed by German employees and the media, some of which characterised Vodafone's manoeuvres as an example of pernicious free market capitalism (Halsall, 2008). That was until Germany's then chancellor (Gerhard Schroeder) intervened by engaging in talks with the then UK Prime Minister (Tony Blair) that were heightened to an extent that the issue was oftentimes portrayed as a battle between nations (Corrigan, 1999, p. 35). The fifth wave started slowing down in 2000 when the "dot-com" bubble, which involved "exuberant" investment in online businesses (Greenspan, 1996), burst and, in some cases, online businesses fell in value by up to 90% (Valliere & Peterson, 2004) and about 5,000 dot-com companies disappeared by 2001 (Wang, 2007). This wave can be said to have taught employees at least two lessons that instil fears about mergers and acquisitions. One is that international mergers and acquisitions can create a clash of cultures with consequences for the way they work or enjoy work, and the second is that mergers or acquisitions inspired by what is fashionable (such as a product or service boom or bubble) could be doomed, and therefore employees in sectors experiencing a boom or bubble could fear that their jobs remain vulnerable.

The 6th wave

The sixth wave began after economies recovered from around 2003 and an estimated 23,000 mergers or acquisitions took place worldwide (Mohammed, 2008) until the wave peaked in 2007. In contrast to the fifth wave, organizations engaging in mergers or acquisitions are said to have displayed a more risk-averse approach to expansion (Alexandridis, Mavrovitis, & Travlos, 2012) and were less likely to embark on speculation or overconfidence about the financial outcomes of a merger or acquisition (Hayward & Hambrick, 1997). "Hostile" transactions are said to have become less frequent, and about half of the mergers and acquisitions globally are estimated to have occurred across borders (Dealogic, 2007). This wave also included mergers or acquisitions across borders that were inspired by changes in laws or policies within Eastern Europe that deregulated and liberalised economies and markets (Uhlenbruck & De Castro). Whereas in previous waves, manufacturing, minerals, or oil were popular sectors, service organizations such as banking and insurance became popular sectors for mergers or acquisitions (Allen et al., 2011). Other popular sectors were telecommunications (e.g. AT&T and Bellsouth; Comcast and AT&T Broadband & Internet Services), utilities (e.g. Royal Dutch Petroleum and Shell Transport & Trading; Gaz de France and Suez), and technology (e.g. Symantec and Veritas; Cisco and Linksys; eBay and Skype; Google and YouTube; AMD and ATI; HP and Compaq) (Dealogic, 2007). The financial success of mergers and acquisitions is questionable. Alexandridis et al. (2012) found in a sample of 3,206 merger and acquisition cases that, even in the sixth wave (as with many previous waves), many transactions failed to deliver positive returns. The housing bubble of 2007 and the ensuing subprime mortgages of 2008 reduced investors' optimism and slowed down merger and acquisition activities because the crisis had wider financial ramifications when large financial institutions, such as the Lehman Brothers, became bankrupt (Gaughan, 2007). Due to greater globalisation in this wave compared to previous waves, the financial crisis carried a far bigger contagion risk than the previous bubbles, and it quickly sparked a ripple effect through markets in many countries (Allen et al., 2011). Several banks were nationalised in the UK as a rescue mechanism, such as Northern Rock, Bradford and Bingley, and in part the Royal Bank of Scotland (Marshall et al., 2012; Kickert, 2012). Other European governments followed suit with similar bailout actions to minimise the negative impact of failed private banks and the subprime financial crisis on the national economy (Alter & Schuler, 2012). Soon after, Ireland, Greece, and Portugal requested Eurozone help against defaults on sovereign debts and Spain/Italy were also severely vulnerable to defaults (Beirne & Fratzcher, 2013). The recession improved from mid-2009 in the US when GDP growth was reported but, in European countries, only some recovered quickly and to date, some countries are still grappling with the aftermath of that economic crisis (Zoega, 2019). The sixth wave of mergers and acquisitions can be said to have ended around the time of the subprime financial crisis in 2008. This wave can be said to have shaped beliefs among employees that a significant number of mergers and acquisitions end in failure, whether or not this is accurate within a given sector, and that those within financial services or involving international markets are particularly at risk, even if the economic crisis just occurs in some countries.

The 7th wave

The current, seventh wave of merger and acquisitions started in the 2014 (Cordeiro, 2014), although certain analyses seem to suggest it started few years earlier

(Junni & Teerikangas, 2019) and, in 2014, the total value of deals was 3.5 trillion US dollars with over 40,000 deals announced globally (Thomson Reuters, 2015). The trend seemed to continue in 2015, with close to 5 trillion US dollars-worth of assets transferring ownership in around 40,000 deals (Dealogic, 2015). The new wave in the global landscape of mergers and acquisitions has already exceeded 2007 global levels, and is still expected to continue in the coming years (Thomson Reuters, 2015; Bloomberg, 2016; Dealogic, 2015). A feature of the seventh wave is a focus on very large deals (Bloomberg, 2016). By transaction value, the top sectors globally include finance, retail, manufacturing, healthcare, and communications (Bloomberg, 2016), and the most active regions involved in mergers and acquisitions activity are North America and Asia Pacific (Bloomberg, 2016). Recent examples of major deals are Pfizer's acquisition of Hospira Inc for $16.8 billion; Royal Dutch Shell's acquisition of BG Group PLC for $79.3 billion; the merger between H.J. Heinz Co's and Kraft Foods Group Inc for $55.4 billion; Charter Communications Inc's acquisition of Time Warner Cable Inc for $79.2 billion; and Anheuser-Busch InBev SA/NV's merger with SABMiller Plc (Bloomberg, 2016). This wave could be said to have contributed to the narrative among employees of viewing mergers and acquisitions as tending to involve deals of huge value and scale. On one hand, that could make employees feel powerless and without much say about changes that will happen in organizations that are very big and in which policies or practices are set on a grand scale. On the other hand, the trend of mergers and acquisitions as events that remain popular among organizations, and that still happen despite previous waves ending with stock market crashes, economic recessions, or other crises, can make employees feel less fearful about them and potentially more supportive of them. It could help employees feel assured that mergers and acquisitions are common organizational events that might not mean job losses or other negative outcomes. Overall, however, what employees think or feel about mergers and acquisitions doesn't just depend on trends within the seventh wave, but also trends within previous waves.

Trends in entering and exiting mergers or acquisitions

In the previous section, we discussed the seven waves of mergers and acquisitions and we noticed a series of trends emerging in terms of the factors that inspire organizations to enter mergers and acquisitions, which we can call "entry" factors, and factors that inspire them away from mergers or acquisitions, which we can call "exit" factors. We suggest that they shape the way that employees tend to think about them, and the fears or other emotions that they tend to exhibit (see Chapter 3), as well as the tendency among employees to want to quit and work elsewhere (Chapter 4). These factors include economic or societal events that act as triggers, or that signal the likely success or failure of a merger or acquisition. Figure 2.1 illustrates our summary, based on the history of mergers and acquisitions and the entry or exit factors that we noticed from the history of the field. We argue that these trends have shaped public opinion about mergers or acquisitions, and understanding the history will help you understand, psychologically,

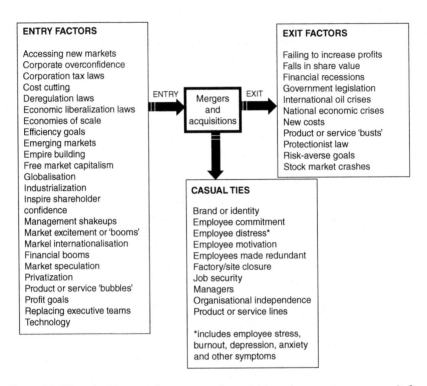

ENTRY FACTORS

Accessing new markets
Corporate overconfidence
Corporation tax laws
Cost cutting
Deregulation laws
Economic liberalization laws
Economies of scale
Efficiency goals
Emerging markets
Empire building
Free market capitalism
Globalisation
Industrialization
Inspire shareholder
confidence
Management shakeups
Market excitement or 'booms'
Markel internationalisation
Financial booms
Market speculation
Privatization
Product or service 'bubbles'
Profit goals
Replacing executive teams
Technology

ENTRY → Mergers and acquisitions → EXIT

EXIT FACTORS

Failing to increase profits
Falls in share value
Financial recessions
Government legislation
International oil crises
National economic crises
New costs
Product or service 'busts'
Protectionist law
Risk-averse goals
Stock market crashes

CASUAL TIES

Brand or identity
Employee commitment
Employee distress*
Employee motivation
Employees made redundant
Factory/site closure
Job security
Managers
Organisational independence
Product or service lines

*includes employee stress, burnout, depression, anxiety and other symptoms

Figure 2.1 How the history of mergers and acquisitions (common entry or exit factors and casualties) can shape employees' fears, uncertainties, quitting intentions, and other phenomena discussed within this book

why employees have fears or uncertainties about them, or what we can call potential psychological (human) casualties, such as job losses. Figure 2.1 will also summarise some of these psychological casualty factors, and we explore several of them in greater detail across this book.

Entry and exit factors in mergers or acquisitions, and common casualties

What we call "entry factors" are common goals or trends that inspire organizations to embark on a merger or acquisition, and we can deduce these from our historical overview, summarised earlier in this chapter. One of the most common entry factors is the desire to increase profits and history shows that organizations have achieved it by pursuing certain complementary goals (Berkovitch & Narayanan, 1993). One example is increasing profits by accessing new markets nationally, such as a bank that acquires a chain of real estate agencies as a way of accessing customers on the property market, allowing the bank's current operations (staff selling mortgages) to access new types of consumers (people who need a mortgage but who do not currently bank with them). Organizations also often use mergers or acquisitions as a way of accessing markets in other countries (market internationalisation), and this is a common method of increasing profits (Srivastava, Shervani, & Fahey, 1988). An example is a hotel chain that acquires independently owned hotels in other countries, rebrands them, and the chain is thus able to access customers internationally. The idea of emerging markets, such as the idea that previously communist, protectionist, or developing countries are open to free market capitalism, globalisation, or industrialisation can also motivate organizations to embark on mergers or acquisitions involving companies in countries that are new to certain product or service sectors (Lebedev, Peng, Xie, & Stevens, 2015).

Another common reason why organizations embark on a merger or acquisition is the idea that an intended company is potentially profitable, but it needs a new executive team (Walsh & Kosnik, 1993). An example is a company that embarks on an acquisition then instigates a management shakeup as a way of restoring excitement or confidence about the company on the stock market. The companies pursuing such acquisitions are usually private equity firms, such as Carlyle Group or Blackstone Group, and have a buy-to-sell approach to their acquisitions. One example is the acquisition of United Defense Industries by Carlyle Group in 1997 (Pasztor, 1997). After its initial public offering at the New York Stock Exchange (Kelly, 2001), the fund exited the defence company in 2004 (United Defense Industries, 2004). Corporation tax laws can also motivate organizations to embark on mergers or acquisitions, such as laws that provide tax discounts or rebates to organizations entering certain sectors (e.g. energy efficiency or social care) (Coffee, Lowenstein, & Rose-Ackerman, 1988). Cost cutting is another common motivator for mergers or acquisitions (Chatterjee, 1986). An example is a supermarket chain that acquires a large cattle ranch business as a way of reducing the cost of beef. Deregulation laws or public policies can also motivate organizations to merge with or acquire organizations that provide products or services that were previously restricted (Boateng, Qian, & Tianle, 2008). An example is a conglomerate that acquires a house-building business after the government announces a relaxation in house-building laws, such as allowing houses to be constructed on land that was previously protected as greenbelt land. Other laws or public policies that can motivate organizations to embark on a merger or acquisition are those that liberalise the economy or encourage privatisation (Uhlenbruck & De Castro, 2000). An example is a law that allows the privatisation of an airline that was previously government-run, which inspires a private organization to acquire the airline. The principle of economies of scale can also motivate mergers or acquisitions (Lambrecht, 2004). Imagine an industrial bakery that sells pastries to cafés at the cost of £0.55 per pastry for orders of 50 to 119 pastries, or £0.35 for orders of 120 or more pastries. A chain of three cafés buys 90 pastries a day at the cost of £49.50, then sells them for £1.99 each, yielding a daily profit of £129.60. The chain works out that among the advantages of acquiring another café will be being able to buy the pastries cheaper by increasing their order to 120 pastries a day, raising the profit from £1.44 to £1.64 per pastry. Another motive for mergers or acquisitions is the desire to improve efficiency (Maksimovic & Phillips, 2001). An example is an online retailer that acquires a logistics company as a way of improving the speed with which customers receive their products. A sense of market excitement or a product or service "boom" is another common factor that motivates mergers or acquisitions (Lusyana & Sherif, 2016; Kumar & Sharma, 2019). An example is a food manufacturer inspired by the "clean eating" trend to acquire a gluten-free food brand. Financial booms that boost average wages or employment rates can increase consumer spending which, in turn, can motivate mergers with or acquisitions of businesses in retail (Carlson, 1991). Product or service "bubbles" are contexts where there are speedy rises in the profitability of certain products or services, often linked with heavily optimistic predictions about the future and therefore a motivation for a merger or acquisition (Lovallo & Kahneman, 2003). An example is an organization that sees other organizations making a lot of money on selling a certain type of insurance, based on recent rises in the numbers of customers buying that type of insurance, and assuming that the number of customers will continue to rise and, therefore, that acquiring an insurance underwriting business that provides that type of insurance is a good idea.

We notice that some entry factors seem primarily driven by an organization's circumstances or goals such as cost-cutting, economies of scale, empire building, efficiency goals, overconfidence, and inspiring shareholder confidence. These entry factors can therefore be relevant within any type of organization or sector, and we theorise that employees form their expectations about the likely success or failure of a merger or acquisition driven by these factors on a case-by-case basis. We theorise that employees remember past experiences or attitudes (including anecdotes by employees in other organizations and media reports), and that employees with negative memories or impressions about these types of mergers or acquisitions are more likely to be uncertain or cynical about the organization's ability to cut costs or improve efficiency through a merger or acquisition. In Chapter 3, we will discuss the types of negative emotions that employees exhibit and extrapolate the relevance of uncertainty and cynicism in employees' negative emotions. Chapter 4 will then discuss factors that shape employees' support for or resistance against a merger or acquisition. In subsequent chapters we will discuss the relevance of group processes of "us versus them," and culture as factors that fuel employees' resistance against a merger or acquisition. This chapter has thus helped you understand how history can contribute to employees' emotions about mergers and acquisitions, as well as their behavioural reactions – such as supporting or resisting them.

In contrast to an entry factor, an "exit factor" is something that tends to trigger the dissolution of a merger or acquisition, which we can deduce from history. A common exit factor for many mergers or acquisitions is failing to increase profits (Ravenscraft & Scherer, 1987; Kaplan & Weisbach, 1992). An example is Microsoft's exit from its acquisition of Nokia, a mobile phone company, in 2015 (Microsoft, 2016). Microsoft had tried to enter the mobile phone market by launching a Windows phone in 2010 but it did not fare as well as Microsoft hoped. Microsoft acquired Nokia in 2014 and launched a new subsidiary company, Microsoft Mobile. It launched Lumia, a new mobile phone, but its sales were not as good as Microsoft wanted, resulting in Microsoft cutting 15,000 Nokia employees' jobs and selling Nokia to another company in 2016 (Microsoft, 2016). New or unexpected costs could also be another common reason for exits from mergers or acquisitions. An example is Toshiba's failed acquisition of Westinghouse Electric, which specialised in nuclear power. Toshiba hoped that acquiring Westinghouse would allow it to enter markets outside Japan (where Toshiba already had nuclear operations). However, Toshiba encountered higher than expected construction costs (Hals, Yamazaki, & Kelly, 2017). Product or service busts can be another reason why mergers or acquisitions fail, such as when a previously popular sector declines as an opportunity to make profits (CBInsights, 2017). One example is Yahoo's exit from its acquisition of Tumblr, a social networking website. Yahoo had embarked on the acquisition because it wanted to cash in on the rise in successful social media companies but, after failing to hit idealistic sales targets of $100 million a year, Yahoo ended its acquisition of Tumblr with a loss of $712 million (Fiegerman, 2016). Other common reasons for exiting a merger or acquisition are falls in share value or stock market crashes that reduce the value of a company, or financial recessions that make certain products or services less profitable (Peel, 1995). Other reasons include government legislation that introduces regulation within a market, such as classifying a previously unregulated cosmetic or tablet as a pharmaceutical and thereby introducing new costs, regulatory compliance needs, and delays to their manufacturers (CBInsights, 2017). Government legislation introducing protectionist laws can have a similar effect (Heinemann, 2012), such as businesses that sell products manufactured overseas facing new taxes that make the products less profitable. Crises in national economies (e.g. severe inflation) or international economies (e.g. from an oil crises) can have spill-over effects in many sectors because of the rising costs of wages, transport, imports, or foreign exchange. Finally, cultural differences between organizations are another commonly reported exit factor. An example is a difference in the extent to which each side approaches workplace interactions, something that we will discuss further later on in this book. Overall, the history of exit factors in mergers and acquisitions could make employees feel fearful that organizational, national, or global events could inspire an organization to back out of a merger or acquisition (with potential job losses in the process), or cut jobs to maintain profits by reducing staffing costs. This leads to what we can say are employees' ideas, stereotypes, or expectations about common casualties in mergers and acquisitions that further explain why employees tend to have negative emotions and behavioural reactions.

The next few chapters will discuss common human casualties of mergers or acquisitions from a psychological point of view. Although there are many studies about employees' experiences, feelings, and behavioural responses to mergers or acquisitions, this is the first book to help readers understand the overall picture about the psychological impact of mergers or acquisitions on employees by drawing on published evidence. This will be the focus of the next few chapters within this book, starting with our systematic review of published studies showing the range of negative emotions that employees experience about a merger or acquisition in the next chapter.

Conclusion

In this chapter, we discussed the history of mergers and acquisitions, and the way that market bubbles or supportive legislation tended to increase the numbers of mergers and acquisitions, whereas stock market crashes, oil crises, bubble bursts, and other national or global economic events have tended to reduce their numbers. Mergers and acquisitions used to be popular as a way of achieving a monopoly, but competition laws forced organizations to shift to types of deals that use legal loopholes or that involve other countries. We discussed why employees can experience fear and other negative emotions about an impending merger or acquisition within the organization that they work for by looking at the history of mergers and acquisitions nationally or globally, as well as by developing stereotypes from the media or other employees that were inspired by historical events. This leads us to explore the empirical evidence about what emotions employees experience – both positive and negative – through a systematic review of published studies about the topic within Chapter 3.

3 Psychobiology of human emotions, why employees experiencing mergers or acquisitions feel fear, anger, and other negative emotions, and a new assessment toolkit

In Chapter 1, we explored the different types of mergers and acquisitions, helping you understand their structure and objectives from the perspective of businesses and business operations, as well as giving you an appreciation of their complexity as major organizational events. Chapter 1 set the foundation for understanding why mergers and acquisitions can often leave employees feeling confused or uncertain about what is going to happen, and Chapter 2 then helped you understand their history as organizational events that can rise or fall in popularity depending on laws, fertile market conditions, national or global economic crises, and product or service booms or busts. History has shaped the way that the public, including employees, think about mergers or acquisitions as events that could lead to job losses, site closures, culture clashes, or drastic changes in management. Chapter 2 set the foundation for understanding why employees can feel scared about an impending or ongoing merger or acquisition, and why emotions are the focus of this chapter. Emotions are subjective and therefore what matters from a psychological perspective is not the hard fact of whether a merger or acquisition is good or bad, or the actual probability of job losses or other negative outcomes. For some employees a change in management after an acquisition might be great news, whereas for other employees it might be terrible news because they liked the previous management. Therefore, you can see why mergers and acquisitions have a range of emotional outcomes for employees, as you will discover in our systematic review of the published evidence within this chapter. As psychologists, we focus on this human side of mergers and acquisitions not just because it is fascinating but also because there is no known review of employees' emotional reactions to mergers and acquisitions. We use a systematic review method of analysing and synthesising the literature. We argue that understanding employees' emotions is an important gateway to understanding what employees will *do* – something that we briefly discuss towards the end of this chapter, and that we explore further in Chapter 4 (e.g. on employees quitting) and Chapter 5 (e.g. on "us versus them" behaviours). Moreover, what employees feel is important in and of itself because employees' emotions are an important component of their occupational health (Warr, Bindl, Parker, & Inceoglu, 2013;

Bakker & Oerlemans, 2012). We conceptualise mergers or acquisitions as events that trigger strong emotions among many employees, therefore this chapter will help you explore the empirical evidence in the field showing the different types of emotions commonly displayed by employees. The evidence suggests that negative emotions are quite prevalent and they include shock, fear, anger, and uncertainty. We therefore label them, collectively, as "emotional distress." This chapter will then help you understand how to use a new psychometric tool that we have developed from our systematic review, so that you can help organizations and employees measure emotional distress after a merger or acquisition. This chapter will also help you recognise the causes and consequences of employees' emotional distress from a merger or acquisition, including quitting their jobs, looking for another job, withdrawing effort from work, and various counterproductive workplace behaviours. First, let us begin this chapter by understanding what human emotions are.

The psychobiology of human emotions

In human psychology, emotions are also commonly known as "affect," and some authors define an emotion as a person's psychobiological response to an internal or external trigger (Russell & Barrett, 1999; Watson & Tellegen, 1985). The word "psychobiological" means anything happening within a person's mind, brain, and body. Defining emotions biologically might include reactions or processes within cells, organs, across pathways within the body (e.g. the autonomous nervous system), and it can involve hormones or neurotransmitters that change the way that the brain or body reacts. Emotions are therefore partly biological events or processes and partly psychological events or processes, a view proposed by Russell (1980). Emotions can also be defined as the brain and the body's reaction to pleasantness or unpleasantness, and the brain or body's reaction to activation or deactivation (see also Russell, 2003; Mäkikangas, Feldt, & Kinnunen, 2007). The difference between a pleasant and an unpleasant trigger is easy to understand. For example, a pay raise (pleasant) versus a pay cut (unpleasant), or an announcement that jobs are safe (pleasant) versus an announcement that an organization will make some people redundant (unpleasant). Of course, people can vary in what they define as pleasant or unpleasant, and, therefore, what matters in understanding their emotions is their subjective experience of an event. The difference between activation and deactivation is more nuanced in that it concerns psychological or biological events or processes that signify (to a person) the need to behave in a certain way or take action (which is called activation) or no need to take action (which is called deactivation). For example, an employee who reads an email announcing that his organization is about to be acquired by an organization with a reputation for savage cost-cutting might experience faster heartbeats and a feeling within their body of unease, together with shock and fear, which we can call being in a state of emotional activation. An emotion, therefore, is unlikely to be a discrete psychological or biological event, but rather, a summation of how a person's mind, body, and brain have reacted. This is why, within this chapter, we concentrate on theories that acknowledge the psychobiology of human emotions.

What other theories are there about human emotions? There are two broad theoretical perspectives defining human emotions. One theoretical perspective can be called the "individual emotion" approach because it comprises of different theories about different types of emotions as separate entities, each with unique defining characteristics and certain consequences for the people feeling them that mean that different emotions are thought to have different consequences. For example, Ekman (1984, 1999) and Ekman and Friesen (1978) famously researched six basic human emotions that are common across different cultures and languages in terms of how they are expressed or recognised on a face. The six emotions in this body of work are anger, fear, surprise, disgust, sadness, and happiness, contributing a new theory of what are called "primary" human emotions (Ekman, 1984, 1999; see Hofmann & Doan, 2018 for a review). Another example of a theory within the individual emotion approach is research into what can be called more complex or secondary emotions, such as guilt or shame, and the difference between them in a range of circumstances and cultures (Giner-Sorolla, Kamau, & Castano, 2010; Demoulin et al., 2004; Fischer & Manstead, 2000). From the perspective of understanding how to theorise emotions in mergers and acquisitions, it will be very important for future literature to explore each of the most common emotions extensively because that will enrich knowledge about what each emotion means psychologically, biologically, and behaviourally. At present, however, the field is relatively new, therefore examining individual emotions arising from a merger or acquisition is less urgent than a systematic review of all the possible emotions expressed by employees about mergers or acquisitions. To our knowledge, this is the first systematic review of its kind.

In contrast to these theories about specific or individual emotions is a broader, holistic, theoretical perspective which conceptualises emotions in terms of psychobiology. We argue that, because of the wide range of emotions evoked by a merger or acquisition as a triggering event, the state of current research lends itself to this broader, holistic method of understanding emotions. Earlier on in this section we introduced and defined emotions in terms of psychobiology and we discussed an emotion as something that can be manifest within the mind, brain, or body, at the level of cells, organs, pathways, and so on. Psychobiological perspectives about emotions are certainly compatible with both individual theories about emotions and other broader theories about emotions. In the case of mergers and acquisitions, where the current evidence only allows a broad theory about emotions, we can apply a psychobiological perspective called circumplex theory (Russell, 1980; Posner, Russell, & Peterson, 2005) that broadly clusters human emotions in terms of whether they are positive or negative affective states. Circumplex theory argues that we can understand any given emotion in the same way by viewing it as a person's psychological interpretation of certain types of physiological activation within their brain and body. Examples of physiological activation are neural alerts within the brain or stress hormones, such as cortisol, which increases blood glucose levels or adrenaline, which in turn increases heart rate and blood pressure. Physiological activation can be said to alert the brain and the result could be a psychological change in mood, alertness, an emotion, or cognitions, such as memories. Posner et al. (2005) proposed that we can classify what is happening to the brain and body in two ways. We need to classify the "valence" of what is happening by placing a person's psychological and physiological state somewhere on a continuum between positive valence (e.g. pleasure) and negative valence (e.g. displeasure). We also need to classify the "alertness" or "activation" within the person by placing their psychobiological state somewhere on a continuum between low activation or arousal and high activation or arousal. For instance, the circumplex model proposes that happiness and excitement are high in pleasantness and moderate to high in arousal, whereas it proposes that boredom is moderate to high in unpleasantness and low in arousal, while nervousness is high in both arousal and unpleasantness (Posner et al., 2005). The circumplex theory argues that people rarely experience just one emotion at a time and therefore that it is often more accurate to conceptualise a person's emotional state along the two simplified continuums. The circumplex model fits with theories about how people react to stressful situations, such as Selye's theory (1936) of the General Adaptation Syndrome, which likewise explains the body's physical responses, including the production of stress hormones. Emotions and other stress responses could contribute to poor physical or mental health by evoking physiological reactions that reduce immunity, raise fight or flight physiological responses, and make people more susceptible to mental or physical illnesses (Pennebaker, 1995; Stewart-Brown, 1998).

Circumplex theory is supported by evidence from neuroscience and psychopathology (that is, the study of mental disorders), and it is a theory thought to explain why emotions are broadly linked to physical and mental health better than some other theoretical approaches to emotions (Posner et al., 2005). Although neuroscience research has yet to conclusively pinpoint all the brain regions that are responsible for processing emotions, evidence implicates the prefrontal cortex (Bechara, Damasio, Damasio, & Anderson, 1994) and amygdala (Davidson & Irwin, 1999) as areas of the brain that are critical in helping both the perception of emotions and the production of emotional responses. In terms of the continuum of positive to negative valence, the circumplex theory by Posner et al. (2005) implicates the mesolimbic dopamine pathway as an important area of the brain for emotions because it includes nerve cells that release dopamine to other cells. Dopamine is a neurotransmitter that sends signals about reward and other pleasurable states. The mesolimbic dopamine pathway is said, by the circumplex theory, to connect with the hippocampus and amygdala, which have memory and emotional functions, and the prefrontal cortex, which is involved in a range of cognitive processes. In terms of the continuum from low activation or arousal to high activation or arousal, Posner et al. (2005) propose an "arousal network" that starts with a sensory stimulus that activates the thalamus. The thalamus is grey matter within the brain whose function is to relay sensory signals and regulate consciousness, including levels of alertness and sleep. The activation of the thalamus then activates the amygdala, then the parietal cortex, an area of the brain that makes sense of sensory information by classifying it as a sound, smell, taste, or other. The theory suggests that activation of the thalamus also leads to activation of the primary sensory cortex (which is involved in locating touch and other physical sensation on different parts of the body), the association cortex (which is involved in making sense of objects), and the frontal cortex (which regulates motor functions such as body movements, memories about tasks or emotions, and has many dopamine-receptive neural cells). Additionally, circumplex theory suggests that activation of the amygdala and parietal cortex each lead to activation of the reticular network, or neural cells from many different parts of the brain relevant to alertness, which in turn activates the primary sensory cortex, the association cortex, and the frontal cortex. Circumplex theory is supported by evidence in many ways, but we must also note the limitations of methods common in cognitive neuroscience. Brain imaging techniques, like functional magnetic resonance imaging, are not always reliable in showing a cause and effect connection between the brain and emotions (Vul, Harris, Winkielman, & Pashler, 2009).

The crucial take-home message, in applying the circumplex theory to understanding how employees react to mergers or acquisitions, is that emotionally relevant stimuli trigger a complex series of brain reactions. These, in turn, trigger a wide variety of psychological reactions (e.g. cognitive processes such as memory, emotions), physiological reactions (e.g. a higher heart rate or blood sugar to energise the body), and physical reactions (e.g. running away, quitting a job, having an argument with another employee). It explains why employees could experience many different emotions simultaneously after a merger or acquisition, and why the range of emotions should be broadly conceptualised as negative or positive. This chapter sets the foundation for understanding the wide range of consequences of mergers or acquisitions discussed in subsequent chapters.

Systematic review of emotions in mergers or acquisitions

Let us now explore the wide range of emotions observed among employees about mergers or acquisitions by researchers who have published their results. We use a technique called a systematic review as a step towards a comprehensive overview of all the literature within the field. Published literature shows that employees experience a range of emotions before, during, and after a merger or acquisition. Table 3.1, which follows, summarises published studies about the topic, giving you an overview of what type of industry the merger or acquisition involved, how many employees took part in the research, what type of method the researchers used, and what their results show. Giving employees a questionnaire survey is one example of cross-sectional research. It is so called because it captures psychological concepts in one segment of time. Observational studies and interviews also tend to capture one segment of time, but the difference between them and cross-sectional research is that observational and interview studies tend to gather qualitative data or quantitative data that is much more basic than many cross-sectional surveys. Longitudinal research can be a survey, an observational study, or an interview study conducted across two or more time points. An example of longitudinal research is asking employees to fill in a questionnaire just before a merger, just after, and a few months later. From the perspective of examining employees' emotions about mergers and acquisitions, each method has its advantages and disadvantages. For example, surveys can provide rich data about different emotions using valid and reliable measurement methods that have been developed in previous research (though not all researchers use such measures). However, surveys provide researchers with employees' subjective responses to questions whose answers they might feel the need to impression manage. Many researchers in psychology or related fields offer survey respondents anonymity and/or confidentiality, but some employees could still feel uncomfortable about admitting to feeling distressed or having negative emotions because of the possible stigma. Surveys, therefore, might capture an underestimate of the emotions experienced by employees, or they might tend to find that employees who are concerned about confidentiality are less likely to express negative emotions. Observational studies can be useful in allowing researchers to analyse behaviour or events in their natural environment in a way that is relatively objective. However, the validity of observational research can depend on the researcher's expertise, neutrality, and behaviour of the researcher as well as what they are looking for or measuring. Its reliability can depend on whether or not organizations or employees modify their behaviour or events because a researcher is present. Interview research has some advantages, such as allowing employees to freely express concepts that might not be captured in a structured survey, but it has the disadvantages of poor validity and reliability due to small or unrepresentative sample sizes, a lack of quantifiable data, and small quantities of qualitative data that cannot be used to analyse statistical effects including testing the probability of hypotheses or analysing the strength of effects or associations. Interview research does not reveal causality, and neither does cross-sectional or observational research (the latter two of which tend to show only prevalence, correlations, trends, or associations among data but not causality). Longitudinal research is useful in providing data that can be compared across two or more time points, which is useful in analysing increments or decrements in psychological concept and causality. For example, testing an emotion before and after an acquisition, and analysing many employees' data to test the probability that the emotion changed, can show us that the acquisition caused an increase in the emotion and, therefore, longitudinal research is one of the only few ways of testing causality. However, what counts as a cause can be difficult to pinpoint in cases where other factors change at the same time as the cause changes. The other method that can tell us about causality is an experiment which is, defined simply, a type of study that compares the same outcome in people who are in different categories (or different levels of one independent variable) or the same people at different time points. Complex experiments test how different independent variables interact in predicting an outcome, also called a dependent variable. Good experiments require tight controls which can be accomplished in laboratory human research, but rarely in natural settings such as mergers and acquisitions, and this is why they are relatively rare in the latter context. Looking at Table 3.1,

Table 3.1 Systematic review of emotions in mergers and acquisitions

Emotion	Ref.	Research design	Industry and number of employees or other workers	Methodology
Mergers and acquisitions (M&As) change employees' feelings of commitment to the organization.	Armstrong-Stassen and Cameron (2003)	Longitudinal research	159 Healthcare	Quantitative
	Shimei and Yaodong (2013)	Cross-sectional research	210 Multi-sector	Quantitative
	Rafferty and Restubog (2010)	Longitudinal research	155 Real estate	Quantitative
	Kovoor-Misra and Smith (2011)	Cross-sectional research	71 Multi-sector/ CEOs	Quantitative
	Bartunek and Franzak (1988)	Longitudinal research	473 NGOs	Quantitative
	Schweiger and Denisi (1991)	Longitudinal research	147 Manufacturing	Quantitative
	Cartwright and Cooper (1993)	Cross-sectional research	157 Financial	Quantitative
	Weber (1996)	Cross-sectional	129 Multi-sector/ Management	Quantitative
	Terry, Carey, and Callan (2001)	Cross-sectional research	445 Aviation	Quantitative
	Cartwright, Tytherleigh, and Robertson (2007)	Longitudinal research	336 Higher education	Quantitative
	Klendauer and Deller (2009)	Cross-sectional research	128 Multi-sector/ Management	Quantitative
	Joslin, Waters, and Dudgeon (2010)	Cross-sectional research	250 Communication	Quantitative
	Nikolaou, Vakola, and Bourantas (2011)	Cross-sectional research	327/285 Technology	Quantitative
	Michela and Vena (2012)	Cross-sectional research	62 Banking	Quantitative
M&As change employees' emotional attachment to the organization	Chun and Davies (2010)	Cross-sectional research	128 Technology	Quantitative
M&As make employees feel hopeful	Burlew, Pederson, and Bradley (1994)	Structured interviews	6 Retail	Quantitative

(Continued)

Table 3.1 (Continued)

Emotion	Ref.	Research design	Industry and number of employees or other workers	Methodology
M&As change employees' feelings of motivation at work	Clarke and Salleh (2011)	Observational/ Semi-structured interviews	33 Financial	Qualitative
	Teerikangas (2012)	Observational/ Interviews	141 Multi-sector	Qualitative
M&As make employees angry	Burlew et al. (1994)	Structured interviews	6 Retail	Qualitative
M&As make employees feel anxious	Empson (2001)	Observational/ Semi-structured interviews	92 Consulting	Qualitative
	Styhre, Börjesson, and Wickenberg (2006)	Interviews	28 Automotive/ Healthcare	Qualitative
	Rafferty and Restubog (2010)	Longitudinal research	155 Real estate	Quantitative
	Lupina-Wegener (2013)	Semi-structured interviews	6 Financial	Qualitative
	Maguire and Phillips (2008)	Interviews	15 Financial	Qualitative
	Astrachan (2004)	Cross-sectional research	119 Higher education	Quantitative
	Lawlor (2013)	Observational/ Semi-structured interviews	41 Higher education	Qualitative
	Drori, Wrzesniewski, and Ellis (2013)	Semi-structured interviews	41 Information technology	Qualitative/ Other
M&As make employees feel betrayed	Brown and Humphreys (2003)	Semi-structured interviews	75 Higher education	Qualitative
	Searle and Ball (2004)	Interviews	6 Food industry	Qualitative
	Teram (2010)	Observational study/ Interviews	Hotels & Restaurants	Qualitative
M&As make employees feel burnout	Idel et al. (2003)	Longitudinal research	93 Healthcare	Quantitative
	Armstrong-Stassen and Cameron (2003)	Longitudinal research	159 Healthcare	Quantitative

(*Continued*)

Emotion	Ref.	Research design	Industry and number of employees or other workers	Methodology
M&As make employees feel confused	McEntire and Bentley (1996)	Interviews	63 Travel/Tourism	Qualitative
	Shearer, Hames, and Runge (2001)	Observational study/ Interviews	Chemical	Qualitative
	Carter and Pavur (2003)	Observational study/ Interviews	12 Manufacturing	Qualitative
	Lundbäck and Hört (2005)	Observational study/ Interviews	65 Automotive	Qualitative
M&As make employees feel emotionally distressed	Idel et al. (2003)	Longitudinal research	93 Healthcare	Quantitative
	Barratt-Pugh, Bahn, and Gakere (2013)	Semi-structured interviews	302 Public sector	Qualitative
M&As make employees feel fearful	Kavanagh and Ashkanasy (2006)	Observational/ Interviews	123 Higher education	Qualitative
	Meyer (2006)	Semi-structured interviews	49 Financial	Qualitative
	Clark, Gioia, Ketchen, and Thomas (2010)	Semi-structured interviews	33 Healthcare	Qualitative
	Goddard and Palmer (2010)	Unstructured interviews	49 Healthcare	Qualitative
	Junni (2011)	Cross-sectional research	103 Multi-sector	Quantitative
	Mirc (2012)	Interviews	25 Recruitment	Qualitative
M&As make employees feel frustrated	Greenwood, Hinings, and Brown (1994)	Semi-structured interviews	59–44 Financial	Qualitative
	Siegel (2000)	Interviews	28 Financial	Qualitative
	Minbaeva and Muratbekova-Touron (2011)	Interviews	Utilities	Qualitative
	Langley et al. (2012)	Interviews	18/21 Healthcare	Qualitative
	Shearer et al. (2001)	Observational study/ Interviews	Chemical	Qualitative

(*Continued*)

Table 3.1 (Continued)

Emotion	Ref.	Research design	Industry and number of employees or other workers	Methodology
M&As make employees feel insecure	Bartels, Douwes, de Jong, and Pruyn (2006)	Cross-sectional research	250 Public sector	Quantitative
	Guerrero (2008)	Longitudinal	56 Industrial	Quantitative
M&As give employees other types of negative emotions	Vaara (2000)	Semi-structured interviews	208 Multi-sector/ Management	Qualitative
	Fugate, Kinicki, and Scheck (2002)	Longitudinal research	81 Airline	Quantitative
	van Dick, Wagner, and Lemmer (2004)	Cross-sectional research	459 Healthcare	Quantitative
M&As make employees feel psychologically distressed	Joslin et al. (2010)	Cross-sectional research	250 Communication	Quantitative
M&As make employees feel resentment	Lee, Kim, Kim, Kwon, and Cho (2013)	Cross-sectional research	271 Technology	Quantitative
	Clarke and Salleh (2011)	Semi-structured interviews	33 Financial	Qualitative
M&As make employees feel shocked	Burlew et al. (1994)	Structured interviews	6 Retail	Qualitative
M&As make employees feel stressed	Terry and Callan (1998)	Cross-sectional research	1104 Healthcare	Quantitative
	Schweiger and Denisi (1991)	Longitudinal research	147 Manufacturing	Quantitative
	Amiot, Terry, Jimmieson, and Callan (2006)	Longitudinal research	220 Airline	Quantitative
	Cartwright and Cooper (1993)	Cross-sectional	157 Financial	Quantitative
	Greenwood et al. (1994)	Semi-structured interviews	59–44 Financial	Qualitative
	Harwood and Ashleigh (2005)	Observational/ Interviews	33 Healthcare	Qualitative
	Dumond (2005)	Cross-sectional research	238 Public sector	Quantitative
	Cartwright et al. (2007)	Longitudinal research	336 Higher education	Quantitative
	Makri and Hantzi (2012)	Cross-sectional research	140 Not reported	Quantitative

Emotion	Ref.	Research design	Industry and number of employees or other workers	Methodology
M&As make employees feel suspicious	Burlew et al. (1994)	Structured interviews	6 Retail	Qualitative
M&As make employees feel tense	Maguire and Phillips (2008)	Interviews	15 Financial	Qualitative
M&As make employees feel threatened	Amiot, Terry, and Callan (2007)	Longitudinal research	215 Airline	Quantitative
	Zhou, Shin, and Cannella (2008)	Cross-sectional research	403 Multi-sector	Quantitative
	Clark et al. (2010)	Semi-structured interviews	33 Healthcare	Qualitative
	van Vuuren, Beelen, and de Jong (2010)	Semi-structured interviews	31 Higher education	Qualitative
	Lupina-Wegener, Schneider, and van Dick (2011)	Semi-structured interviews	37/890 Healthcare	Qualitative
	Jacobs, Oliver, and Heracleous (2013)	Experimental	Telecom	Qualitative
M&As make employees feel uneasy	Burlew et al. (1994)	Structured interviews	6 Retail	Qualitative
M&As make employees feel worried	Terry and Callan (1998)	Cross-sectional research	1104 Healthcare	Quantitative
	Kovoor-Misra and Smith (2011)	Cross-sectional research	19 Retail	Quantitative
M&As affect whether employees feel included	Harwood and Ashleigh (2005)	Observational/ Interviews	33 Healthcare	Qualitative
	Bellou (2007)	Cross-sectional research	255 Multi-sector	Quantitative
M&As affect employees' feelings of psychological safety	Nemanich and Vera (2009)	Cross-sectional research	453 Industrial	Quantitative
M&As affect employees' feelings of satisfaction	Schweiger and Denisi (1991)	Longitudinal research	147 Manufacturing	Quantitative
	Cartwright and Cooper (1993)	Cross-sectional research	157 Financial	Quantitative
	Peck, Towell, and Gulliver (2001)	Longitudinal research	143 Healthcare	Quantitative

(*Continued*)

Table 3.1 (Continued)

Emotion	Ref.	Research design	Industry and number of employees or other workers	Methodology
	Gulliver, Towell, and Peck (2003)	Longitudinal research	86 Healthcare	Quantitative
	Brown and Humphreys (2003)	Semi-structured interviews	75 Higher education	Qualitative
	van Dick, Wagner, and Lemmer (2004)	Cross-sectional research	459 Healthcare	Quantitative
	Nikandrou and Papalexandris (2007)	Cross-sectional research	135 Multi-sector	Quantitative
	Guerrero (2008)	Longitudinal research	56 Industrial	Quantitative
	Nikolaou et al. (2011)	Cross-sectional research	327/285 Technology	Quantitative
	Colman and Lunnan (2011)	Interviews	47 Technology	Qualitative
	Covin, Sightler, Kolenko, and Tudor (1996)	Cross-sectional research	2845 Manufacturing	Quantitative
	Fischer, Greitemeyer, Omay, and Frey (2007)	Cross-sectional research	82 Higher education	Quantitative
	Wickramasinghe and Karunaratne (2009)	Cross-sectional research	109 Financial	Quantitative
	Marmenout (2010)	Cross-sectional research	81 Higher education	Quantitative
M&As make employees feel depressed	Väänänen, Ahola, Koskinen, Pahkin, and Kouvonen (2011)	Longitudinal research	6511 Multi-sector	Quantitative
M&As make employees feel devalued	Ray and McGee (2006)	Interviews	46 Healthcare	Qualitative
	Collins and Wickham (2002)	Interviews	53 Retail/Financial	Qualitative
	van Dijk and van Dick (2009)	Semi-structured interviews	23 Legal services	Qualitative
	Piekkari, Vaara, Tienari, and Säntti (2005)	Ethnography/ Unstructured interviews	8 Financial	Qualitative
	Vaara, Tienari, Piekkari, and Säntti (2005)	Observational study/ Interviews	24 Financial	Qualitative

Emotion	Ref.	Research design	Industry and number of employees or other workers	Methodology
M&As make employees feel disappointed	Searle and Ball (2004)	Interviews	6 Food industry	Qualitative
	Kiessling, Harvey, and Moeller (2012)	Cross-sectional research	92 Multi-sector	Quantitative
M&As make employees feel emotionally exhausted	Terry et al. (2001)	Cross-sectional research	445 Airline	Quantitative
	Peck et al. (2001)	Longitudinal research	143 Healthcare	Quantitative
	Väänänen, Pahkin, Kalimo, and Buunk (2004)	Longitudinal research	7850 Multi-sector	Quantitative
M&As make employees feel gloomy	Randall and Procter (2013)	Cross-sectional research	20 Public sector	Qualitative/ N/A
M&As make employees feel helpless	Fried, Tiegs, Naughton, and Ashforth (1996)	Longitudinal research	91 Services industry	Quantitative
M&As make employees feel hurt	Burlew et al. (1994)	Structured interviews	6 Retail	Qualitative
M&As make employees feel isolated	Harwood and Ashleigh (2005)	Observational/ Interviews	33 Healthcare	Qualitative
	Langley et al. (2012)	Interviews	18/21 Healthcare	Qualitative
M&As make employees feel demoralised	Siegel (2000)	Interviews	28 Financial	Qualitative
	Goddard and Palmer (2010)	Unstructured interviews	49 Healthcare	Qualitative
M&As make employees feel nostalgic	Lawlor (2013)	Observational/ Semi-structured interviews	41 Higher education	Qualitative
M&As make employees feel overloaded	Makri and Ntalianis (2015)	Cross-sectional research	140 Financial	Quantitative
M&As make employees feel rejected	Burlew et al. (1994)	Structured interviews	6 Retail	Qualitative
	Searle and Ball (2004)	Interviews	6 Food industry	Qualitative
M&As make employees feel sadness	Lawlor (2013)	Observational/ Semi-structured interviews	41 Higher education	Qualitative
M&As make employees feel various forms of affect	Bhal, Bhaskar, and Ratnam (2009)	Cross-sectional research	225 Financial	Quantitative
	Jetten, Duck, Terry, and O'Brien (2002)	Cross-sectional research	153 Higher education	Quantitative

you can see that only one study has used an experiment, and that most of the existing research into employees' emotions about a merger or acquisition use cross-sectional, observational, interview, or longitudinal methods.

We can extrapolate from the various studies (see Table 3.1) that common emotional reactions to mergers or acquisitions among employees are anger, anxiety, resentment, hope, motivation, shock, anxiety, worry, excitement, changing feelings of commitment or emotional attachment, feeling burnout, betrayal, confusion, distressed, afraid, frustrated, insecure, stressed, suspicious, threatened, excluded, uneasy, disappointed, psychologically unsafe, depressed, nostalgic, tense, overloaded, sad, and other largely negative emotions.

Here are some examples illustrating the methods and findings of research within the field. Aside from the common emotions of fear, anger, and confusion, which are unsurprising emotional reactions (see Chapter 2), let us look at some less easily predicted but common emotional reactions such as employees' feelings of commitment towards and motivation within the organization. Terry et al. (2001) carried out a cross-sectional study among 445 employees in a merged airline to explore their responses from an intergroup perspective. They analysed the differences in terms of affective commitment and the study compared low-status and high-status employees – a statistical technique called ANOVA (analysis of variance). ANOVA tests whether two or more groups of people differ significantly on a certain dimension of interest. Results showed that employees with a low status in the merged organization were less committed to the organization compared to the employees in the high-status position. Another study (Klendauer & Deller, 2009) was conducted among 128 managers from 37 companies involved in domestic or cross-border mergers and acquisitions. Correlational analysis by the authors showed that perceptions of distributive, procedural, and interactional justice were positively associated with employees' feelings of effective commitment to the organization. Another study involving 160 employees in a cross-border acquisition between an American and a German firm (Chun & Davies, 2010) showed that tenure negatively correlated with employee emotional attachment. That is, the longer the employee has worked for the organization, the less they were emotionally attached to the organization after the acquisition. The authors also explored the relevance of the corporate reputation of the firm. Corporate reputation was conceptualised in terms of warmth (i.e. the belief that the organization is caring and supportive), integrity (i.e. the belief that the organization is being honest in its interactions with employees), empathy (i.e. the belief that the organization can understand employees' feelings and needs), and conscientiousness (i.e. the belief that the organization provides security to employees and is a reliable firm). The four measures of corporate reputation were found to be positively associated with emotional attachment. Interviews with employees in a merger between two banking institutions following a restructuring (Clarke & Salleh, 2011) revealed that employees lost their motivation, and they felt worried and had emotional strain. These effects were still felt by the employees ten months after the restructuring measures had been taken.

Burnout and emotional distress also appear to be common emotional responses among employees to changes brought about by a merger or an acquisition

(Idel et al., 2003). In a study among 93 nurses from two hospitals in Israel, Idel et al. collected response data when the merger was announced and six months after the merger's completion. While from time one to time two authors found no significant difference in terms of burnout or stress, they observed a significant difference between groups of nurses. More specifically, nurses who had to relocate to the new hospital were more emotionally distressed than the employees who did not have to relocate. Employees who felt more stressed by the merger and threatened by its outcomes also felt more burned out, had more adjustment difficulties, and cited lack of physical or mental strength. The regression analysis carried out by Armstrong-Stassen and Cameron (2003) in a similar study setting (i.e. a hospital merger) showed that burned-out employees were unable to make use of control-oriented coping strategies. Prior coping resources facilitated the use of control-oriented coping. Control-oriented coping involves thinking in positive terms about a stressful situation, having a problem-solving approach to the stressful situation, and seeking help or information (Latack, 1986). Prior coping resources were conceptualised as personal control (i.e. employees felt like they were capable of manage the merger situation), organizational support (i.e. the perception that the organization addresses employees' feelings and needs and provides a sense of psychological safety), and affective commitment. Therefore, organizations need to provide a sense of psychological safety in order to make sure employees have the necessary resources to manage stressful situations in mergers and acquisitions. A healthy environment where employees feel understood, are empowered to voice their opinions, and are included in the decision-making process with a leader that has a transformational style were found to be associated with innovation success, efficiency, and a feedback learning culture (Nemanich & Vera, 2009).

Therefore, we can conclude from the systematic review of many published studies that employees experiencing mergers and acquisitions frequently experience negative emotions such as fear, anger, confusion, distress, lower attachment to the organization, feeling demoralised, devalued, and uncertain. Few studies show positive emotions, but we must note that there might be what is called a "bias" within the literature in what emotions researchers decide to measure, and in what studies tend to be published. It may be that few researchers decide to conduct research into positive emotions about mergers or acquisitions. We therefore recommend that researchers start measuring a range of both positive and negative emotions, and publishing data about the prevalence of each among employees experiencing a merger or acquisition. Until such studies are published in the future, we have developed a tool that captures the emotions discovered during the systematic review that consultants and other practitioners can use to assess employees' emotional reactions to a merger or acquisition.

How to assess employees' emotions about a merger or acquisition

Based on the emotions uncovered in our systematic review, we have developed an assessment tool that you can use to test the range and severity of emotions experienced by employees after a merger or acquisition. For example, you may be a human resource professional, manager, occupational health professional, or consultant tasked with investigating how employees feel about a merger or acquisition. It is important for you to measure employees' emotional responses to mergers or acquisitions on a continuum, across different time points, and to use a tool such as our new Employee Emotion Assessment Toolkit (EEAT; Kamau & Oancea, 2020b). We also recommend that you supplement this with a measure of a range of positive emotions so that you gain a balanced view of both positive and negative emotions. The EEAT is derived from our systematic review of published studies, but we noted the infrequency of research about positive emotions and called for further research about both positive and negative emotions among employees experiencing a merger or acquisition.

The EEAT is a useful method of troubleshooting employees' emotions after the announcement of a merger or acquisition, and throughout the process. Ideally, we recommend using the troubleshooting toolkit as a self-assessment method that you ask employees to use as way of identifying and monitoring their emotional responses in a way that remains confidential to them. You should, of course, then provide appropriate support for the employees, such as through group support sessions, peer-to-peer support, and management interventions (e.g. giving employees more information or allowing them to be involved in planning the merger or acquisition as a way of addressing their fears, uncertainties, or anger). Alternatively, when used as a group troubleshooting toolkit, we recommend ensuring that employees are able to self-assess their emotions confidentially and anonymously, with data analysed only as group metrics (average score per organization, department, team, job role, etc.).

Employee Emotion Assessment Toolkit (EEAT)

Copyright notice

Instructions to researchers or consultants getting organization-level data

Present each employee with the following questionnaire in paper format or as an online survey that they will fill in individually, confidentially, and anonymously. This will maximise employees' honesty about their emotions. We recommend you provide an anonymous drop-off box in which employees can post their paper questionnaires. If you administer the questionnaire online, we recommend that you do not request an employee's name or identifying details. You will then need to input the data into a statistical software package (e.g. SPSS) to reverse-code the appropriate items, and analyse organization-level trends. When you present the questionnaire, please omit [R] to prevent employees from being aware that some items are reverse-coded.

Instructions to researchers or consultants getting individual-level data

To assess employees' emotions as individuals, we recommend that you present each employee with the following questionnaire in paper format. Allow them to complete it privately and code the questionnaire such that an independent person (e.g. a consultant, and not the employee's manager) is able to match the questionnaire with an employee to maximise employees' honesty about their emotions and to assure them that their questionnaire will not be used for adverse reasons (e.g. making redundancy decisions). You will then need to manually reverse-code the data and calculate each employee's score or, alternatively, process all employees' scores and reverse-code appropriate items using a software package such as SPSS. When you present the questionnaire, please omit [R] to prevent employees from being aware that some items are reverse-coded.

Employee Emotion Assessment Toolkit (EEAT)

Instructions to employees

Your organization is currently undergoing a merger or acquisition. Think about how this makes you feel, on average, on a scale from 0 to 6. Give each item a number (0, 1, 2, 3, 4, 5, or 6):

Never	*Very rarely*	*Rarely*	*Sometimes*	*Often*	*Very often*	*Always*
0	1	2	3	4	5	6

1 The merger or acquisition makes me feel angry. [R]
2 The merger or acquisition makes me feel anxious. [R]
3 The merger or acquisition makes me feel betrayed. [R}
4 The merger or acquisition makes me feel burnout. [R]

5   The merger or acquisition makes me feel confused. [R]
6   The merger or acquisition makes me feel emotionally distressed. [R]
7   The merger or acquisition makes me feel fearful. [R]
8   The merger or acquisition makes me feel frustrated [R]
9   The merger or acquisition makes me feel hopeful.
10   The merger or acquisition makes me feel excluded. [R]
11   The merger or acquisition makes me feel insecure. [R]
12   The merger or acquisition makes me feel emotionally attached to this organization.
13   The merger or acquisition makes me feel committed to working here.
14   The merger or acquisition makes me feel motivated.
15   The merger or acquisition makes me feel negative emotions. [R]
16   The merger or acquisition makes me feel psychologically safe.
17   The merger or acquisition makes me feel psychologically distressed. [R]
18   The merger or acquisition makes me feel resentful. [R]
19   The merger or acquisition makes me feel satisfied.
20   The merger or acquisition makes me feel shocked. [R]
21   The merger or acquisition makes me feel stressed. [R]
22   The merger or acquisition makes me feel suspicious. [R]
23   The merger or acquisition makes me feel tense. [R]
24   The merger or acquisition makes me feel threatened. [R]
25   The merger or acquisition makes me feel uneasy. [R]
26   The merger or acquisition makes me feel worried. [R]

Employee Emotion Assessment Toolkit (EEAT)

Scoring instructions

These instructions should not be shown to employees while they are filling in the questionnaire. First, reverse-code the items labelled [R], such that an employee who scores 0 gets 6, 1 gets 5, 2 gets 4, 3 gets 3, 4 get 2, 5 gets 1, and 6 gets 0. Then add up each employee's total score. Next, divide the employee's total score by 26, and round the result to the nearest whole number. Finally, place the employee in one of the following six categories. For example, an employee scoring an average of 3.2 should be placed in Category III, and an employee scoring an average of 5.6 should be placed in Category VI, and so on.

Category 0	*Category I*	*Category II*	*Category III*	*Category IV*	*Category V*	*Category VI*
Employee has no positive emotions about the merger or acquisition	Employee very rarely has positive emotions about the merger or acquisition	Employee rarely has positive emotions about the merger or acquisition	Employee sometimes has positive emotions about the merger or acquisition	Employee often has positive emotions about the merger or acquisition	Employee very often has positive emotions about the merger or acquisition	Employee always has positive emotions about the merger or acquisition

Let us now turn to the consequences of negative emotions experienced by employees for their behaviour at work and attitudes towards their jobs during or after a merger or acquisition.

Consequences of emotions in mergers and acquisitions

We can understand the consequences of the emotions experienced by employees during mergers or acquisitions by integrating the circumplex theory of emotions with theories and evidence about how people respond to emotions, including the results of our systematic review that we summarised earlier. Recall that, in circumplex theory, emotions can be understood as biopsychological states that fall somewhere on two continuums of valence (or pleasure to displeasure) and activation (from low to high arousal) (Russell, 1980; Posner et al., 2005). There is not enough research within the field of mergers or acquisitions to justify cat-egorising the emotions expressed by employees in terms of valence and activation because this might vary from one employee to another, but we can conceptualise the emotions in terms of the extent to which they are positive or negative. In the previous section, we discussed evidence showing that employees have many neg-ative emotions about mergers and acquisitions, although we do call for further research measuring positive emotions as well. We argue that an employee's emo-tional responses to a merger or acquisition start with their cognitive appraisal of the event, just as many other emotions do (Lazarus, Kanner, & Folkman, 1980; Smith & Ellsworth, 1985). An example of a cognitive appraisal is an employee thinking of a merger or acquisition as a threat to their job security. A common theme within the published evidence is that employees often think of mergers or acquisitions as threatening events because they make them feel very uncertain about the new management team (Shearer et al., 2001), new work procedures, systems or routines, and their own status within the new organization (Terry et al., 2001). When employees then experience negative emotions such as anger, shock, fear, or uncertainty, it is plausible that, by applying Carver's (2006) theory of approach/avoidance, we can extrapolate the likely consequences of negative emotions. Carver's theory suggests that when people experience negative psy-chobiological reactions they handle this by behaving in a way that deals with the trigger of the reactions (approaching it), or by going away from the trigger (avoiding it) in an attempt to reduce its unpleasant psychobiological effects. We can argue that employees feeling positive emotions about a merger or acquisition are more likely to engage in approach behaviours, such as taking part in activities connected with the event and staying employed in the organization. In con-trast, employees who experience negative emotions might feel more motivated to withdraw from the organization by going absent from work, looking for another job, and quitting. This extends the work of Gray (1990, 1994), who proposed that people have a behavioural activation system and a behavioural inhibition system (BAS, BIS; see also Carver & White, 1994, who developed questionnaires to measure them)x, and the idea that some people have an overactive or under-active BAS or BIS can explain individual differences among people including differences in how employees react to their emotions about a merger or acquisition. It is important to note that Carver (2006) did not apply the circumplex theory of emotions in developing his approach-avoidance perspective and, in fact, Carver proposed the approach-avoidance perspective as an alternative, but we argue that the two theories are not actually conceptually irreconcilable. The circumplex theory is backed by considerable brain-based evidence and Carver's perspective (together with the BAS/BIS approach) is also supported by brain-based evidence (e.g. Sutton & Davidson, 1997; Barros-Loscertales, Meseguer, & Sanjuan, 2006). The problem with theoretically separating circumplex theory from the approach/avoidance perspective, or the BAS/BIS perspective, is that it is simply too early in cognitive neuroscience as a field to eliminate either theoretical perspective because much of the evidence from neuroscience is correlational rather than causal (Vul et al., 2009). Neuroscience can tell us about the areas of the brain that are activated in certain situations or when people are experiencing certain emotions, but future evidence is needed combining neuroscience with other areas of biology and psychology, including testing causal effects on behaviours in the workplace. Current evidence does not allow us to conclusively say that one theory, and not the other, is correct. The approach-avoidance perspective fits with the broader physiological theory that parts of the brain and the sympathetic nervous system have two parallel processes – fight versus flight (e.g. Jansen, Nguyen, Karpitskiy, Mettenleiter, & Loewy, 1995). Again, this is an idea that is conceptually compatible with the circumplex theory, which draws from a wide array of evidence from neuroscience and physiology. We can liken Carver's concept of "approach" to a "fight" response, and we can liken "avoidance" with a "flight" response. Although Gray (1990) argued that the BAS/BIS are *in addition* to the fight-flight system, we argue that there is insufficient evidence to support this view. We can conclude that the approach-avoidance, BAS/BIS, and circumplex perspectives *are* compatible with general evidence from neuroscience and human physiology, justifying an integrated approach to conceptualising emotions and their potential behavioural outcomes. In other words, the two sets of theories explain emotions in ways that are not mutually exclusive. Circumplex theory explains what emotions are whereas the approach-avoidance perspective explains what emotions do.

In order to understand what emotions do, recall that some emotions activate the mesolimbic dopamine pathway, which is associated with positive feelings such as being rewarded (Posner et al., 2005). In contrast, negative emotions activate areas of the brain associated with pain (Shackman et al., 2011). This view of emotions as broadly positive or broadly negative physiological states is supported by a meta-analysis of 397 studies that used positron emission tomography or functional magnetic resonance imaging (fMRI) studies (Lindquist, Satpute, Wager, Weber, & Feldman Barrett, 2016). We propose that when mergers or acquisitions evoke positive emotions, this involves a set of enjoyable psychological and physiological reactions that motivate employees to engage in "approach" behaviours such as spending effort on the job, and organizational citizenship behaviours such as being helpful to other employees, volunteering, and working overtime. Negative emotional states involve reactions within the brain and body that in turn activate behavioural inhibition because wider evidence shows that people avoid stimuli with negative consequences, such as pain or punishment (Murphy, Nimmo-Smith, & Lawrence, 2003). Drawing on the circumplex theory and other evidence from neuroscience and physiology, we propose that when mergers or acquisitions evoke negative emotions, this involves a set of unpleasant reactions within the brain and body (e.g. the production of stress hormones) that encourage employees to engage in avoidant behaviours such as looking for other jobs, going absent from work, missing meetings, and so on. We suggest that employees who feel negative emotions such as shock, anger, or disappointment about a merger or acquisition are also likely to start withdrawing further investment in their current jobs in anticipation of the loss of rewards from that job. Behaviours associated with emotions are often reward-seeking or self-preserving (Watson, Wiese, Vaidya, & Tellegen, 1999; Carver & Harmon-Jones, 2009; Carver, 2006; Citron, Gray, Critchley, Weekes, & Ferstl, 2014), therefore employees might react to mergers or acquisitions in ways that are maladaptive (e.g. aggression, going absent from work) because of feeling overwhelmed by unpleasant physiological and brain-based responses. Negative emotions motivate people to engage in behaviours that help them restore wellbeing (Fredrickson, 2001), therefore negative emotions could be quite motivating for employees in encouraging them to move away from the stimuli causing unpleasant physiological and brain-based responses. It is therefore unsurprising that staff turnover is a common consequence of mergers or acquisitions, and we will explore this in greater detail later on in this book.

Negative emotions are also associated with counterproductive workplace behaviours such as silence, social withdrawal, and effort withdrawal (Warr et al., 2013). Anxiety can make employees avoidant (Aldao, Nolen-Hoeksema, & Schweizer, 2010), and fear or feeling threatened can make employees "freeze" and behave defensively (Blanchard, Hynd, Minke, Minemoto, & Blanchard, 2001). Frustration and feeling insecure or betrayed can make employees deliberately delay job tasks, search for distractions (Harrington, 2005), and ruminate (Rachman, 2010). Uncertainty can prompt un-collaborative workplace behaviour, interpersonal conflict with other coworkers, dips in job satisfaction, and make employees plan to leave an organization (Marmenout, 2010). Mistrust is another negative emotion that pervades mergers and acquisitions, and it can threaten the success of the merger or acquisition by hindering the smooth integration of the combining teams (Vaara, Tienari, & Säntti, 2003; Monin, Noorderhaven, Vaara, & Kroon, 2013). It is important to give employees assurances that reduce or eliminate negative emotions about a merger or acquisition (e.g. ambiguity, uncertainty, and feelings of job insecurity), without which they may "jump ship" by going back on the job market or else psychologically withdraw from work by. minimising job effort, being hostile to colleagues, or unresponsive to communications, etc. Not *all* employees will react to a merger or acquisition in the same way, even if we focus on just one emotional response. For example, whereas some studies show lower organizational commitment (Terry et al.,

2001), other studies shows that commitment does not change (Cartwright & Cooper, 1993). Therefore, researchers, consultants, and other practitioners need to troubleshoot employees' emotional responses to a merger or acquisition using methods that identify emotions at the individual level and then, subsequently, troubleshoot average emotions across organizations, job roles, teams, etc. across different time points.

Recall the new assessment tool that we have created to measure employees' emotional responses to a merger or acquisition, the Employee Emotion Assessment Toolkit (EEAT; Kamau & Oancea, 2019). This is based on our systematic review of commonly occurring emotions. Look back at the scoring instructions and the categories within the assessment tool. As a general rule of thumb, we argue that employees in Category 0 and I are most at risk of engaging in avoidant behaviours. Employees who feel highly anxious, shocked, resentful, threatened, distressed, etc. are more likely to protect themselves psychologically by planning to switch jobs, going absent, or by avoiding meetings or interactions that remind them of problems connected with the merger or acquisition (Fried et al., 1996; Ray & McGee, 2006). Therefore, if resources are low, this rule of thumb can be used to identify which employees are most in need of interventions such as one-to-one meetings that help prevent staff turnover. This make sense from a behaviourist perspective (Russell & Barrett, 1999; Warr et al., 2013) because people generally react to unpleasant situations or stimuli by leaving or avoiding the situations or stimuli in the future; therefore, it is unsurprising that employees who feel strong negative emotions about a merger or acquisition are most at risk of leaving or disengaging. We argue that employees in Category V and VI are most likely to engage in approach behaviours. Therefore, initiatives whose aim is to galvanise staff to get on board with a merger or acquisition could succeed by encouraging employees in these categories to inspire their colleagues. Of course, categorising employees according to their emotions about a merger or acquisition should not be misused for unethical ends such as making redundancy decisions, and organizations should not exploit employees in category V and VI if in fact their hopeful, optimistic emotions are unfounded (e.g. if job cuts are planned then it is important not to mislead them into thinking otherwise).

We recommend that managers, human resource professionals, occupational health professionals, consultants, other practitioners, and researchers implement interventions that help employees in Category 0, I, or II psychologically "move" into Category III emotions or above. You can do this by helping employees apply sense-making theory (e.g. Marmenout, 2010; Vaara et al., 2003). This theory would mean helping employees try to find meaning and sense of the merger or acquisition by observing cues from the organization(s), other people, and other sources of information, e.g. news reports, rumours about how an acquiring organization behaved in past acquisitions, etc. Ideally, you would help them engage in sense-making by focusing on positive rather than negative cues. What employees perceive to be happening is important because they search the unfolding events for cues that help them make causal explanations about what is happening, like: "*Is the acquiring organization making a site visit on Monday because they are thinking of closing this factory plant, just as they closed two factory plants in their last acquisition?*" Employees who already have negative emotions are probably going to interpret cues by assuming the worst because they interpret what is happening from the lens of emotions such as worry or insecurity (Kovoor-Misra & Smith, 2008; Guerrero, 2008). In this example, the explanation might be that the acquiring organization wants to make the site visit because it wants to keep the factory plant, rather than close it, but the lack of discernible cues (e.g. e-mails explaining the purpose of the visit) can cause employees more anxiety, distress, or insecurity if they already have these sorts of negative emotions about the acquisition. The approach of understanding how positively or negatively employees feel about a merger or acquisition is useful because the intensity of the emotions that employees feel determines how intensely they engage in approach or avoidant behaviours during a merger or acquisition (Gable & Harmon-Jones, 2010).

Not all negative emotions about a merger or acquisition lead to avoidant behaviours. Anger can inspire employees to engage in approach behaviours such as asking questions or trying to contribute to the fate of the merger or acquisition because, in general situations, brain-imaging studies show that anger activates the anterior cerebral region, an area commonly associated with approach behaviours (Carver & Harmon-Jones, 2009). Negative emotions that are highly arousing can actually lead to action, whereas other types of negative emotions elicit avoidance (Warr et al., 2013). It is therefore important to give employees who are angry the opportunity to engage in positive approach behaviours by consulting them and involving them in decision-making about what is going to happen as much as possible. On the whole, we encourage you to both understand employees' emotions about a merger and acquisition *and* help them "move" from negative emotions to less extremely negative or more positive emotions. This is important in helping to prevent counterproductive workplace behaviours such as withdrawal of effort, absence, and other methods that employees can use a way of coping with the negative emotions.

Conclusion

This chapter started by discussing the psychobiology of human emotions, including how they are manifest within the mind, brain, and body at the level of cells, neural pathways, and systems or processes within the body. We discussed the circumplex theory of emotions, and its compatibility with other theories of emotions such as the approach-avoidance perspective. This chapter then presented a systematic review of the state of the evidence about the emotions that employees feel in reaction to mergers or acquisitions, with much of the evidence showing that negative emotions, such as uncertainty and fear, are common. We then helped you explore ways of measuring, scoring, and classifying these emotions using the new Employee Emotion Assessment Toolkit (EEAT) if you are a manager, human resource professional, occupational health professional, consultant, or another type of practitioner (including organizational psychologists) involved with a merger or acquisition. Finally, we discussed the behavioural consequences of employees experiencing negative emotions about mergers or acquisitions, such as withdrawal or avoidance by quitting the organization or looking for another job. We will now explore employees' quitting intentions, resistance, and support (or lack of support for a merger or acquisition) in more detail in Chapter 4.

4   What makes employees support or resist a merger or acquisition, and what makes them want to quit?

In Chapters 1 and 2 we explored different types of mergers and acquisitions, and their history as organizational events that have a reputation for cutting costs by making people redundant, closing sites, and making drastic changes to the people managing an organization. Chapter 2 also discussed how mergers and acquisitions have a reputation for failing for financial and economic reasons such as a national recession, a stock market crash, or changes in what is popular with consumers or investors. Although many mergers and acquisitions succeed, it is understandable that employees may be more aware of those that failed, such as through the news, personal experience, or anecdotal evidence from other people. This can explain why many employees have negative emotions and expectations about them (see Chapter 3). Although many mergers and acquisitions have positive outcomes, it is understandable that, as the review of the evidence in Chapter 3 showed, employees experience negative emotions such as feeling afraid, uncertain, betrayed, and distressed, and some react by withdrawing the amount of effort they put into the job or quitting. The negative emotions include feeling threatened, uncertain, and mistrustful, driven by fears about redundancies or drastic changes in their job role and working practices. This raises the question of what the consequences are for employees' behaviour, as well as their support for or resistance against a merger or acquisition. This chapter fills the gap within the literature by providing a comprehensive, up-to-date review of the state of the evidence about how or when employees react to mergers or acquisitions by engaging in behaviours that support or resist an ongoing merger or acquisition. This chapter discusses evidence from the published literature about both positive and negative behavioural responses and attitudes that signify behavioural responses, such as intentions to quit among employees and managers, as well as the organizational or psychological factors that act as antecedents or correlates of the behavioural responses.

What makes employees support or resist a merger or acquisition?

One of the challenges that organizations may have when they are embarking on a merger or acquisition is persuading employees to support the idea. There are a number of published studies that collected data from employees or people involved with an organization that can tell us about what makes employees supportive or unsupportive of a merger or acquisition. The first implication of the evidence is that a leader's style of leadership during a merger or acquisition matters in helping employees support it. Shearer et al. (2001) conducted an observational study and collected interview data from the management team of a newly merged organization within the chemical industry in the United States. The study found that Chief Executive Officers (CEOs) played a crucial role in cultivating supportive behaviours among employees. The factors that influenced the extent to which employees shared and embraced the CEO's vision included: consistent organizational cultural values after the merger, structural changes, employment practices, and the CEO's leadership style. Chapter 7 will discuss the importance of leaders further, helping you learn about the characteristics of a leadership style that sets out a vision that inspires employees to support that vision. A limitation of Shearer et al.'s study is that, in reality, a CEO might have very little influence over employees "below" the level of an executive board or senior management. Each of these leaders might have a different leadership style, and therefore research is needed to tell us the extent to which the average leadership style in the organization matters. A point related to leadership is that the trustworthiness of the people managing an organization matters, and it can be related to the extent to which employees are satisfied with their jobs or the organization they work for (Nikolaou et al., 2011). Nikandrou and Papalexandris (2007) conducted a cross-sectional study of 200 employees that went through mergers and acquisitions in Greece. The study found that employees were more likely to be supportive (e.g. loyal and compliant) when their level of satisfaction was high. The study also suggested that the extent to which employees perceive the people managing an organization as trustworthy helps in cultivating their support for the merger or acquisition. However, it is plausible that the statistical relationship between employees' satisfaction and their supportiveness for a merger or acquisition depends on the type of satisfaction, and on factors that shape that satisfaction (e.g. job security, job role certainty). Additionally, job satisfaction after a merger or acquisition is not a static concept. It can change with time. Some studies suggest that employees' satisfaction with their jobs consistently declines for a few years after a merger or acquisition has taken place (Amiot et al., 2006; Amiot et al., 2007; Guerrero, 2008; Peck et al., 2001), whereas some research suggests that job satisfaction slowly increases across about two years after (Gulliver et al., 2003). Employees' support for a merger or acquisition might therefore rise or fall with time, depending on changes in their level of job satisfaction.

The second implication of the evidence is that the way that employees think of the two organizations involved as a good fit matters in cultivating employees' support for a merger or acquisition. Gleibs, Täuber, Viki, and Giessner (2013) conducted a cross-sectional study from 316 students at higher education institutions that were merging in the Netherlands, as well as an experiment with 173 MBA students. The study found that the extent to which the people perceived the two organizations as a good fit was significantly related to their support for the merger. Gleibs et al. suggested that when people perceive two organizations as a good fit this increases their positive emotions about a merger, and that in turn increases their support for the merger. However, it is not clear from the evidence what factors influence employees' perceptions of fit in different types of organizations and sectors (beyond higher education institutions and simulated organizations), therefore research is needed to examine how employees form stereotypes about the other organization involved in a merger or acquisition in a variety of real settings. It is also possible that negative emotions shape the way that employees show supportive behaviour towards a merger or acquisition. For example, Marmenout's (2010) evidence based on an experiment involving 81 students in Switzerland suggests that the more uncertain people feel about a merger or acquisition, the less willing they are to collaborate about it. Chapter 5 will discuss the importance of group processes (of which group stereotyping is an example), and employees' perceptions of "us versus them" in mergers and acquisitions. Evidence that some employees hold attitudes of "us versus them" when they are dealing with or thinking of employees from the partner organization involved in a merger or acquisition include Brown and Humphreys' (2003) interviews with 75 employees in a merged organization in the UK. The study found that employees in each of the former organizations thought of the other employees as very different from themselves and relationships across the two sets of employees became competitive and discriminatory. The way that employees from the two partner organizations view each other could be influenced by group processes (see Chapter 5). Further empirical evidence should thus explore what variables shape employees' perceptions of fit between organizations.

The third implication of the evidence is that the relative size or status of an organization, compared to the partner with which it is merging or acquiring (or by which it is being acquired), matters in cultivating support for a merger or acquisition. Giessner, Viki, Otten, Terry, and Täuber (2006) conducted two experiments involving 148 students in Austria and 129 students in the United Kingdom. The study suggests that when people are in an organization that has a high status they are more supportive of a merger in which the lower status organization's values, practices, and other norms are assimilated by the high-status organization. Status in the study by Giessner et al. (2006) was conceptualized in terms of the organization's reputation and economic factors. The study suggests that when people are in the lower-status organization among two organizations involved in a merger or an acquisition, they are more supportive of process that involves integration, equality, and transformation rather than assimilation. Empson's (2001) observational and interview-based study of 92 employees in UK organizations involved in mergers and acquisitions found that the employees feared being "contaminated" by the bad reputation of the partner organization, suggesting that employees who consider their organization to be of higher status want to assimilate rather than integrate with the lower-status organization because of reputational concerns.

The literature on the power relations between the groups after the merger or the acquisitions confirm this proposition. Specifically, employees who perceive the two partner organizations as dissimilar and are in the low-status (i.e. low domi-nance) organization appear to be less likely to identify with the new organization after a merger or acquisition (van Knippenberg, van Knippenberg, Monden, & de Lima, 2002). van Knippenberg et al.'s research involved 373 and 122 employ-ees in two merged public organizations. Therefore, employees in high- or low-status organizations can hold prejudiced views about the partner organization in a merger or acquisition. Employees can construe a merger or acquisition as not being conducive to growth but a deterioration of image and professional-ism, together with the addition of "low-calibre people" (McEntire & Bentley, 1996; Weber & Camerer, 2003), which can explain why employees fear being associated with a seemingly "downmarket" organization and why they might avoid being "contaminated" (Empson, 2001). Instead of cooperating, relations between the two sets of employees can become quite competitive and discrimi-natory (Brown & Humphreys, 2003). A limitation of the study by Giessner et al.'s (2006) is that an experiment involving students probably does not capture enough of the complex factors facing employees in real organizations, including the notion of status based on a reputation with customers, investors, or the stock market. It is thus important for evidence to tell us about the factors that are the best determinants of an organization's status from the perspective of employees in real organizations. A point related to status is an organization's size. Wicker and Kauma (1974) conducted a cross-sectional study in the United States that involved collecting data from 233 church members after two local religious insti-tutions became integrated. The study found that members of the smaller-sized church were less supportive of the integration compared to the members of the larger church, which suggests that employees in the smaller organization are less likely to support a merger or acquisition. A limitation of this study is that mem-bers of an institution might not be psychologically comparable to employees of an institution because, for the latter, pay and job security are at stake. Therefore, more evidence is needed to clarify the impact of an organization's size on employ-ees in mergers or acquisitions.

Other studies support the idea that an organization's status is important, including Terry and Callan's (1998) cross-sectional study of 1,104 hospital employees in Australia whose hospitals were about to merge. Terry and Callan defined status by taking into account factors such as prestige and job opportuni-ties. The study found that employees in the lower-status hospital showed stronger signs of favouring their own hospital, and the bias was related to the employees' perceptions of the merger as a threatening event. Similarly, Amiot et al. (2007) found, in a cross-sectional study conducted three and 24 months after a merger, that employees in the low-status organization showed more signs of ingroup bias than employees in the high-status organization. A limitation of these studies is that they assume that there is consensus among employees about which of two organizations has higher status. Different employees might use different facts (or illusions) to define the status of their organization, e.g. the physical size, market share, financial productivity, length of time trading, popularity in a niche sense (e.g. winning industry awards), how ethical or green the organization is, and so on. Some employees might use one of these things to define status, whereas other employees will use a combination of two or more things to define status. It is also plausible that some employees define status in terms of the competence of the workforce in each organization, but perceptions of competence might be biased by group processes of "us versus them." Weber and Camerer's (2003) experimental study of students at two universities in the United States suggests that people blame the members of the merger or acquisition partner, and they blame difficulties on a lack of competence on the latter. Therefore, the relative status of two organizations can often be ambiguous and open to the subjective interpretations of employees which, in turn, can be shaped or made complex by a variety of group processes (see Chapter 5).

The fourth implication of the evidence is that getting employees directly involved with helping an organization transition into a merger or acquisition cultivates their support for it. Basinger and Peterson (2008) conducted interviews of 20 employees in a merged public sector organization within the United States. The study found that employees who were directly involved in the merger or transition process embraced the change and were accepting of the merger. The study found that employees who were not involved in the merger process felt that the change was unnecessary and they disagreed with it. A limitation of this study is that the data are few and qualitative, which means that it cannot tell us about the size or statistical significance of the differences between employees who are and are not involved with the transition process. A related point is that getting employees to trust and become committed to preserving the relationship between the two organizations cultivates their support for a merger or acquisition (Wittmann, Hunt, & Arnett, 2009). It is plausible that employees' feelings of trust influence the way that they interact with and evaluate the relationship with the partner organization (Dirks & Ferrin, 2001). Wittmann et al.'s study involved 47 members of the Association of Strategic Alliance Professionals (ASAP) from several countries, but their views about what works in cultivating employees' support should be corroborated by testing the views by collecting data from employees.

In summary, factors that shape employees' support for a merger or acquisition are:

- A CEO with a visionary leadership style.
- Having trustworthy leaders in the organization.
- Having a good fit between two organizations.
- Being the higher status or bigger organization.
- Being directly involved in the transition process.
- Trusting the merger or acquisition process.

On the other hand, employees can respond to a merger or acquisition by resisting it or engaging in a variety of actions or thoughts that demonstrate their resistance such as protesting or neglecting their duties (Nikandrou & Papalexandris, 2007), deliberately withholding valuable information and refusing collaboration with other employees (Empson, 2001), being reluctant to learn from other employees (Apfelthaler, Muller, & Rehder, 2002), behaving in a hostile way, or having cultural clashes or conflicts (Goddard & Palmer, 2010; Vaara, Sarala, Stahl, & Björkman, 2012). Conflict can arise about a wide range of issues such as the timing of the reorganization to the way that changes are communicated or implemented (Quah & Young, 2005). Employees' resistance behaviours after a merger or acquisition, such as being reluctant to cooperate, can be harmful to the organization because knowledge transfer is an important way that integration can happen (Vaara et al., 2012). Table 4.1 summarises some of the evidence about resistant behaviours among employees and factors that contribute to them:

Table 4.1 Factors that contribute to employees' resistance towards a merger or acquisition

Authors	Type of study	Findings
van Oudenhoven & de Boer, 1995	Experiment carried with managers from Dutch organizations	The researchers carried out an experiment among managers in Dutch organizations. The study found that a high degree of integration makes employees engage in actions resisting the changes, especially if there is high cultural dissimilarity between the two organizations.
McEntire & Bentley, 1996	Interview/ observational study in United States	The study suggested that some employees resisted working with each other, showed biased attitudes, and imposed their own approaches or norms. Factors that contributed to resistance behaviour were reputational gaps, lack of information, and appearance.
Apfelthaler et al., 2002	Case study in Austria and United States	The study collected data from 20 managers in a merged organization, and the evidence suggested that an organization can resist learning from the organization it is acquiring (and vice versa). The interview data suggested that the two did not consider it necessary to learn from one another.
Quah & Young, 2005	Observational/ interview-based study in United States	The researchers collected interview data from 32 managers and employees, and found that the acquired firm's management team showed resistance behaviours. The study suggested that employees who were not senior managers tended to show resistance behaviour during the middle phases of the post-acquisition process and that resistance declined with time.

Authors	Type of study	Findings
van Dijk & van Dick, 2009	Observational/interviews in Australia	The researchers collected data from 23 employees involved in a merger or acquisition and found that employees who had the greatest resistance were those who felt a lower sense of identification with the new organization. Employees engaged in resistance by psychologically changing the categorisation that was salient or important to them, changing the value that they associated with the categorisation, promoting the old organization's identity, and negating the partner organization.
Teram, 2010	Observational/interview study in United States	The researchers collected interview data from employees in a public US organization, and the results suggested that the employees expressed resistance by refusing to let go of what they felt were characteristics typical of the organizations before they engaged in the merger or acquisition.
Jetten & Hutchison, 2011	Cross-sectional study in United Kingdom	The researchers collected data from two defence organizations in the United Kingdom (one with 308 employees, the other had 498 employees). The study suggested that employees want to protect their organization's history and therefore perceptions that a merger will harm historical continuity predict employees' resistance to a merger or acquisition.

A limitation of some of these studies is that they do not necessarily tell us the extent to which employees who feel resistant towards a merger or acquisition express their resistance in behavioural terms and, if so, what the behaviours involve. There is a hint from the evidence that one type of resistance involves employees refusing to learn from other employees in the partner organization and refusing to give away information that the latter need (e.g. McEntire & Bentley, 1996; Apfelthaler et al., 2002). For example, Empson's (2001) observational and interview-based study of 92 employees in UK organizations involved in mergers and acquisitions found that the employees dismissed the relevance of the knowledge of employees from the partner organization. Similarly, Chua and Goh's (2009) observational and interview study of 28 employees within a research and development department of a merged organization in Singapore found that employees in the organization that was engaging in the acquisition were dismissive of the relevance of employees' knowledge within the acquired organization. They made almost no attempt to study the latter's knowledge base. A cross-sectional study of 123 employees in Finland found that mistrust, organizational politics, and conflicting views correlates negatively with knowledge transfer (Vaara et al., 2012). Resistance that takes the form of refusing to learn from employees in the partner organization could be symptomatic of the deliberate reduction by employees in their productivity, which is said to occur after mergers or acquisitions (Cording, Harrison, Hoskisson, & Jonsen, 2014; Chung, Du, & Choi, 2014), as well as the rise in conflict-related behaviour and an unwillingness to collaborate that is observed among some employees after mergers or acquisitions (Marmenout, 2010). Employees' use of knowledge as a point of resistance is thus common after a merger or acquisition, and this is something that Chapter 8 will explore in further detail.

Another point of resistance could be in the sense of employees trying to keep the old organization's culture and refusing to accept cultural changes after a merger or acquisition. Sarala's (2010) study about employees who had experienced acquisitions found that the more employees engaged in cultural preservation (be they within the acquiring or the acquired organization), the more conflict there was after the acquisition. Cultural preservation could be symptomatic of a wider problem in which employees persist in maintaining their old organization's values or identity. Ailon-Souday and Kunda's (2003) study of a merger involving US and Israeli companies conducted interviews with employees who suggested that they were persistently trying to maintain a boundary that demarcated the two organizations and trying to assert their old organization's authority. Those boundaries might have involved or been made worse by employees drawing on country-based categorisation. Tienari, Søderberg, Holgersson, and Vaara's (2005) interviews of 40 employees in merged organizations from Denmark, Sweden, and Finland found that employees constructed ideas of "us" and "them" using national categories. Viewing two organizations as culturally dissimilar is something that employees can harness as a political tool with which to resist changes during a merger or acquisition, as Vaara's (2000) semi-structured interviews with 200 employees in two financial companies from Finland and Sweden suggested. In Sarala's study, conflict included employees experiencing or showing difficulties with cooperation, having differences in opinion, and feeling mistrust towards other employees. Future research should thus evaluate the relative importance of different types of psychological resistance in predicting, for example, grievances, conflict, or intentions to quit. Future research should also clarify whether organizations that engage in a high degree of consultation before a merger or acquisition have employees whose level of resistance after a merger or acquisition is high or low. Nonetheless, we can summarise the factors that contribute to employees' resistance as follows:

- The two organizations are trying to integrate each other to a great extent.
- The two organizations have very different cultures or reputations.
- Employees are not kept well informed about the merger or acquisition.
- Not seeing learning between the two organizations as necessary.

- Being a manager.
- Not feeling a sense of belonging within the new organization.
- Holding persistent stereotypes about the two organizations.
- Feeling that a merger or acquisition will undermine an organization's history.

Resistance and low support for a merger or acquisition could contribute to employees intending to leave an organization by going on the job market in the hope of getting employed elsewhere. The next section will discuss factors that contribute to employees' intentions to quit after a merger or acquisition.

Why employees want to quit after a merger or acquisition

The topic of employees quitting (engaging in turnover) or intending to quit after a merger or acquisition is one which is popular within the published literature. The first implication is that employees are more likely to quit after a merger or acquisition if they feel psychologically disengaged and if they feel that the organization has broken a psychological contract with them (that is, the employees' explicit or tacit expectations). Rafferty and Restubog's (2010) longitudinal study of 155 employees in the Philippines found that the more employees felt psychologically disengaged the more they had the intention to quit, although the concept of "psychological engagement" might co-vary so closely with intentions to quit in a way that creates statistical multi-collinearity problems. Some factors make employees more likely to psychologically distance themselves or feel disengaged from an organization (Murray, Derrick, Leder, & Holmes, 2008; Murray, Holmes, & Collins, 2006). One of the things that might make employees feel psychologically disengaged from an organization is feeling the merger or acquisition has led to a breach in the promises that the organization made to the employee explicitly or tacitly. Evidence suggests that employees can view a merger or acquisition as a betrayal (Brown & Humphreys, 2003) and that the new organization has failed to fulfil its promises (Linde & Schalk, 2008), and this could make employees feel that they have to engage in compensatory actions to restore a sense of justice (Mahony & Klass, 2008; Darley & Pittman, 2003). The problem might be worse among organizations that do not deliver promises to employees. Cording et al.'s (2014) study of 129 employees that went through a merger or acquisition found that employee productivity was higher among organizations that had under-promised relative to those that over-promised. Organizations that had more consistency between their values and their practices were also more strongly associated with employee productivity. Employees sometimes react to broken promises by intending to quit the organization (Rafferty & Restubog, 2010). Bellou (2008) found, in a cross-sectional study in Greece, that the extent to which restaurant employees felt that their psychological contract had been breached after an acquisition had an impact on their intentions to move jobs as well as their civic virtue behaviour (e.g. doing favours or volunteering within the organization). It is plausible that employees' expectations about the psychological contract in the future are also important. A change within the organization can make employees feel uncertain about its future actions and it can make employees fear that their job responsibilities or performance evaluations will change (Michela & Vena, 2012). A limitation with the study by Bellou (2008) is that the relevance of the psychological contract as a predictor of wanting to quit might depend on other factors, for example how dependent an employee is on the job. Some employees might have a high level of dependence on an organization and, for such employees, what might matter is not the psychological contract as a whole, but their level of certainty or uncertainty about job security after the merger or acquisition. Michela and Vena (2012) found that some employees are more psychologically dependent on an organization than others and that, for highly dependent employees, their level of uncertainty predicted their level of commitment to the organization. In short, we can conclude that employees who feel less psychologically engaged with an organization are more likely to want to quit after a merger or acquisition, and the reason why employees feel disengaged is believing that the organization has broken a psychological contract *or* feeling vulnerable or uncertain about one's job security.

A second implication is that – on average – employees are more likely to want to quit if a merger or acquisition presents few or no career development opportunities. Chung et al. (2014) conducted a study of 174 employees in a merged organization in China and found that the more the organization provided employees with training opportunities and job security, the higher was task performance after the merger. Likewise, evidence from 200 employees in Greece suggests that training and development practices are positively associated with the effectiveness and performance of an organization, such as in terms of employee productivity, the quality of customer service and innovation (Nikandrou & Papalexandris, 2007). Mergers and acquisitions can create a lot of ambiguity and volatility about the scope of an employee's work and his or her future within the organization (Marmenout, 2010). The purpose of a merger or acquisition is often unclear to employees (Eriksson & Sundgren, 2005), and there are questions about whether organizations give employees enough information about a prospective merger or acquisition (Rafferty & Restubog, 2010). Searle and Ball (2004) interviewed six employees who were going through an acquisition and the results suggest that employees felt uncertain, which made them vigilant about information they received about the acquisition, and they felt powerlessness, which made them engage in gossip about poor treatment by managers. Not having enough information can prompt employees to want to quit after the merger or acquisition is announced (Schweiger & Denisi, 1991), or even some years after (Hambrick & Cannella, 1993). This could be because employees have fears about the impact of a merger or acquisition on their careers and personal experiences at work, such as what their job entails, what promotional opportunities exist, how much freedom they have to make decisions within the job, and how much they can progress in their career. Employees can choose to look for other career options outside the merged organization because the merger or acquisition threatens their job role clarity, job autonomy, or status within the organization (Hambrick & Cannella, 1993; Lubatkin, Schweiger, & Weber, 1999; Krug & Nigh, 2001; Li, 2008).

Fried et al.'s (1996) longitudinal study of 91 employees in an acquired Filipino company found that employees who do not feel that the merger or acquisition gives them career development opportunities are likely to withdraw from work and develop the intentions to quit the organization. However, there might be variation among employees in what they count as sufficient career development opportunities and the relevance of this variable could depend on what employees feel they were promised, or what they feel they can reasonably expect. One of the sources of information that employees use to gauge the career opportunities on offers appears to be the kind of language used by either of the organizations involved in the merger or acquisition. Piekkari et al. (2005) conducted unstructured interviews with eight employees in a financial organization that was formed after a merger between a Finnish and a Swedish organization. The study found that the kind of corporate language used by either of the merging organizations had implications for employees in terms of their career path and professional requirements. This created tension which seemed to have influenced some employees' intentions to quit. A limitation of this study is the sample size, and ambiguity in whether the eight employees' experiences were representative of the experiences of other employees.

A third implication is that employees are more likely to want to quit if they feel that the merger or acquisition deprives them of benefits that employees in the other organization have, and if they feel that there is unfairness between the two organizations in the way that job cuts or other negative things are distributed. Lee et al. (2013) conducted a cross-sectional survey of 271 employees in a merged organization in South Korea. They found that employees who felt more deprived than other employees had greater intentions to quit the organization. A limitation of this study is that the sources of deprivation can vary among employees and therefore there might not be a way of defining relative deprivation after a merger or acquisition in a way that is generalizable. For example, some employees might compare the parental leave allowance within the two organizations, whereas employees who are not intending to be parents might not feel deprived by the parental leave policy. Related to the idea of perceived deprivation is the idea that employees who perceive unfairness in the way that an organization is distributing punitive measures, such as job cuts, are more likely to want to quit. Fried et al. also found that the more employees felt that employee termination procedures were unfair, the more likely they were to psychologically withdraw from work, but clarity is needed about whether these results apply to organizations where redundancy procedures are governed by national laws.

A fourth implication is that the more employees feel a sense of identification (belonging or loyalty) with the organization after it has embarked on a merger or acquisition the less likely they are to want to quit. Feelings of belonging can play an important role in helping employees cope with a merger or acquisition, perhaps because it tallies with seeking support from other employees. Terry, Callan, and Sartori's (1996) cross-sectional study of 662 employees in a merged airline in Australia found that social support was among the strategies that the employees used to cope. Makri and Hantzi (2012) conducted a cross-sectional survey of 140 employees in Greece and found that the more strongly employees felt they identify with the organization after a merger or acquisition, the less likely they were to intend to quit. A study by van Dick et al. (2004) in Germany also found similar results. The importance of identity is something that studies in other areas of the field have found. Lipponen, Olkkonen, and Moilanen's (2004) cross-sectional study of 189 employees in Finland found that developing a psychological bond or identity with the new organization (after a merger or acquisition) has a positive impact on the extent to which employees behave in a way that benefits the organization, even if it is beyond their job role. Similarly, other evidence from 459 employees in a merged organization in Germany suggests that identification is positively related with the rate at which employees engage in organizational citizenship behaviours as evidence (van Dick et al., 2004). Another study by Smith, da Cunha, Giangreco, Vasilaki, and Carugat (2013) interviewed employees in a merged organization (comprising of organizations from Finland and Sweden). The study found that some employees did not develop a sense of shared fate and similarity with the employees of the merging organization. The study suggested that the more the employees from the two sets of organizations interacted, the more they found reasons to view each other as different. Employees can perceive such differentiation by persistently challenging the partner organization's work procedures and decisions (Colman & Lunnan, 2011), being dismissive of them, and imposing their own solutions (Chua & Goh, 2009; McEntire & Bentley, 1996). A limitation of these studies is that they do not tell us about what causes employees to develop a sense of identification with an organization after a merger or acquisition, and whether some causes are more important than others. A sense of belonging with an organization might be less likely among employees who feel uncertain about what is going to happen to their jobs or job roles after the merger or acquisition, and therefore uncertainty might make employees want to quit. Marmenout (2010) conducted an experiment among 81 students in Switzerland using hypothetical situations and the results showed that the more the perceived uncertainty about the situation, the greater are the intentions to leave and the lower the willingness to collaborate. A limitation of this study is the fact that the experiment was scenario-based and it did not involve employees, therefore, additional evidence is needed to clarify the correlation between uncertainty and quitting intentions after a merger or acquisition.

In summary, factors that increase employees' intentions to quit an organization after a merger or acquisition include:

- Feeling psychologically disengaged.
- Perceiving a breach in their psychological contract.
- Feeling dependent on the organization, yet uncertain about job security.
- Few or no opportunities to develop their careers.
- Unfairness in what employees in the two organizations have.
- Unfairness in job cuts or redundancies.
- Low feelings of belonging to the organization.

This raises questions about what makes employees want to switch jobs more generally (in any organization), and what this can tell us about why mergers or acquisitions inspire employees to want to quit. A meta-analysis of 316 studies about employee voluntary turnover by Rubenstein, Eberly, Lee, and Mitchell (2017) found that the antecedents of employee turnover include an employees' personality, aspects of the job, whether an employee has traditional attitudes about work (e.g. believing that workers should remain in the same organization for as long as possible), the external job market, context, and having an attitude of withdrawing from the organization. In terms of personality characteristics that predict turnover, Rubenstein et al.'s meta-analysis found that employees who have an external locus of control (e.g. blaming experiences on other people) and who are more externally motivated are more likely to quit an organization. That is compared to those with an internal locus of control (e.g. blaming themselves for experiences) who, when they experience work-related stress, try to overcome the obstacles and stay in the organization. In terms of context, Rubenstein et al. found that factors that were important in contributing to employees' decisions to quit an organization were: a negative working climate, stressful experiences within the organization, and poor support from the organization. These superseded positive aspects such as the reputation benefits that employees can get from working in a prestigious organization.

Rubenstein et al.'s (2017) meta-analysis also found that other strong predictors of employee turnover were job satisfaction and commitment to the organization. Feeling committed to an organization is one of the best predictors of voluntary employee turnover, and such commitment can be shaped by a variety of factors. Porter, Steers, Mowday, and Boulian (1974) suggest that organizational commitment is related to how strongly employees identify with the organization, how much they believe in and accept goals and values, and how willing they are to expend effort in remaining within the organization. Evidence suggests that employees can fail to develop a sense of "we" within an organization after a merger or acquisition (van Knippenberg et al., 2002). One leading perspective about what constitutes commitment is Meyer and Allen's (1991) model, which postulates that there are three components of organizational commitment: affective, continuance, and normative commitment, rooted in the multidimensional. Affective commitment is an employee's emotional attachment to, sense of belonging with, and involvement in the organization. Continuance commitment is based on the costs that an employee thinks are associated with leaving an organization, and normative commitment is about feeling obligated to remain in the organization. Meyer & Allen's model suggests affective commitment correlates positively with normative commitment, but negatively with continuance commitment. This means that the more employees feel emotionally connected to an organization, the more they also tend to feel obliged or bound to stay within the organization. The sense of fear and uncertainty about the merger or the acquisition leads to decreases in organizational commitment (Schweiger & Denisi, 1991) and Koch and Steers (1976) suggest that organizational commitment is a bigger predictor of quitting intentions than job satisfaction (Steers, 1975). Employees who are not committed to the organization are likely to underperform, quit the job, not show up, be late at work, or experience stress and work-family conflicts (Steers, 1977; Mathieu & Zajac, 1990; Meyer, Stanley, Herscovitch, & Topolnytsky, 2002; Cohen & Freund, 2005). Conversely, evidence suggests that the more employees have affective commitment towards the organization, the more they engage in voluntary behaviours such as organizational citizenship and behaviours that help an organization but are not part of their job role (Williams & Anderson, 1991). As well as feelings of commitment being an important predictor of employees' intentions to quit, job satisfaction was found by meta-analysis to be an important predictor of employee turnover (Boswell, Boudreau, & Tichy, 2005; Judge, 1993). Literature about mergers and acquisitions supports the idea that job satisfaction is related to not just quitting intentions but also counterproductive behaviours (Tett & Meyer, 1993).

Rubenstein et al.'s (2017) meta-analysis is important in providing an overview of the psychology of employees' voluntary turnover, but it raises the question of whether mergers or acquisitions inspire more employees to want to quit, and whether this is because they make employees more pessimistic than they usually would be. The announcement of a merger or acquisition can cause an abrupt shift in how employees view their work and the organization (Schweiger & Denisi, 1991). Many employees feel uncertainty and cynicism (see Chapter 3) about a merger or acquisition, and we suggest that this can make employees more pessimistic about whether stressors within the organization will change. Evidence shows that employees tend to have low levels of job satisfaction after a merger or acquisition, and this persists months into the integration stage (Schweiger & Denisi, 1991), and even two (Amiot et al., 2007) or three years (Guerrero, 2008) after the implementation of merger- or acquisition-related changes. This could be because a merger or acquisition creates a real or perceived climate that prompts employees to go back on the job market. Negative expectations about mergers or acquisitions as prone to failure (see Chapter 2) could make employees less likely to view their jobs in positive terms and more likely to focus on signs that negative changes are going to happen such as job cuts or relocation. For example, employees can develop the idea that a merger or acquisition will result in being asked to relocate to another region inside or outside the country based on knowledge about relocations in other cases of mergers or acquisitions. Relocation can be quite common, with a case study by Stovel and Savage (2006) in the United Kingdom showing that there was an increase in the number of employees who were geographically transferred at time points that coincided with a merger or acquisition. Stovel & Savage examined historical records about the bank Lloyds, its mergers or acquisitions, and the work histories of 2,500 employees. During a merger or acquisition, employees might also be more likely to experience unfamiliar stressors (e.g. redundancy consultations, a new management team), and this could increase their stress levels, making their overall attitudes about the working environment more unpleasant and their expectations of positive prospects more pessimistic. Research should clarify why withdrawal behaviour and turnover intentions are common behavioural coping devices that employees use after mergers or acquisitions (Fried et al., 1996). A meta-analysis replicating that done by Rubenstein et al. (2017) can tell us more about why mergers or acquisitions inspire so many employees to quit an organization. Such research should clarify the impact of different types of mergers or acquisitions (see Chapter 1) and employees' personal expectations about whether mergers or acquisitions are likely to succeed or fail.

Organizations suffer when employees leave because the costs include the recruitment, selection, and training of replacement employees (Allen, Bryant, & Vardaman, 2010). Whereas some authors suggest that voluntary staff turnover has positive consequences such as "value creation" within the new organization (Papadakis, 2005), other evidence points to negative consequences. Cording and colleagues (2008) found that employee turnover had a negative effect on the financial performance of an organization after an acquisition. Organizations also suffer when employees leave because this means that they have lost the abilities, expertise, and experience of people whose tacit knowledge about the organization cannot be easily replaced, and the losses in social capital or reputation could lead to low morale among the remaining employees (Dess & Shaw, 2001; McElroy, Morrow, & Rude, 2001; Felps et al., 2009). As well as employees' quitting intentions being notable as a frequent topic within the merger and acquisition literature, managers' intentions to quit are also frequently researched. The risk of departures by top management employees is said to be even higher than that of other employees (Hambrick & Cannella, 1993). The next section will discuss factors that contribute to managers' intentions to quit after a merger or acquisition, and other types of behavioural responses among managers.

What makes managers want to quit and what are other common behaviours?

Voluntary turnover is a common escape route for not just many employees after a merger or acquisition, but also for many managers (Walsh & Kosnik, 1993). In a study examining the rate of quitting by managers within top management teams by Hambrick & Cannella, 1993), the results showed that 67% of the executives within the acquired organization quit within four years. Another study by Walsh (1988) found an average management turnover rate of 59% across five years in various types of mergers or acquisitions. Walsh found that market extension acquisitions have the highest turnover rates; a market acquisition involves organizations in similar industries but selling in different geographic markets (Walsh, 1988). In such acquisitions, the rate of quitting by top management is 37% in year one and rises up to 64% in year five (Walsh, 1988). The first implication from the evidence is therefore that some managers quit, and that the rate of quitting rises over five years. However, it is important for further evidence to clarify whether the rates of management turnover over five years are equivalent or higher than they would be without the merger or acquisition.

A related implication is evidence that the greater the number of managers who quit an organization during or after a merger or acquisition, the more negative the outcomes are for the merged or acquired/acquiring organization. Ellis, Reus, and Lamont (2009) conducted a longitudinal survey of 62 employees in the United States, and the study suggested that retaining managers significantly predicted the amount of value that was created during and after a merger or acquisition. Another study by Kiessling et al. (2012) collected cross-sectional data from 92 employees in managerial positions, and the study suggests that retaining managers is positively correlated with the performance of an organization after a merger or acquisition. Similarly, 29 case studies about mergers and acquisitions by Butler, Perryman, and Ranft (2012) found that the more senior managers quit within an acquired organization, the worse is the organization's performance after the acquisition. The problem with these studies, however, is that they do not compare the impact of managers quitting alongside the impact of non-managers quitting. It could therefore be that *any* kind of staff turnover is negatively correlated with good outcomes after a merger or acquisition and, therefore, that retaining managers is no more important than retaining other types of staff. The impact of managers quitting might also be neutral in some cases, with a meta-analysis by Butler et al. (2012) finding that there is a negative or neutral relationship between management turnover rates and financial performance measures such as return on equity or assets.

The second implication is that cultural differences between organizations, and removing managerial autonomy, can contribute to managers quitting during or after a merger or acquisition (Lubatkin et al., 1999). Lubatkin et al. conducted a longitudinal study of 69 CEOs and 36 senior vice presidents of companies that went through mergers or acquisitions in the United States. The study found that cultural differences significantly predicted the likelihood of these senior managers quitting the organization within the first year, and having their autonomy removed predicted their likelihood of quitting within four years. A related piece of evidence is that by Krug and Nigh (2001), who conducted a cross-sectional study of 284 executives in the United States, representing 142 merger or acquisition cases. The study found that some of the key reasons why executives quit were: a lack of leadership or direction, dishonesty, low morale, and loss in job status. The study also suggested that the executives were more likely to quit if they felt alienated from the top management team over time. A limitation with these studies is that they tacitly assume that managers or executives are unique, psychologically, when in fact the factors that make them quit (e.g. feeling alienated, reduced job autonomy, cultural differences, or low morale) are the same factors that could make non-managers quit.

A third implication is that some managers psychologically withdraw from work after a merger or acquisition, and their behaviour is governed by the emotions that they have. A cross-sectional study of two mergers in India suggests that the emotions that managers have about a merger or acquisition shape the way that they behave (Bhal et al., 2009). For example, some studies suggest that managers tend to withdraw psychologically from work and remain largely passive after a merger or acquisition (Choi, Holmberg, Löwstedt, & Brommels, 2011). Choi et al.'s study of 22 employees suggest that there is the perception of managers as people who prefer to "wait out the storm" after an initial enthusiasm for the change. A limitation with these studies is that adequate comparisons of managers and non-managers are necessary to show how they differ from other employees in the emotions that they experience, and in the type or extent of their psychological withdrawal. For example, job satisfaction is an important antecedent of the decision by senior managers to stay in the organization after a merger or acquisition (Krug & Nigh, 2001), as well as an antecedent of supportive, compliant behaviour or resistive behaviour (Nikandrou & Papalexandris, 2007), but these findings echo those of studies about employees who are not managers.

Among those managers who do not quit after a merger or acquisition, the evidence suggests that managers vary in their approaches to managing. In the previous section we saw evidence that leadership during a merger or acquisition matters in inspiring and instilling trust among employees, but do leaders play an important role in protecting employees from harm during a merger or acquisition? The fourth implication within the current section concerns evidence that protective managers are beneficial to employees. Case studies of two acquisitions by a company in Norway by Colman and Lunnan (2011) suggested that in the acquisition that resulted in successful integration, the managers behaved protectively towards employees, shielding them from harm during the acquisition. The study found that in the other company where the acquisition led to less successful integration, managers behaved confrontationally in the process of shielding their employees from harm, and the employees in that company were unhappy about the merger, with the study suggesting that there was noise and conflict about it. A limitation of generalising this study is that in some mergers or acquisitions, managers might not have much power or say over the future of the employees that they manage, therefore they may not have the opportunity to behave protectively. It also raises the question of whether what matters is not so much how protective managers are, but rather conditions that allow any positive attitudes, policies, or practices about managing employees. It is also important to recognise the isolation that managers can feel because of practices such as the use of confidentiality agreements within mergers or acquisitions agreements. Harwood and Ashleigh (2005) interviewed 33 managers in a merging healthcare organization and found that the use of confidentiality agreements led to feelings of inclusion, membership, belonging, responsibility, and exclusivity on one hand, but feelings of being isolated on the other hand. This can also create a boundary dividing managers and non-managers.

A fifth implication of the evidence is that managers who behave in a way that prioritises their own personal interests, and managers who fail to intervene effectively when intervention is required, can hinder the success of a merger or acquisition (Meyer, 2006). Meyer conducted interviews of 49 employees in Norway and found that if managers behave egocentrically, this can hinder the success of a merger or acquisition, and the study suggested that such egocentricity is a bigger problem than resistance against a merger or acquisition from employees. This study was limited because it involved qualitative data that cannot tell us about the statistical effect size or significance of the impact of managers' self-interested behaviour on the outcomes of a merger or acquisition. The problem of some managers construing mergers or acquisitions from an egocentric point of view is one which has been noted in other research. Vaara, Junni, Sarala, Ehrnrooth, and Koveshniko (2014) conducted a cross-sectional study from 92 managers involved in mergers and acquisitions in Finland. The study suggested that managers tend to take credit for successes and failures, which might fuel the illusion that needs, wants, and priorities during mergers and acquisitions revolve around managers. Managers might have developed this idea from the fact that many organizations *do* blame or credit them for negative and positive outcomes (respectively). The idea that managers behave egocentrically during or after a merger or acquisition is not a firm fact. Other research suggests that managers try to behave equitably in allocating resources after a merger or acquisition. For instance, a case study involving two European logistics companies that were merging involved interviews of managers at three time points, and the study found that the managers' concerns about equality shaped their decisions about how to allocate resources (Monin et al., 2013). A related point of evidence is that suggesting that managers try to create homogeneity (similarity) across the two partner organizations involved in a merger or acquisition. Langley et al. (2012) interviewed 18 and 21 employees in two merged organizations, and found that employees felt under pressure from managers to have a sense of sameness. Golden-Biddle et al.'s study also suggested that employees react to managers' efforts to create homogenous identity across the two organizations by trying to differentiate themselves within the new entity. On the other hand, other evidence suggests that managers (as well as other employees) constantly negotiate around organizational boundaries when it comes to deciding how to implement best practice, transfer information, and assess performance (Drori et al., 2013). Drori et al.'s study was comprised of interviews of 41 employees in a merged organization in the United States and found that the boundary negotiations involved managers or employees expressing acceptance or rejection of various practices, beliefs, and values. Therefore, whereas some managers do behave egocentrically after a merger or acquisition, other managers might not; whereas some managers try to achieve equality and homogeneity across the two organizations, others omit or include organizational boundaries in different circumstances.

In summary, the evidence from this section suggests that, during mergers or acquisitions:

- Some managers quit.
- Quitting by managers is associated with negative organizational outcomes.
- Some managers behave protectively, shielding their employees from harm.
- Some managers behave confrontationally while trying to protect employees.
- Some managers behave egocentrically, taking credit for successes or failures.
- Some managers fail to intervene when their intervention is needed.
- Managers' emotions shape the way that they behave.

Therefore, many managers quit after a merger or acquisition, and this has negative consequences for organizations – but this is a similar effect that non-managerial voluntary staff turnover has on consequences for organizations. In that sense, managers are not unique or special employees, but the breadth of literature about the impact of their quitting on how mergers or acquisitions fare could be because managers (as a sample) receive more interest from researchers than non-managers. However, there are ways in which managers have a unique position within an organization that makes their reaction to a merger or acquisition different from that of a non-manager. That includes being in a position to protect his or her employees from harm during the organizational changes and to intervene. Managers can also have the unique privilege of being able to behave egocentrically (e.g. taking credit for their team's successes). Managers can also be more vulnerable than non-managers in that more senior managers might blame them for their team's failures, and they therefore might feel more vulnerable to negative consequences after a merger or acquisition. These are possibilities that future research should investigate.

Conclusions

This chapter has discussed evidence about how employees respond to mergers or acquisitions, behaviourally speaking. This chapter started by examining what makes employees supportive or resistant towards a merger or acquisition. The first implication of the evidence was that a leader's style of leadership during a merger or acquisition matters in helping employees support it. The second implication of the evidence was that the way that employees think of the two organizations involved as a good fit matters in cultivating employees' support for a merger or acquisition. The third implication of the evidence was that the relative size or status of an organization, compared to the partner with which it is merging or acquiring (or by which it is being acquired), matters in cultivating support for a merger or acquisition. The fourth implication of the evidence was that getting employees directly involved with helping an organization transition into a merger or acquisition cultivates their support for it. Instead of supporting a merger or acquisition, employees can respond by resisting the change by engaging in a variety of actions that demonstrate their resistance. The evidence shows that employees are most likely to engage in resistance behaviour when: the two organizations are trying to integrate each other to a great extent; when the two organizations have very different cultures or reputations; when the employees are not kept well informed about the merger or acquisition; when employees do not see learning between the two organizations as necessary; if they are a manager; if they do not feel a sense of belonging within the new organization; if they hold persistent stereotypes about the two organizations; and if they feel that the merger or acquisition will undermine the organization's history.

This chapter then examined evidence about why employees want to quit after a merger or acquisition. The first implication is that employees are more likely to quit after a merger or acquisition if they feel psychologically disengaged and if they feel that the organization has broken a psychological contract with them. A second implication is that – on average – employees are more likely to want to quit if a merger or acquisition presents few or no career development opportunities. A third implication is that employees are more likely to want to quit if they feel that the merger or acquisition deprives them of benefits that employees in the other organization have, and if they feel that there is unfairness between the two organizations in the way that job cuts or other negative things are distributed. A fourth implication is that the more employees feel a sense of identification (belonging or loyalty) with the organization after it has embarked on a merger or acquisition, the less likely they are to want to quit. Other predictors of employee turnover are job satisfaction, commitment to the organization, an employees' personality, aspects of the job, whether an employee has traditional attitudes about work (e.g. believing that workers should remain in the same organization for as long as possible), the external job market, context, and having an attitude of withdrawing from the organization. This chapter then examined the evidence about what makes managers want to quit, because a notable proportion of managers do quit after a merger or acquisition and evidence shows that the rate of quitting rises over five years. One implication is that the greater the number of managers who quit an organization during or after a merger or acquisition, the more negative the outcomes are for the merged or acquired/acquiring organization, but this can be true about non-managerial turnover. The second implication is that cultural differences between organizations, and removing managerial autonomy, can contribute to managers quitting during or after a merger or acquisition. A third implication is that some managers psychologically withdraw from work after a merger or acquisition, and their behaviour is governed by the emotions that they have. The fourth implication is evidence that protective managers are beneficial to employees. A fifth implication of the evidence is that managers who behave in a way that prioritises their own personal interests, and managers who fail to intervene effectively when intervention is required, can hinder the success of a merger or acquisition.

Mergers and acquisitions thus lead to employees and managers behaving supportively in some cases, but most of the evidence points towards quitting, quitting intentions and resistance behaviours as more common outcomes. Resistance behaviours are often inspired by attitudes among employees of "us versus them," which Chapter 5 will discuss.

5 Why employees experiencing mergers and acquisitions think and act in terms of group dynamics of "us versus them"

Mergers and acquisitions can elicit a mentality among employees of "us versus them." This is because the psychology sub-field of group processes and intergroup relations tells us that social situations which put people into groups elicit a sense of belonging and identity for people within one's group but rivalry, hostility, or discrimination towards people outside the group or the outgroup (Tajfel & Turner, 1979; Turner, Hogg, Oakes, Reicher, & Wetherell, 1987). Employees could therefore respond to a merger or acquisition by seeing employees from the partner organization as "not one of us." The field of group processes and intergroup relations is based on social identity theory (Tajfel & Turner, 1979) and self-categorisation theory (Turner et al., 1987). The merger and acquisition literature frequently applies these theories to examine how employees react, think, and behave (Amiot et al., 2007; Bartels et al., 2006; Boen, Vanbeselaere, Brebels, Huybens, & Millet, 2007; Edwards & Edwards, 2012; Fischer et al., 2007; Giessner & Mummendey, 2008; Giessner et al., 2006; Giessner, Ullrich, & van Dick, 2012; Gleibs, Mummendey, & Noack, 2008; Hogg & Terry, 2000; Jetten, Duck, et al., 2002; Panchal & Cartwright, 2001; Terry & Callan, 1998; Terry et al., 2001; Ullrich, Wieseke, & van Dick, 2005; van Dick et al., 2004; van Knippenberg et al., 2002; van Leeuwen, van Knippenberg, & Ellemers, 2003). This chapter discusses these theories and evidence about how employees react to mergers and acquisitions from the lens of ingroups versus outgroups. We will start by providing an introduction to social identity theory, then self-categorisation theory, followed by a review of the evidence about "us versus them" attitudes or behaviours after mergers or acquisitions. We will discuss literature showing the implications of employees' perceptions of continuity in the identity of the organization after a merger or acquisition (e.g. Jetten, O'Brien, & Trindall, 2002; van Knippenberg et al., 2002), and evidence of the impact of status differences between organizations on negative consequences for employees (e.g. Terry et al., 2001) and organizations (e.g. Goddard & Palmer, 2010). We will also discuss the relevance of employees' emotions for intergroup rivalry after mergers or acquisitions, drawing on literature showing the prevalence of threat or uncertainty and other emotions (Buono, Bowditch, & Lewis, 1985) and Rousseau, 1998).

Introduction to social identity theory

Social identity theory (Tajfel & Turner, 1979) and self-categorisation theory (Turner et al., 1987) are two "sister" theories in social psychology that have spanned a large amount of research and evidence from both basic and applied psychology, including organizational psychology. Social identity theory was inspired by Tajfel's (1970) experiments into something called the "minimal group paradigm." In these experiments, researchers show that simply putting people into a group influences their attitudes and behaviours towards people inside or outside the group. This is no matter how trivial (minimal) the reasons for the group's existence, such as the tossing of a coin, and even if the people in the group are strangers to each other. In the real world, where social groups often have stronger bonds, groups have an even more powerful effect on their members. Social identity theory argues that belonging to a group makes people engage in a number of attitudes, behaviours, and tendencies. This includes favouring fellow members of one's group (ingroup members) and discriminating against members outside one's group (outgroup members). This means that when a merger or acquisition is underway, employees can think of themselves and their colleagues along the lines of "us" and "them." For instance, they can categorise other employees, managers, policies, or activities in terms of whether they belong to the "ingroup" (the old organization) or the "outgroup" (the partner organization involved in the merger or acquisition). We suggest that ingroup bias in mergers and acquisitions could take various forms such as behavioural bias (e.g. allocating a bigger budget to the ingroup), attitudinal bias (e.g. stereotyping the ingroup as better skilled or more knowledgeable), collective self-esteem bias (e.g. valuing the ingroup more highly), and so on. Likewise, it is plausible that outgroup discrimination in mergers and acquisitions can take various forms such as behavioural discrimination (e.g. placing more outgroup employees in the list of people to be made redundant after a merger or acquisition), attitudinal discrimination (e.g. thinking of outgroup managers as less trustworthy or competent), collective self-esteem-based discrimination (e.g. viewing the outgroup as a lower status brand), and so on.

Tajfel and Turner's (1979) social identity theory argues that people often compare the ingroup and the outgroup, therefore a sense of competitiveness permeates relations between people in different groups. This suggests that employees can frequently compare what benefits or losses they have received from a merger or acquisition, and what benefits or losses employees in the partner organization have received. Social identity theory tells us that people want to feel that the ingroup is better than the outgroup, and they engage in behaviours or hold attitudes that create as much "distance" or "differentiation" as possible between the ingroup and outgroup. This means that employees could strive to accentuate the differences between them and employees in the partner organization, such as by engaging in resource allocation that puts their ingroup in a better position than the partner organization. This is plausible considering that experiments using something called the "minimal group paradigm" (Tajfel et al., 1971;

Vaughan, Tajfel, & Williams, 1981) found that people have such a desire to make the ingroup better than the outgroup that their behaviour shows a preference for something called a "maximum difference" strategy over a "maximum outcome" strategy. For example, if employee A belongs to organization A (the ingroup), and A is asked to choose between (1) allocating a £1,500 marketing budget to organization A and a £1,000 marketing budget to organization B, or (2) allocating a £2,000 marketing budget to organization A and a £1,800 marketing budget to organization B, evidence from the experiments suggests that people tend to choose option 1 instead of option 2. In other words, people who are competing with an outgroup tend to use a maximum difference strategy instead of a maximum outcome strategy when allocating resources to themselves and the outgroup. As you can see, the difference in 1 is £500 whereas the difference in 2 is £200. The minimal group paradigm suggests that people prefer a bigger gap between the ingroup and outgroup over the alternative of getting more for the ingroup but achieving a smaller gap when comparing the ingroup and the outgroup.

Translating the experimental evidence about how people tend to think or behave when they are within a group suggests that employees could, after a merger or acquisition, perceive employees from a partner organization as "them," hold prejudiced views against them, give them fewer resources or opportunities, and so on. These sorts of behaviours and attitudes are at odds with the purpose of most mergers or acquisitions (see Chapter 1), therefore organizations need to be aware about the psychology of intergroup rivalry. Although chief executives and other members of an organization's senior management would like to think that the official strategy of the merger or acquisition governs the behaviour or attitudes of employees at ground level, the reality might be quite different. What is more, it is important to note that the "group" can be not just organization A versus B, but also managers versus non-managers, or human resources staff versus other employees. We believe that overcoming the powerful impact of group processes is an important step in helping mergers and acquisitions become successful.

Something that organizations undergoing a merger or acquisition can do is to understand why group differences are active, and help employees reconfigure their ideas about "us versus them" by emphasising the identity of the post-merger or post-acquisition organization as "all of us." Additionally, another strategy is for organizations to help deactivate the relevance of group memberships within the organization by making each employee's individuality more relevant and accentuated. Social identity theory (Tajfel & Turner, 1979) tells us that group memberships are not always relevant to how people think or behave in every social situation. People can fluctuate between thinking of themselves as individuals (e.g. I am extroverted, I am funny) and thinking of themselves as members of social groups (e.g. I am a Genex employee, I am an accountant). In order to develop interventions against intergroup rivalry after a merger or acquisition, organizations therefore need to understand self-categorisation theory – a theory that explains what social or psychological conditions make people mentally activate their group memberships.

Introduction to self-categorisation theory

Turner et al. (1987) expounded on social identity theory by developing self-categorisation theory, a perspective that explains how people cognitively navigate social situations and decide whether or not their group membership is relevant to the way that they will think about or behave towards other people. Self-categorisation theory argues that the psychological activation or deactivation of a group membership within someone's mind depends on the literal social context, e.g. who else is in the room and whether their group membership is clear or ambiguous (see an illustrative example in Berry & Kamau, 2013). By psychological activation or deactivation, the theory means in the cognitive sense of someone's thoughts, attention, and mental decision-making processes. Self-categorisation theory argues that whether group membership is relevant or irrelevant in a certain situation depends on the comparisons that someone makes with other people, e.g. *"Bearing in mind what I know about what type of person is a prototypical member of my ingroup, and what type of person is a prototypical member of the outgroup, can I tell who in this room is an ingroup or outgroup member, and how similar or different am I from them?"* Self-categorisation theory suggests that a person psychologically activates their group membership and thinks or behaves in ways that are governed by their group membership *if* there is a clear contrast between the ingroup and outgroup. This is called the meta-contrast principle. Self-categorisation theory defines the meta contrast principle as an algebraic equation with which you can metaphorically understand the cognitive processes at work. McGarty (1999) explains the algebraic equation thus:

> "The formula for the meta-contrast ratio is shown in [the equation] . . . where n_d is the number of relevant dimensions; n_x is the number of members of some category X; n_y is the number of members outside category X; and the x and y values are the positions of a member of one or the other category on a particular dimension. When the value of this ratio is greater than 1 then category x will be perceived to be an entitative category."
>
> (McGarty, 1999)

You will seldom need to use the meta-contrast equation in practice, but what is important is to recognise the complexity of self-categorisation. What McGarty's (1999) quote means is that in a given situation, people decide whether or not there is a division of "us versus them" (an entitative category) by considering whether the characteristics of the people around them show a clear division of "us versus them." The equation suggests that people decide this by taking into consideration the numbers of people in the room or place, and the number of dimensions upon which they are judging people's characteristics. Brown (2001) presents a textual version of the meta-contrast principle that simplifies the equation in a way that focuses on the difference between oneself and the most prototypical member of the ingroup, and the difference between the most prototypical member of an ingroup and the most prototypical member of an outgroup. Let us imagine a fictional employee, Jacob, who is an engineer. Jacob's self-concept (his idea of himself) comprises of several group memberships that matter to him, as well several personal characteristics that define his sense of who he is. Figure 5.1, which follows, illustrates the group elements of Jacob's self-concept within the areas shaded in black. The area shaded grey represents Jacob's personal characteristics, such as being an introvert, enjoying solo fishing, being good at drawing, and so on.

We see from the figure that Jacob's group memberships are shown in areas shaded black, and the more important a particular identity is to Jacob (and thus the more similar Jacob feels to the most prototypical member of that ingroup), the larger the area shaded black. For example, Jacob's gender identity as a man is quite important to him, and therefore when he is in a room full of men and women, he will probably notice how similar he is to the other men in the room, how different he is from women, and he will thus feel a sense of belonging to men. Applying social identity theory and self-categorisation theory means that being a man will probably govern Jacob's behaviour in the room. He might act in ways that he feels are typical of a man (e.g. being chivalrous towards women) or he might hold stereotypical views (e.g. thinking that men will want to talk about Premier League football and women will want to discuss cake baking or knitting). We also see that Jacob's professional identity as an engineer is very important to him, and therefore he feels very similar to what he feels is a typical engineer. This means that, even in a room full of men and women, Jacob might focus on his identity as an engineer if he sees clear differences between people who are engineers and people who are not. For example, in a room full of 20 people there

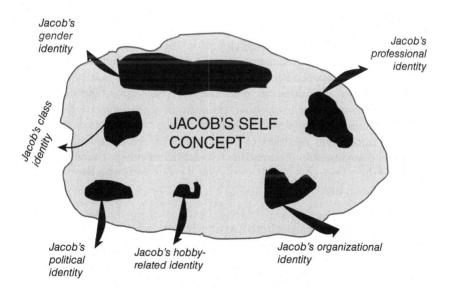

Figure 5.1 A metaphor illustrating group memberships within Jacob's self-concept

might be a group of ten people convened at the corner of the room who Jacob realises are all engineers, and therefore, what might matter to him is who is and is not an engineer – rather than who is and is not male. This means that, after a merger or acquisition, organization A versus B will be psychologically relevant to employees if the circumstances make it the most salient basis for categorising one-self and other people. The concept of "us versus them" after a merger or acquisition can also be based on other groupings, e.g. "IT staff versus other staff" and "managers versus non-managers," and these can actually unite employees from across organizations A and B depending on the circumstances.

Self-categorisation theory argues that what is in a given person's self-concept varies from person to person, and it depends on someone's history and habits as well as who else is in a given situation. As you can see from the figure, Jacob has several group identities that are important to him and therefore, whenever he is in a social situation – even at work – he has the option of activating any one or none of these group identities. Let us recall the meta contrast ratio and understand what it means for Jacob. Brown (2000) simplified this ratio as comprising of two components. One component, the denominator, is the difference between the self (e.g. Jacob) and the most prototypical member of the ingroup (e.g. Bodega, the organization where Jacob works). The second component, the numerator, is the difference between the most prototypical member of the ingroup (e.g. an employee who best embodies a typical employee in Bodega) and the most prototypical member of the outgroup (e.g. an employee who best embodies a typical employee in the organization acquiring Bodega, Zunicon). If the numera-tor is greater than the denominator, which means that the intergroup differ-ences between Bodega and Zunicon are greater than the intragroup differences within either, the meta contrast principle would predict that Jacob will activate his organizational identity as a Bodega employee. His attitudes or behaviours will exhibit ingroup bias favouring employees in Bodega, and he will engage in outgroup discrimination against employees in Zunicon, such as not including their ideas in projects or nominating them for redundancy. The greater the intra-group differences between Bodega and Zunicon, the bigger these problems. Put simply, mergers or acquisitions are most likely to evoke ingroup bias or outgroup discrimination when they involve two very different organizations and employees who view themselves as typical employees within the "old" organization.

Having understood the theories that explain how people think and behave when group membership is potentially relevant, let us now examine evidence of "us versus them" attitudes or behaviours among employees who have undergone a merger or acquisition.

Evidence of "us versus them" attitudes or behaviours in merged or acquired organizations

Social identity theory and self-categorisation theory have been used to study employees undergoing mergers and acquisitions (Amiot et al., 2007; Bartels et al., 2006; Boen et al., 2007; Edwards & Edwards, 2012; Fischer et al., 2007;

Giessner & Mummendey, 2008; Giessner et al., 2006; Giessner et al., 2012; Gleibs et al., 2008; Hogg & Terry, 2000; Jetten, Duck, et al., 2002; Panchal & Cartwright, 2001; Terry & Callan, 1998; Terry et al., 2001; Ullrich et al., 2005; van Dick et al., 2004; van Knippenberg et al., 2002; van Leeuwen et al., 2003). These theories are commonly called group processes and intergroup relations theories, and they are influential within many psychological studies about mergers and acquisitions. They are useful theories when researchers examine how organizational identity, self-categorisation, ingroup bias, outgroup discrimination, and other group processes govern employees' attitudes and behaviours towards other employees after a merger or acquisition. This chapter will not review the application of social identity theory and self-categorisation theory within studies about mergers or acquisitions because reviews exist in previous literature (e.g. Giessner, 2011). What this chapter will do is help you understand some key conclusions from the literature that can help organizations prevent "us versus them" attitudes or behaviours among employees.

Lesson 1 – Beware of the psychological power of the "old" organization after a merger or acquisition

Employees can hold on to their feelings of affiliation with the pre-merged or pre-acquired organization because the salience of the "old" organization might remain powerful, especially if the old logo, team, clients, and physical location are unchanged. Studies have found that the extent to which employees feel they belong to the new organization after a merger or acquisition is often lower than their feelings of belonging towards the old organization (Boen et al., 2007; van Knippenberg et al., 2002; van Leeuwen et al., 2003; van Dick et al., 2004; Gleibs et al., 2008; Giessner, Ullrich, & van Dick, 2012). The problem can be compounded by a lack of rebranding or integration of the two organizations. In a replication of the minimal group paradigm, van Leeuwen et al. (2003) found that the more a new group was perceived as a continuation of the old group, the more people displayed ingroup bias. In a study of employees' perceptions of a merged organization in banking, Gaertner, Dovidio, and Bachman (1996) suggests that the more the employees perceived the two organizations as one group, the lower their levels of intergroup anxiety were, whereas the more they perceived the organizations as two separate groups, the higher their level of intergroup bias. Therefore, it is important to understand the power of the old organization, and the relevance of employees' emotions (e.g. feeling threatened or fearful) as cognitions that fuel attitudes or behaviours of "us versus them" in mergers and acquisitions.

Lesson 2 – Rebrand and integrate the two organizations after a merger or acquisition

Evidence shows that there are psychological and organizational benefits of embracing the new organization after a merger or acquisition. If employees develop a strong organizational identity relating to the new organization after the merger or acquisition, research shows that this is conducive to successful integration outcomes (Gleibs, Noack, & Mummendey, 2010). Evidence shows that when employees believe they share a common future in the new organization it increases their level of commitment and engagement, which leads to better workplace cooperation (Kramer, 1991; Tyler, 1999), organizational citizenship behaviour (Dutton, Dukerich, & Harquail, 1994), support for the organization (Mael & Ashforth, 1995), and lower staff turnover (Mael & Ashforth, 1995; Tyler, 1999). It also improves perceptions of fairness and smooth adjustment (Amiot et al., 2007), commitment, job satisfaction, and wellbeing (Terry et al., 2001).

Applying theories about social identity and self-categorisation suggests that mergers and acquisitions should ideally result in the formation of a new organization with a new name, and with physical and psychological integration of employees as a way of minimising ingroup bias associated with the old organizations. Without that, self-categorisation processes can encourage employees to defend perceived threats to their old organizational identity and stereotype or allocate unfavourable traits to the outgroup as a way of defending their old organizational identity (Deaux & Emswiller, 1974; Hewstone & Jaspars, 1982; Deschamps & Clemence, 1987). However, while rebranding and physical/psychological integration is feasible in some types of mergers, it is less likely to be possible in cases of mergers or acquisitions where the two organizations retain their former branding and physical/staffing infrastructure. Creating a unified organizational identity can also be made difficult by real or perceived differences in the status or power of the two organizations involved in a merger or acquisition.

Lesson 3 – Beware of the impact of status differences between the two organizations

Mergers and acquisitions are very rarely of equals, and therefore the process of forming a new organizational identity is often made difficult by the difference in status between the two organizations (Amiot et al., 2007; Boen et al., 2007; Ellemers et al., 1992). For example, even in a merger that is supposedly of equals, one organization might have a higher financial status or a better reputation than the other, a more recognisable brand or a bigger share of the consumer market. One organization might also have to compromise by moving its staff to the other's locations. Organizations going through an acquisition are also often subsumed by the identity of the organization taking them over. Therefore, status can determine how much employees identify with the new organization blending the two (van Knippenberg et al., 2002). Employees from the high-status organization (e.g. the acquirer, or – in a merger – the more profitable or well-known of the two organizations) might view themselves as the dominant of the two organizations. This could give them the advantage of being in a position of assimilating the lower-status organization and dominating the new organization's brand, operations, location, and so on. Being in the dominant organization might make employees from the high-status organization more willing to embrace a merger or acquisition. Research suggests that employees from the low-status organization tend to perceive the merger or acquisition as unfair (Amiot et al., 2007). They can feel attached to their old organizational identity and uncertain about embracing a new one. Evidence shows that status differentials in mergers or acquisitions correlate with ingroup bias, affective responses, and perceptions of stability and threat (Terry & Callan, 1998). Employees from low-status groups often hold onto reasons why they differ from other groups by choosing "status irrelevant" dimensions of comparison (Terry & Callan, 1998). For example, employees in a small web company about to be acquired by a technological giant can think of themselves as doing well in being innovative, small, and friendly.

In research aimed at examining the ingroup bias in response to an anticipated merger between two hospitals, Terry and Callan (1998) found that the low-status employees rated themselves more positively on status-irrelevant dimensions than the high-status group rated them, and moreover, that the low-status group derogated the high-status group on the status-irrelevant dimensions. Also, employees of the low-status group rated the high-status group on the status-irrelevant dimensions more negatively than the high-status group rated themselves. In this study, the authors operationalised status dimensions in terms of high prestige, challenging job opportunities, and high variety in patient care, while the status-irrelevant dimensions, in terms of inter alia, good relations between staff, good communication by management, and relaxed work environment. The low-status group thus viewed the other group as having superior competence level, and the ingroup as higher on scales that defined interpersonal relations. Similar findings were also obtained by Terry et al. (2001) in the case of a newly merged airline company, where the low-status employees viewed their merger partner higher in technical expertise and professional attitudes, and described their ingroup as higher on communication skills, hard work, and administrative efficiency.

We know from the field of group processes and social cognition that, within a prototypically homogenous and cohesive group, group members seek to differentiate themselves from the outgroup and increase similarities within the ingroup (Fiske & Taylor, 1991; Hamilton & Sherman, 1996; Hamilton, Sherman, & Lickel, 1998; Sherman, Hamilton, & Lewis, 1999; Hogg & Terry, 2000). Employees in a lower-status organization can tend to view the differences between the two organizations as more pronounced than employees from the more dominant organization (van Knippenberg et al., 2002). Making group processes even more difficult is the fact that employees can influence each other and views among ingroup members can converge (Keltner & Haidt, 1999; McHugo, Lanzetta, Sullivan, Masters, & Englis, 1985; van der Schalk et al., 2011). That process can amplify beliefs among employees that there are substantial differences between the two organizations involved in the merger or acquisition, and employees from both sides can end up sharing the same belief about which organization is of higher status than the other. Empirical evidence shows that groups tend to recognize their respective status (Blake & Mouton, 1985; Buono et al., 1985; Schweiger, Ivancevich, & Power, 1987; Terry & Callan, 1998; Terry et al., 2001), cognitively legitimise (Halsall, 2008; Roundy, 2010; Vaara, Tienari, &

Laurila, 2006; Vaara & Tienari, 2011; Zhu & McKenna, 2012) and dominant groups perpetuate a reality that confirms their sense of being higher in the hierarchy (Deschamps & Clémence, 1987; Pettigrew, 1979). Several empirical studies also suggest that employees from both the low- and high-status organizations can hold similar views about the status each group holds in the post-merger or post-acquisition organization (Bastien, 1987; Blake & Mouton, 1985; Buono et al., 1985; Gaertner et al., 1996). As social dominance theory proposes (Sidanius & Pratto, 1999), groups can create a mythical reality that enhances or attenuates hierarchical differences between them and other groups (Pratto, Sidanius, Stallworth, & Malle, 1994).

Evidence (e.g. Terry et al., 2001; Amiot et al., 2007) shows that status differentials can arise even in mergers "of equals." This may be because status can be defined in different ways. Haunschild, Davis-Blake, and Fichman (1994) and Terry and Callan (1998) defined status in terms of technical skills, while in a laboratory experiment, Boen et al. (2007) manipulated the status by informing participants about their pre-merger performance. Other studies define status in terms of dominance akin to power (van Knippenberg et al., 2002). In their empirical study of one merger of two local government organizations and one merger of two secondary education institutions, van Knippenberg et al. (2002) operationalised status in terms of prestige, and questionnaire items referred to the level of influence in the merger process by the merger partners. Status can also be defined in terms of the resources held by each organization, because these can shape hierarchy within the new organization (Clegg, 1989; Vaara et al., 2005). Resources can be tangible, such as money, property and staff, or intangible, such as what is known as social capital or cultural capital (Bourdieu, 1984, 1986, 1989).

Lesson 4 – Being in the lower-status organizations can reduce job satisfaction and esteem

We discussed the concept of status earlier and concluded that status differences can antagonise intergroup relations (Bastien, 1987; Vaara et al., 2003). Status is relevant not just because of group processes and their related concepts, such as organizational identity, but also because status differences are an important antecedent to job satisfaction (Terry et al., 2001; Amiot et al., 2007; Makri & Hantzi, 2012). Employees of low-status organizations tend to feel less satisfied with their jobs than employees from high-status organizations. Status is also relevant to how satisfied employees are with a merger or acquisition. Covin et al. (1996) devised items to measure satisfaction such as "*The atmosphere at the organization is becoming similar to 'the good old days,'*" or "*All things considered, the merger should not have taken place*" (Buono, Bowditch, & Lewis, 1988). Evidence shows that employees with the acquiring organization display higher levels of satisfaction than the employees of the acquired organization (Terry et al., 2001).

Belonging to the lower-status organization after a merger or acquisition can also reduce employees' sense of esteem at work. People want to be associated with groups that have a positive identity (Tajfel & Turner, 1979) or what is sometimes called a sense of "positive distinctiveness" (Abrams & Hogg, 1988). This means that people want to be associated with groups that are popular or doing well because this adds value to their sense of self, contributing to what is known as "collective self-esteem" (Luhtanen & Crocker, 1992). A loss of group status can reduce collective self-esteem (Lupina-Wegener et al., 2011; Piekkari et al., 2005; Vaara, 2000). When people are trying hard to maintain group boundaries, this can make them behave competitively or uncooperatively, which can jeopardize the success of a merger or acquisition (Empson, 2001).

Lesson 5 – Emotions fuel intergroup rivalry between the two organizations

In the previous chapter we discussed how employees display feelings of anger, anxiety, confusion, insecurity, shock, resentment, and resistance. It is plausible that some of these emotions arise from the anticipation of intergroup rivalry, and that emotions fuel a sense of "us versus them." For example, employees feel that a merger or acquisition threatens their previous organizational identity (Terry et al., 2001; Haunschild et al., 1994; Rousseau, 1998). Group processes can also encourage feelings of mistrust and uncertainty about the intentions of the outgroup, strengthening the psychological boundaries between the two groups and the old organizational identity (Hogg & Terry, 2000), explaining why research observes anxiety, trauma (Scwheiger et al., 1987), threat, and uncertainty (Haunschild et al., 1994; Terry et al., 2001) among employees after mergers and acquisitions. Also, status differences between the organizations involved in a merger or acquisition can make employees feel pessimistic. An experiment by Fischer et al. (2007) found that an organization's status predicted employees' satisfaction with a merger, and that employees in the low-status organization were more pessimistic in believing that the merger was not beneficial in the long term.

We believe that group processes exacerbate employees' emotions about mergers or acquisitions, and that emotions fuel group processes evoking intergroup rivalry. Evidence shows that employees can feel betrayed, deceived, or exploited by either the acquiring organization (Brown & Humphreys, 2003) or their own organization (Searle & Ball, 2004). Employees often also feel that HR policies are applied inconsistently (Teram, 2010), and that mergers or acquisitions are seen by employees as threatening events. Feelings of threat are often connected with group identity and the self-esteem that people derive from their group membership (Amiot et al., 2007; Colman & Lunnan, 2011), as well as the sense of structure, meaning, and security that membership to a group provides (Spicer, 2011) and the potential loss of material or symbolic resources held by the group (Smith et al., 2013). Threat in mergers and acquisitions literature has also been framed in terms of existential risks posed on the groups involved (van Vuuren et al., 2010; Clark et al., 2010; Lupina-Wegener et al., 2011), and in terms of the need to compete for resources and power (Smith et al., 2013).

Employees feel threatened by fears that the central, distinctive, and enduring aspects of their organization are going to disintegrate (Jacobs et al., 2013), and that embedded ways of thinking, values, and beliefs central to their old organization are in jeopardy from a merger or acquisition (Spicer, 2011; Colman & Lunnan, 2011). If an outgroup organization has very different values or beliefs, this can make employees feel threatened. Dissimilar outgroups challenge the validity of on an ingroup's values and the threats that this poses to the self-esteem of ingroup members can make them behave defensively and reject or ridicule the outgroup (Greenberg et al., 1990; Greenberg, Solomon, & Pyszczynski, 1997; Solomon, Greenberg, & Pyszczynski, 1991). They can also perceive interactions with the outgroup as a sign of submission and a threat to their old group identity (Smith et al., 2013). Threat is linked with the urge to eliminate the source of threat through fight, flight, or freeze responses (Blanchard et al., 2001), therefore, consultants and researchers working with employees experiencing a merger or acquisition really need to understand the far-reaching consequences of threat as a form of affect. We recommend assessing the extent to which employees perceive a merger or acquisition as a threat using available scales (e.g. Zhou et al., 2008). Other emotions can make employees feel even more threatened. For instance, ambiguity about the impact of the merger or acquisition on their career progression, rewards, and job security can make them interpret information about the merger or acquisition in threatening terms (Goddard & Palmer, 2010; Lupina-Wegener, 2013; Burlew et al., 1994; Clark et al., 2010; Kovoor-Misra & Smith, 2008).

As well as threat, group processes can explain other common emotions in mergers or acquisitions. For instance, uncertainty and anxiety (see Chapter 3) are common. This could be because employees feel unsure about their future in the new organization (Searle & Ball, 2004) and its rewarding prospects, because people joining a new group are more likely to develop a sense of belonging if the group is rewarding (Kamau, 2013). It can also be because mergers or acquisitions force changes in what an organization stands for, as well as its culture, meaning that even those factors that are not necessarily related to social identity, self-categorisation, or other group processes can be interpreted from the lens of group processes. The introduction of strict new working arrangements or standards (Kavanagh & Ashkanasy, 2006) can make employees feel overwhelmed by new targets and expectations (Drori et al., 2013), and create a sense of cultural anxiety about what their organization stands for, making employees wonder, "*What are the organization's values or norms now, and where do I fit in?*" Styhre et al. (2006) wrote about cultural anxiety in mergers and acquisitions as an effective response to changes within the organizational reality. Styhre et al. studied the emotional experience of employees in two merger cases (Astra with Zeneca, and Ford with Volvo) and found differences among the cultures of the different organizations. They found that employees became anxious as a result of the culture clash because previously familiar and established procedures, practices, or norms were now potentially contentious. Employees were also made anxious by differences in management, mistrust, inequality among employees, a short-term financial focus by the organization, and a clash of individualist versus collectivist cultural values. The literature also suggests that some employees fear "cultural contamination" of their organization's public image. Employees in high-status organizations can fear being associated with a "downmarket" organization or having their public image "contaminated" by a less savvy or trendy organization that will hurt their reputation (Junni, 2011; Mirc, 2012). Therefore, emotions such as anxiety about a merger or acquisition can be understood from a group processes perspective.

By considering the role of emotions within an organization's understanding of "us versus them" attitudes or behaviours, you will be bridging two very different fields of psychology – but this is necessary within applied areas of the subject, such as in helping employees and organizations who have experienced a merger or acquisition. Just as meta-approach is encouraged more generally within the field (Grant & Pollock, 2011), we call for this kind of "meta-approach" to understanding the cognitive processes that underpin employees' perceptions about their new and old organization. In other words, although self-categorisation theory and social identity theory do not explicitly discuss the role of emotions, it is important to acknowledge the importance of fear, shock, anger, and other types of affect as cognitions that can fuel the fire of "us versus them." Although several attempts have been made to bridge different theoretical frameworks, these have focused on bridging the psychological and non-psychological literature and on specific outcomes, such as employee health and wellbeing (e.g. van Oudenhoven & de Boer, 1995; Citera & Stuhlmacher, 2001), and how employees interpret power differentials (Haunschild et al., 1994; Terry & Callan, 1998; Boen et al., 2007; van Knippenberg et al., 2002).

We therefore urge researchers examining intergroup rivalry after mergers and acquisitions to include measurements of employees' emotions. For instance, it is plausible that employees experience fear that their previous organizational identity will be undermined by the merger or acquisition, so they fail to engage in self-categorisations of "we" (in the superordinate sense of embracing both organizations) and zoom instead to the previous organizational identity in their search for positive distinctiveness, which they connect with their self-efficacy, self-worth, and self-consistency (Millwar & Kyriakidou, 2004; Ashforth & Mael, 1989). Emotions can thus fuel employees' self-categorisations of themselves and others after a merger or acquisition in terms of "us versus them."

Conclusions

This chapter helped you explore theories about group processes and intergroup relations – social identity theory and self-categorisation theory. These theories helped you discover why employees can react to mergers and acquisitions from the lens of "us versus them" or "ingroups versus outgroups." In this chapter, we explored key concepts within these theories, such as the meta-contrast principle and its implications for how people evaluate the relevance of their group membership in different social situations. We then gave you an overview of the evidence about "us versus them" attitudes or behaviours after mergers or acquisitions, such as the power of the old organization, especially when employees feel that there is continuity in the identity of the organization after a merger or acquisition. We then discussed evidence of the impact of status differences on employees after mergers or acquisitions, and the relevance of employees' emotions as cognitions that fuel a sense of intergroup rivalry. We also discussed the impact of group processes on emotions, such as threat and employees' pessimism about a merger or acquisition. By understanding the importance of group processes and intergroup relations in the attitudes and behaviours of employees, you can help organizations (and employees) take preventative steps. Effectively rebranding and integrating two organizations after a merger or acquisition is important not just because it reduces the chances of intergroup rivalry within the new organization, but also because it improves employees' commitment and satisfaction. This leads us to explore some of the ways that cultural differences between organizations can have an impact on the way that employees interact in Chapter 6.

6 Why cultural differences in nonverbal language and workplace interactions create problems among employees experiencing mergers and acquisitions

Mergers or acquisitions that involve a clash of culture are more likely to fail (Schoenberg, 2006), and cultural clashes can be understood by considering factors that increase interpersonal conflict or misunderstandings among employees. Culture can be defined in terms of the objects, values, and behaviours that are considered normal in a particular country, industry, or organization. Defining culture in organizational psychology requires an understanding of practices (e.g. business procedures), language (e.g. nonverbal behaviour), artefacts (e.g. office décor), branding (e.g. imagery in advertisements), symbolism (e.g. beliefs or values), and so on. Nonverbal language is one of the most important determinants of how well employees interact and communicate with each other, yet it is a topic that is almost non-existent within previous literature about mergers and acquisitions. Interpersonal communication between employees involves not just what they say to each other, but how they say it, e.g. eye contact, facial expressions, voice pitch, clothing style, walking style, posture, the wording of emails, and more. Such nonverbal behaviour is said to be one of the most important elements of human communication (DePaulo, 1992). Cultural similarity can shape how employees perceive each other and whether they interpret certain behaviour as normal versus abnormal, polite versus or rude, typical versus bullying. Many studies have found that nonverbal aspects of interpersonal communication predict good-quality workplace relations, perceptions among employees, positive attitudes towards employees, their chances of promotion, their sales performance, and other workplace outcomes (see Kamau, 2009, for a review). Cultural norms are important because culture shapes the "rules" or "dialects" that are considered normal or expected in nonverbal communication (Ekman & Davidson, 1994; Elfenbein, Beaupré, Lévesque, & Hess, 2007; Matsumoto et al., 2005). These norms are often familiar to people inside a culture but, to outsiders, the norms can be unfamiliar (Richardson & McKenna, 2006), creating the potential for problems such as conflict or misunderstandings among employees after mergers or acquisitions that involve organizations from different cultures in terms of nation or sector. It is also plausible that cultural clashes can occur even among mergers or acquisitions within the same country or sector because different organizations can have different cultural norms. Mergers or acquisitions might thus be seen by employees as events that pose a threat to their organization's cultural values (e.g. the way that managers and employees interact), and this might prompt employees to resist a merger or acquisition because of the threat it poses to their workplace culture. This chapter will discuss the relevance of cultural norms about nonverbal language to mergers and acquisitions, and the possible impact of employees misunderstanding messages or attitudes conveyed by other employees, increasing the chances of workplace hostility, hyper-vigilance, or paranoia and other negative outcomes. This chapter will also discuss the potential impact of cultural differences in nonverbal language on the likelihood of employees experiencing stress, depression, and burnout after a merger or acquisition. We will discuss laboratory research from neuroscience showing that when people misunderstand or make errors in nonverbal communication, there is evidence that this activates distress signals within the brain (Kim, Liss, Rao, Singer, & Compton, 2012; Klucharev, Hytonen, Rijpkema, Smidts, & Fernandez, 2009). Cultural differences could be one of the reasons why employees going through a merger or acquisition are at higher risk of depression (Cartwright & Cooper, 1993; Joslin et al., 2010; Cartwright et al., 2007; Väänänen et al., 2011) and emotional exhaustion (Väänänen et al., 2004). This chapter will then examine further directions for research in this field, and ways that organizations can prevent problems arising from cultural differences among employees by helping them develop intercultural competence. It is important to remember that mergers or acquisitions across cultures have many advantages, therefore, this chapter encourages organizations to learn about the potential pitfalls then take steps to prevent cultural differences from having a negative impact on employees. Organizations should be aware of the potential pitfalls but they should not avoid entering into cross-cultural mergers or acquisitions.

How cultural differences among employees hinder mergers and acquisitions

Studies about organizations that have been through a cross-cultural merger or acquisition show that many experience cultural differences in how employees interact or behave and there are consequences for conflict, trust, and integration among employees. Ailon-Souday and Kunda's (2003) ethnographic study found that, in a case of an American organization acquired by an Israeli organization, there were cultural differences among employees in their formal or informal behaviour at work, and in their deference towards managers or people in authority. The study suggested that Israeli workers had a more informal working culture than American employees. The cultural differences were exacerbated by language differences, and the employees categorising each other as Americans or Israelis (Ailon-Souday and Kunda, 2003). It is possible that the Israeli employees might have faced problems such as finding that their informal behaviour within the workplace was misunderstood or negatively evaluated by American employees who were more accustomed to formal workplace norms. Likewise, the American employees might have experienced negative outcomes from Israeli employees for their formality, such as being misunderstood as unfriendly or hostile. Another study by Frederick and Rodriguez (1994) found that, after an acquisition of a German company by a Spanish company, employees in the two companies had cultural differences in their working practices. The study found that German workers had rigid, procedural, detail-focused approaches to working whereas Spanish workers had more relaxed, flexible, and accommodating working practices. The study suggested that the cultural differences eventually fuelled mistrust among the employees, particularly towards people in management. It is plausible that mistrust arises from managers and employees misinterpreting each other because of cultural differences. Brannen and Salk's (2000) study found that, after a merger between a German and a Japanese organization, conflict arose because of cultural differences in the two organization's norms about decision-making, ideas about work, how employees perceived their job roles, language, and market orientation. For example, the study found that Japanese employees tended to work late, while German employees tended to leave work at 5 pm. It is possible that employees do misinterpret each other's behaviour – for example, the Japanese workers might have thought of the German workers as uncommitted or not hardworking enough because they did not work late, with potential negative consequences for job appraisals and promotions. Brannen and Salk's study found that German employees tended to feel more empowered to make decisions or solve problems independently, suggesting that this might create conflict between them and Japanese managers who might negatively evaluate independent decision-making as insubordination or disrespect.

Another example of how cultural differences can have an impact on employees after a merger or acquisition is a study by Styhre et al. (2006), who conducted qualitative interviews of some employees at AstraZeneca (the result of a merger between the Swedish company Astra with the British company Zeneca), and Volvo (a Swedish company) acquired by Ford (a US company). The study suggested that US and Swedish cultures have different management cultures, for example, an employee from Volvo said, "The American culture and our culture – it is actually a culture shock. They want to control from the top what we do, and they think that if you can control something, that's great. We never think in those terms at Volvo" (Styhre et al., 2006, p. 1300). Another example suggesting that Swedish employees perceived cultural differences in the management style of US-based Ford company, suggesting that it is a top-down, hierarchical management style, was a designer at Volvo who said:

> We Swedes are used to taking responsibility and being given responsibility, that is why we have a flat organization structure. In the US you never do more than what the boss tells you to. If you do, you're out, even if you do a good thing, because you pose a threat to your boss. You must never by-pass your boss. You ask your boss who in turn asks his or her boss. And don't you forget anyone. We do not have such a society. Here, any employee can, more or less, walk up to the CEO and complain about me, or anyone else. It is an opportunity, but not in the US . . . It is a good thing because it makes all people feel commitment.
>
> (A Volvo employee on the management style within the US Ford company, which acquired Volvo; Styhre et al., 2006, p. 1300)

It is plausible that cross-cultural mergers or acquisitions with companies consisting of the sort of hierarchical management style described in Styhre et al. could make workers from cultures with less power distance between managers and non-managers feel bullied or micro-managed, possibly escalating into filing a grievance, quitting, or taking industrial action. However, it is important to note that the top-down culture described by employees as the culture of the US-based Ford company (Styhre et al., 2006) may be a culture unique to Ford, rather than all US companies. A different study of a US company within the automobile sector found that the US company in that case had a more informal, less top-down management approach, showing that cultural differences in mergers or acquisitions arise not just from national differences, but also from differences between organizations (Badrtalei & Bates, 2007).

Badrtalei and Bates (2007) discussed the 1998 merger between the German company Daimler-Benz and the US company Chrysler. The two companies are said by Badrtalei & Bates to have had different cultures in terms of workplace formality and independence in decision-making, with Daimler-Benz having a formal culture of using titles, formal names, and wearing suits with ties, in contrast to Chrysler's casual interactions, clothing, and a less-hierarchical approach to decision-making. A related point is that, whereas all Daimler-Benz employees were accustomed to flying first class, only some employees at Chrysler were allowed to fly first class, and this caused a lot of conflict that Badrtalei & Bates say took six month to resolve. Chrysler's executives were paid substantially more in basic salaries and bonuses than Daimler-Benz executives, but decision-making in the latter company was more formal and hierarchical. Another cultural difference suggested by Badrtalei & Bates was that, whereas German culture made it normal for Daimler-Benz employees to drink wine with lunch, alcohol was banned in Chrysler. Therefore, the cultural differences in the case of Daimler-Benz and Chrysler arose from a mix of organizational and national factors. The merged DaimlerChrysler was controversial among shareholders who argued that it was a merger of equals on paper, but a takeover of Chrysler by Daimler in practice; they filed a class-action lawsuit and won a settlement of $300 million in 2003 (English, 2003). The merger led to many job cuts, losses, and management changeovers that Badrtalei & Bates blame, in part, on cultural differences. DaimlerChrysler eventually sold off Chrysler in 2007 but, without empirical data about the impact of cultural differences on the merger's failure, we cannot conclusively say that culture was the only or biggest contributor to the merger's ending. There are other factors to consider, such as market variables within the automobile industry, competition, and business decisions after the DaimlerChrysler merger that may have led the merger to fail. However, it is plausible that cultural differences make executives, shareholders, and employees more pessimistic about other problems with an organization, hastening the ending of the merger or acquisition.

Cultural differences in how employees dress and behave have also been noted in other studies. Buono et al. (1985) suggested that cultural differences become salient after mergers or acquisitions in ways that are both intangible (e.g. norms and values) and tangible (e.g. objects, as the layout of offices, décor, dress code, etiquette, and so on). McEntire and Bentley's (1996) study of a merger observed cultural differences in terms of the structure of offices, décor, employees' style of clothing and grooming, length of men's hair, beards, and clothing fabric. The study found that the way employees spoke was a source of conflict and derogatory behaviour among employees of the two organizations involved in the merger.

Despite such fascinating insights into the presence of cultural differences in the way that employees from different organizations behave or interact, there is very little in-depth empirical research about cultural differences in nonverbal language within cases of mergers or acquisitions across or within countries. The studies that we review hint at the fact that, in workplace interactions, what is important is not just *what* an employee says but also *how* they say it. When two people are speaking to each other, their eye contact, tone of voice, posture, hand gestures, facial expressions, and other nonverbal language cues or signals matter (DePaulo, 1992). Countries, regions, industries, and organizations can differ in what is considered normal or good nonverbal language. Culture can thus determine whether an employee's behaviour is perceived and evaluated positively (e.g. being liked or promoted) or whether the same behaviour, from the lens of a different culture, leads the employee to be perceived negatively or penalised (e.g. being seen as incompetent or having their job at risk). We will now explore the concept of nonverbal language in more detail, helping you understand why it is an important yet neglected topic within the psychology of mergers and acquisitions.

Why do cultural differences in nonverbal language matter in mergers or acquisitions?

It is plausible that employees use nonverbal language to help them establish successful working relationships with new managers or colleagues after a merger or acquisition. Research shows that people use nonverbal language (e.g. eye contact, posture, clothing, accent) to help them come across as competent, likeable, respectable, committed, and so on – something called impression management and is defined as the manipulation of one's nonverbal behaviour to achieve a mental, material or social goal (Leary & Kowalski, 1990). Studies show that employees who use impression management strategies have higher chances of positive outcomes such as having their work colleagues or managers rate them as likeable, competent, or promotable (Bolino & Turnley, 2003; Leary & Kowalski, 1990; Rosenfeld, Giacalone, & Riordan, 1995; see Kamau, 2009, for a review). Being able to convey a positive impression through nonverbal language can therefore help employees get along with each other, like each other and work well on projects after mergers or acquisitions that combine teams from different organizations or port managers or executive teams across organizations. A merger or acquisition that combines organizations with different cultural practices can make it difficult for employees to be understood by other employees, managers, or clients. This, in turn, can hinder the goals that employees have within their work, such as being persuasive, being seen as competent, being trusted, or having one's leadership role respected. There are many studies about how employees use nonverbal behaviour to achieve goals such as closing a sale (Leigh & Summers, 2002), gaining promotion (Westphal & Stern, 2007), influencing their manager's or supervisors' ratings of them (Vilela, González, Ferrín, & del Río Araújo, 2007), and gaining positive performance evaluations (Gordon, 1996; Bolino & Turnley, 2003). Impression management is thus important because nonverbal communication contributes to how people perceive an employee's competence, power, likeability, and reciprocal liking (see Kamau, 2009, for a review). An impression management strategy is a complex cluster of different verbal and nonverbal signals to other people (e.g. certain facial expressions, clothing styles, attitudes) and there are many possible impression management strategies that employees in many organizations use, each with a variety of possible goals and outcomes (Rosenfeld et al., 1995). A merger or acquisition that introduces cultural differences can thus disrupt the outcomes that employees achieve from speaking with colleagues, managers or clients, yet there is very little research about this. Remember that culture can be defined in many ways, e.g. industry, region, social class, ethnicity, nation, political or economic climate, and so on. Therefore, what matters is whether the cultural differences hinder employees' optimal ability to speak to each other, influence each other, lead or follow each other, and work with each other. Here are some possible examples:

Table 6.1 How cross-cultural mergers or acquisitions can hinder employees' achievement of workplace goals

Example	Cultural norms in Organization A	Cultural norms in Organization B	The impact of the cultural differences
Imagine Harry, a factory manager in a chemicals manufacturing company (Organization A). A then acquires Organization B, a lorry company that delivers large chemicals to customers who order them. After the acquisition, Harry is transferred to work in Organization B.	In Organization A, Harry is a factory manager. He has to very closely manage all operations within the factory, and he has to be consulted about most or all decisions by factory supervisors. Harry behaves decisively and uses nonverbal language that conveys his sense of authority over the factory. Harry often raises his voice and he comes across as impatient and abrupt. Employees in Organization A usually respond to Harry's demeanour by complying with him. It is also "normal" for supervisors and managers in all parts of Organization A to behave like Harry.	In Organization B, the lorry drivers are accustomed to working independently and managing their own work, which they have done within Organization B for many years. The people who have had the role of their manager usually focus their time on strategy (e.g. increasing orders from customers or winning new customers, financial accounting, and marketing). The culture within Organization B is one in which managers or supervisors behave politely towards employees, and where authoritarian behaviour is rare or unheard of.	In his first week as a manager in Organization B, Harry calls a staff meeting and the lorry drivers are shocked by Harry's nonverbal language. They become hostile when he shouts, and they start losing respect for him when he behaves abruptly. Harry then starts micromanaging the lorry drivers by phoning them often, sending them many emails, and asking them to inform him about every aspect of their work. The lorry drivers become angry, upset, and distressed. They join together and approach the human resources department and their union representative, asking for Harry to be removed as their manager. Harry becomes confused and upset when he hears this and he feels stressed.

Conclusion: In this example, we can see that the cultural differences have hindered Harry's goals of being a competent, respected manager in an environment that is not hostile (from his perspective). The cultural differences have also hindered the lorry drivers' goals of working independently in a working environment that is not hostile. Of course, objectively speaking, we can see that Harry's managerial style is actually not a good one and that the culture in Organization A of allowing shouting or abrupt behaviour is probably quite harmful to the wellbeing of workers subjected to such behaviour. Nonetheless, the cross-cultural acquisition leaves both Harry and the lorry drivers feeling unhappy and unable to fulfil their workplace goals properly.

Example	Cultural norms in Organization A	Cultural norms in Organization B	The impact of the cultural differences
Imagine Shihoko, a product designer within an engineering company in Nagoya, Japan (Organization A). The company is merging with an engineering company in London, England (Organization B) and Shihoko is asked to work in B for six months to help with the merger.	Shihoko, like most employees in Organization A, behaves deferentially towards her manager and any employee who is older, because of Japanese cultural norms. When they have team meetings, Shihoko and other employees agree with everything their manager says, and they seldom express doubts or disagreement with their manager's ideas or plans. Shihoko's manager rewards her nonverbal behaviour by approving her application for promotion. During her appraisal meeting, her manager tells her that he is very pleased with her performance at work.	In Organization B, it is normal for employees to furiously debate ideas during team meetings. Managers in Organization B like employees to come up with alternative ideas or suggestions about why an idea is wrong or flawed. Employees often sigh, roll their eyes, fold their arms, or laugh loudly during team meetings, and the manager does not construe that as a sign of disrespect. The manager rewards employees who are the most vocal during debates in team meetings by approving their application for promotion. Disagreeable behaviour is construed positively in Organization B.	When Shihoko has a meeting with her manager in Organization B, she is quiet and deferential, which makes her manager think that she might not be competent enough for the job. During the team meetings, Shihoko nods when the manager speaks and stays quiet during the debate because she wants the manager to see her as someone who complies with his ideas. Shihoko's compliant and quiet behaviour makes other employees start to doubt her capability as a product designer. Because Shihoko does not animate her facial expressions or laugh loudly, they start gossiping about whether or not they can trust her. During her appraisal, Shihoko's manager tells her that her performance requires improvement and that he may terminate her contract, which makes Shihoko feel shocked, confused, and upset.

Conclusion: In this example, we can see that Shihoko, despite being a competent product designer, is misunderstood in Organization B and has a negative appraisal by her manager because of cultural differences in what nonverbal behaviour is expected of employees there. The goals she achieved in Organization A (e.g. being liked by her manager, promoted, and having a secure job) are goals she does not achieve because the manager's expectations in Organization B are shaped by cultural norms about how a competent employee behaves. Of course, objectively speaking, the manager in Organization B should be more sympathetic about the fact that Shihoko's behaviour is shaped by cultural norms in Japanese workplaces, and it is wrong to give a negative appraisal or threaten her with job insecurity. The employees should also not be gossiping about her, but should make an effort to familiarise themselves with cultural norms against animated or loud nonverbal language in other cultures. Likewise, the manager in Organization A should not punish employees who disagree with his ideas. However, we can see that the cross-cultural merger leaves both Shihoko and the manager in Organization A feeling that each has failed to meet the expectations of the other.

We can therefore see why nonverbal language is an important aspect of employees' interactions with other employees in any organizational context, including organizations that have undergone a merger or acquisition, and that includes employees of any level (e.g. managers, senior executives). It is here that culture enters into the equation because the suitability of certain types of nonverbal communication, particularly those that form part of an impression management strategy, depends on social or organizational cultural norms (see Kamau, 2009, for a review). For instance, even just focusing on facial expressions alone, experiments suggest that people from different cultures have different "dialects" about how to animate one's face when expressing certain types of emotions (Elfenbein et al., 2007). In Shihoko's case within the example in Table 6.1, maintaining a neutral facial expression and not laughing loudly is normal and expected in Organization A, but seen as unusual in Organization B. Cultural norms can determine what employees think other employees' facial expressions mean because of variations in how emotions such as fear, anger, happiness, sadness, disgust, and surprise are expressed (Ekman and Friesen's, 1971; Russell, 1991). There is also ample evidence that different cultures vary in their norms about level of "nonverbal expressiveness" that is expected during social interactions or the extent to which someone conveys emotion nonverbally (Friedman, Prince, Riggio, & DiMatteo, 1980; Richmond, McCroskey, & Johnson, 2003). Nonverbal expressiveness involves animating one's facial expressions, varying one's vocal pitch, using a lot of eye contact while talking, displaying frequent positive cues such as smiling or laughing, and avoiding the display of negative cues such as frowning. The amount of nonverbal expressiveness that is seen as "normal" or "good" during social interactions varies from culture to culture (DePaulo, 1992; Matsumoto et al., 2005). Evidence shows that people unfamiliar with a culture are often unaware or confused about what sorts of nonverbal signals produce positive or negative reactions, including misinterpreting nonverbally expressive behaviour as rude, uncouth, or obnoxious (Spong & Kamau, 2012). Remember that cultural differences exist not just between countries but also within countries, such as comparing different sectors (Drory & Zaidman, 2007). Therefore, defining a merger or acquisition as a cross-cultural merger or acquisition requires an understanding of all relevant cultural norms.

Let us revisit the concept of impression management strategies and recall that employees use nonverbal language in order to achieve certain workplace goals. Research shows that some impression management strategies or clusters of nonverbal behaviour can backfire in some cultures and in some types of organizations, yet lead to positive results in other cultural contexts (see Kamau, 2009, for a review). This section will discuss way in which cross-cultural mergers or acquisitions can inhibit employees' success at meeting goals such as being liked, promoted, seen as competent workers, and respected by other employees. For instance, consider the goal that many employees have of being liked at work, being seen as a high performer, and getting promoted. Evidence shows that ingratiation is an impression management strategy used by employees in many workplaces to achieve these goals (Gordon, 1996). Examples of ingratiating behaviour are being agreeable, conforming to others' opinions or requests, doing favours outside one's job description, and flattering them. Many studies show that ingratiation does produce positive results for employees in some cultures, but negative results in others (Kamau, 2009). In terms of positive results, a meta-analysis by Gordon (1996) concluded that employees who ingratiate are, on average, better liked by supervisors or managers, and their performance is evaluated more positively (see also a study by Wayne & Liden, 1995). Other evidence shows that employees who engage in ingratiation are more likely to be promoted. Westphal and Stern (2007) conducted a survey of CEOs and managers from Forbes 500 companies and found that the managers' and CEOs' chances of being recommended for board appointments were connected with their display of ingratiatory behaviours such as doing favours, flattering, or agreeing with others. On the contrary, other studies have shown that Northern European workers view people who engage in ingratiation negatively. Peltokorpi (2006) interviewed 30 Danish, Norwegian, Swedish, and Finnish expatriates who were working as managers in Japan. The managers reported feeling shocked that prestige in Japan is associated with age or job rank in the workplace. The Northern European managers said they were dismayed when junior Japanese employees behaved passively or deferentially, and when they kept silent in meetings because of cultural norms discouraging junior employees from presenting their ideas directly to their seniors. In short, in some cultures, ingratiation by employees is expected and it has positive effects (e.g. the USA, Far East), but in other cultures, ingratiation is not expected and it can be counterproductive. A cross-cultural merger or acquisition can thus leave employees who engage in ingratiation unrewarded or even punished for behaviour that is expected of them in their home culture. The cultural differences can leave an employee with unmet goals of being liked, seen as a high-performer, or promoted.

As well as wanting to be liked by colleagues, manager, followers, and clients, another goal that many employees often have is to be respected. Self-promotion is an impression management strategy in which an employee meets the goal of being respected by making other people aware of their individual accomplishments, competencies, and capabilities verbally or nonverbally (Rosenfeld et al., 1995). The success of such behaviour depends on whether the surrounding culture approves or disapproves of people who engage in self-promotion. In collectivistic cultures, there is a strong emphasis on collective accomplishments (Triandis & Gelfand, 1998), therefore some studies suggest that self-promotion can produce negative outcomes in places like China (Kurman, 2001), perhaps because acting as if one is better than or very different from other people is frowned upon. On the other hand, in individualistic cultures such as France, where self-promotion and celebrating individual achievements are expected, employees who act the opposite, such as acting defeated or self-critical as part of an impression management strategy called "supplication," can experience negative outcomes (Chambon, 2005). Another example of a goal that some employees try to meet is appearing powerful, dominant, or having "downward influence" on other employees (Bolino & Turnley, 2003; Rosenfeld et al., 1995). Some employees use intimidating nonverbal behaviours such as seeming aggressive, speaking louder than normal, extending eye contact, narrowing one's eye gaze, expanding one's body in a poise that exaggerates one's physical size (e.g. sitting with extended arms or legs), using a tense voice, and showing negative facial expressions such as sneering or frowning. This is in their attempt to elicit fearful or submissive responses from other employees. Whereas research shows that intimidating nonverbal strategies have positive outcomes in some cultural contexts, e.g. the USA (see Bolino & Turnley, 2003), such behaviour can backfire in culture where honour, dignity, and saving others' "face" or preventing others' embarrassment is expected during social interactions (e.g. China, see Chang & Holt, 1994).

These examples show that nonverbal behaviour that reaps workplace rewards for employees in one culture can, in a different culture, reap negative outcomes. A cross-cultural merger or acquisition that introduces employees to an unfamiliar cultural context, including requiring them to interact through email, Skype, and phone, could result in employees experiencing frequent misunderstandings. Cognitive neuroscience research suggests that misunderstanding nonverbal language elicits distress signals within the brain, therefore organizations need to be aware of the possible impact of cross-cultural mergers or acquisitions on employees' mental health.

Functional magnetic resonance imaging (fMRI) studies show that when people make errors in nonverbal language that involve interpreting faces differently from how other people interpret them, an area of their brain called the rostral cingulate region becomes activated (Klucharev et al., 2009). A similar study by Kim et al.

(2012) used an electroencephalogram (EEG) rather than fMRI because EEG can be more precise in monitoring reactions to errors. Kim et al. found that such errors elicited signals called feedback-related negativity brainwave potential. These are brainwave signals similar to the signals elicited when people experience negative reinforcement (that is, a punishment or the lack of an expected reward). These brain signals are associated with the cingulate cortex, supporting Klucharev et al. and other evidence suggesting that the cingulate cortex is concerned with error-monitoring and responses to many types of punishment or negative reinforcement (e.g. Botvinik et al., 1999). In other words, when people make mistakes in nonverbal language, the effect on their brains is akin to getting punished or not receiving an anticipated reward. It also appears that humans have an area of their brain (the cingulate cortex) that is, at least in part, responsible for interpreting some types of nonverbal language, demonstrating the importance of nonverbal communication within human functioning. For instance, evidence suggests that the dorsal anterior cingulate cortex region of the brain is activated among people who are looking at faces expressing anger, disgust, or disapproval, compared to people looking at neutral faces (Burklund et al., 2007). The anterior cingulate cortex is associated with reactions to social rejection and it can trigger other areas of the brain that signal distress (Eisenberg, Lieberman, & Williams, 2003). The experiment by Eisenberg et al. (2003) monitored participants' fMRI activity while they experienced social rejection and exclusion and found that this activated the anterior cingulate cortex and the right ventral prefrontal cortex, a region of the brain concerned with regulating distress after pain that is activated to help people manage distress. Other studies using a method called facial electromyography (EMG) suggest that seeing negative nonverbal stimuli produces negative effects even if the stimuli are perceived subconsciously (Dimberg, Thunberg, & Elmehed, 2000).

In short, evidence from cognitive neuroscience suggests that making mistakes or receiving negative signals in some types of nonverbal language elicits punishment responses within the brain and, in some circumstances, distress. This raises the question of what this means for employees experiencing cross-cultural differences in nonverbal language during or after a merger or acquisition, in terms of distress and other health outcomes. There is no known cognitive neuroscience evidence about employees experiencing a cross-culture merger or acquisition, but there is evidence that cultural changes after a merger or acquisition contribute towards employees' emotional exhaustion (Väänänen et al., 2004). Research also shows that employees going through a merger or an acquisition are highly vulnerable to depression (Cartwright & Cooper, 1993; Joslin et al., 2010; Cartwright et al., 2007). This can lead employees experiencing a merger or acquisition to engage in maladaptive coping strategies such as excessive consumption of nicotine, alcohol, and food (Cartwright & Cooper, 1993). In the long run, research should examine whether chronic stress from a merger or acquisition raises the risk of negative health outcomes such as cancer, liver disease, and obesity-related diseases. Due to a lack of evidence within the literature, we do not know how much distress employees experience because of cross-cultural differences in nonverbal language, much less whether this causes mental health problems, or whether employees have a higher risk of mental health problems after a cross-cultural merger or acquisition compared to a merger or acquisition within a similar culture. What evidence there is of how people respond to cultural differences suggests that it puts them at risk of mental and physical health problems. Evidence shows that there is a higher prevalence of heart disease among people living in a culture different from their own (Ullman et al., 2011), and there is also a higher prevalence of chronic stress (Segerstrom & Miller, 2004), psychiatric disorders (Patel, 2011), and sickness-related absence from work (Lei, Liang, & Krieger, 2004). During a merger or an acquisition, employees have a significantly higher risk of psychiatric events and onset of depression (Väänänen et al., 2011), therefore, future research is needed to clarify whether cultural differences among employees precipitate mental and physical health problems.

Directions for future research

Without empirical evidence we can only say that culture is only one of many contributing factors to mental or physical health problems among employees because other elements of mergers and acquisitions can precipitate ill health. In terms of culture, the neuroscience and mental/physical health evidence leads us to theorise that mergers and acquisitions involving organizations from different cultures (e.g. different countries, organizations or industries) expose employees to culture-related errors and misunderstandings that elicit negative brain-based outcomes among employees, and these in turn raise their risk of distress. We theorise that cultural differences worsen problems such as intergroup processes highlighting attitudes of "us versus them" (see Chapter 5). Cultural differences could also reduce employees' sense of self-efficacy at work because of misunderstandings that reduce their feelings of exerting enough influence, power, or control over what other employees think of them. Cultural differences can frustrate employees' accomplishment of workplace goals such as being seen as competent, a good leader, productive, and likeable by coworkers, managers, and followers, therefore cross-cultural mergers or acquisitions might have an impact on employees' mental health because of moderating factors such as having a worse chance of getting promoted or getting a positive appraisal. Cross-cultural mergers or acquisitions might also reduce employees' job satisfaction by presenting misunderstandings that reduce the enjoyment and fulfilment that employees get from their workplace interactions. Future research should thus gather empirical evidence about the effects of cross-cultural differences on the health and work of employees in organizations that have undergone a merger or acquisition. For now, organizations need to pre-empt the potential problems by helping their employees learn about the cultural norms, values, and behaviours of employees in other cultures.

Preventing cultural problems in mergers and acquisitions through intercultural competence

It is important to remember that cross-cultural mergers and acquisitions have many advantages, and therefore this chapter should not discourage organizations from engaging in them. The possibility that employees will encounter cultural differences in nonverbal language and other aspects of workplace interactions with potential negative outcomes could be overcome by organizations helping employees learn about the culture of their partner organization, including making them aware of unfamiliar cultural norms about nonverbal language. Organizations often neglect the potential difficulties that could arise from a merger or acquisition and tend to focus on the benefits rather than the downsides (Oancea & Kamau, 2015; Weber & Camerer, 2003). Organizations often do not realise that cultural differences are an important cause of failed mergers or acquisitions (Weber & Camerer, 2003; Vaara, 2000, 2002). Therefore, this chapter helps organizations (and people working with them) to become aware of the potential negative outcomes of cross-cultural mergers or acquisitions for employees' interactions so that they can do something to prevent the negative outcomes.

The concept of "intercultural competence," (Bartel-Radic, 2006) or intercultural communication competence (Bush, Rose, Gilbert, & Ingram, 2001), refers to the ability of a person to be aware of other people's cultural values, norms, and practices. Organizations that help employees develop intercultural competence before a merger or acquisition could help them better understand their new colleagues and adapt their behaviour in a way that is sympathetic to cultural differences. It is plausible that a merger or acquisition can fail not because employees lack the job-relevant competencies, but because of the dynamics of the intercultural experience (Clarke & Hammer, 1995). Employees can develop intercultural competence themselves, but this is less likely among employees with certain personality traits (e.g. low empathy, low emotional stability), a low desire to learn (Martin & Griffiths, 2014; Yoo, Matsumoto, & LeRoux, 2006), and non-critical self-reflection (Liddicoat, 2017). Employees also need enough time if they are expected to develop intercultural competence independently (Hofstede, 1991) because the more employees interact with the unfamiliar culture, the better their intercultural competence (Borghetti, Beaven, & Pugliese, 2015). However, time for employees to learn through experience is a luxury that organizations might not necessarily feel they have after a merger or acquisition. Shareholders and executives might look at initial dips in an organization's performance as a sign that the merger or acquisition was a bad idea, and push for the organization to take drastic action to address profit losses, such as cutting jobs or changing the management. Of course, if the dips in profit were caused by factors arising from cultural differences, time could reverse dips by helping employees develop intercultural competence. However, the point is that organizations might not realise that cultural differences are the explanation for disappointing staff or profit outcomes after a merger or acquisition, therefore, rather than leaving employees to develop intercultural competence independently, it would be more effective for organizations to actively help them. Employees in a merger or acquisition often fear that their cultural norms or values will be replaced (Styhre et al., 2006), therefore organizations should assure employees that the culture after a merger or acquisition will be a synthesis of the two cultures rather than an outright replacement (Oancea & Neundlinger, 2017). Through training or other types of interventions, organizations should help employees develop intercultural competence by learning about the culture of the merging or acquiring/acquired organization, understanding important cultural differences, and accepting that working effectively with other employees will require empathy towards ways of behaving, interacting, or making decisions that are culturally different but not bad or lacking in validity. The process of intercultural learning is essentially a bidirectional process where each person needs to be mindful of their own culture and the culture of other people (Liddicoat, 2017). Through training or other interventions, organizations can help employees develop intercultural competence that will help them compromise or adapt during workplace interactions, processes, and procedures in a way that accommodates the working habits of the different cultures involved in the merger or acquisition.

Conclusions

Culture is defined not just in terms of a country, but also in terms of what is normal within a certain industry or organization. Cross-cultural mergers or acquisitions may involve cultural differences between organizations that increase the chances of negative or unfulfilling interactions among employees. This chapter reviewed research showing that mergers or acquisitions can be marred by conflict, mistrust, or misunderstandings among employees caused by cultural differences in how they behave, interact, or work. This chapter then focused on nonverbal language as a source of cultural differences because it is a neglected, yet important, determinant of employees' interactions with each other, and because culture can determine the meaning or impact of some types of nonverbal language. Cultural differences can make employees suffer unmet workplace goals, interpersonal conflict, and misunderstandings. We discussed literature from neuroscience and other fields supporting the view that problems with nonverbal language can be distressing, and that being in an unfamiliar culture can raise the risk of physical and mental health problems. This chapter then discussed further directions for research in this field, calling for studies into job-related outcomes (e.g. employees' sense of self efficacy at work, promotion) comparing cross-cultural mergers or acquisitions with those that involve organizations with similar cultures. Finally, this chapter discussed how organizations can help employees develop intercultural competence as a way of preventing the potential negative outcomes of cross-cultural mergers or acquisitions. Organizations that join together across different cultures face many advantages, including giving employees the chance to learn about different but more effective or more ethical working practices, and giving the organization a chance to carve a niche within a new consumer market. This chapter should not discourage organizations from engaging in deals with countries, regions, industries, or organizations with different cultural norms. Knowing about the potential negative outcomes of cultural differences can help organizations take preventative steps such as offering employees training that improves their intercultural competence, thus increasing the chances of a successful merger or acquisition. One of the ways that the culture of an organization can be improved is through good leadership, which Chapter 7 will discuss.

7 Good leadership in mergers or acquisitions is about charisma, dynamics with employees, personality, context, and information processing

A merger or an acquisition is a prime example of organizational change, and there are different theories about what style of leadership is appropriate. Leaders need to tackle issues such as the fear that employees have about the unknown – fears that could lead employees to engage in withdrawal behaviours, lack of commitment, and deliberate reduction in productivity (Fried et al., 1996; Choi et al., 2011). There is also the risk that employees will resist the change by engaging in counterproductive behaviours that jeopardize the success of the merger or the acquisition (Empson, 2001; McEntire & Bentley, 1996; Apfelthaler et al., 2002; Quah & Young, 2005; van Dijk & van Dick, 2009; Teram, 2010; Jetten & Hutchinson, 2011). Some authors suggest that during the transition period preceding a merger or acquisition, employees feel a sense of loss and other negative emotions (Appelbaum, Gandell, Yortis, Proper, & Jobin, 2000; Levinson, 1976). Such evidence was discussed in Chapter 3, and it suggests that one role of leaders during mergers or acquisitions is to manage employees' emotions – their fears, uncertainty, anger, and shock – in order to prevent these emotions from having a significant impact on employees' performance, attitudes, and commitment to their jobs. This suggests that the style of leadership needed is one that considers the individual needs of employees, supports them through the change and devises strategies that will help mitigate the impact of the change on employees. There are multiple theories about leadership in organizational change and it is important to extrapolate the extent to which each theory can be applied as a "best practice" viewpoint on good leadership styles during mergers or acquisitions. The first theoretical perspective that we will discuss is the neo-charismatic perspective on leadership. In his seminal work on leadership, Kotter (1996) argued that organizational change demands a strong leader who is capable of championing a new vision in the organization and encouraging people to embrace the change. This view fits with Burns' (1978) classic transformational and transactional leadership theory, which postulates that a transformational leader is someone who inspires and intellectually stimulates employees, harnessing their individual motives or talents, and inspires them by modelling ideal behaviour. Literature suggests that a radical change process, such as a merger or an acquisition, needs such leadership in order for the transformative plans of the organization to be successful (Beer & Nohria, 2000; Cartwright & Cooper, 1993; Appelbaum et al., 2000).

That perspective explains how leaders can convince employees to back a proposed merger or acquisition and get on board with working towards the new organization's goals, but a weakness of this theoretical perspective is that it does not sufficiently address the emotional needs of employees during a merger or acquisition. The second theoretical perspective that we are going to discuss focuses on the idea of a leader's personality traits based on evidence that a leader's personality traits correlate with their effectiveness in leading (Judge & Bono, 2000; Judge, Ilies, Bono, & Gerhard, 2002; Derue, Nahrgang, Wellman, & Humphrey, 2011; Bono & Judge, 2004). In Chapter 3 we discussed research showing that during a merger or acquisition, employees grapple with a sense of uncertainty about their future and other negative emotions, including fears and worries about how the merger or acquisition will change their job security, job role, and job satisfaction, suggesting that a leader needs to be emotionally intelligent, charismatic, and have a nuanced approach to interacting with individual employees. An advantage of the personality perspective is that it explains individual differences among leaders and it discusses both positive *and* negative personality traits, including narcissism and Machiavellianism. A disadvantage of the personality perspective is that it does not sufficiently address contextual factors such as the type of merger or acquisition, or the economic climate (see Chapters 1 and 2). The third theoretical perspective that we are going to discuss addresses both context (to some extent) and leader-employee interactions. Leader-member exchange theory postulates that leaders develop closer exchange relationships with certain followers, while with the rest, the relationship is based on formalized roles of authority and rules (Dansereau, Graen, & Haga, 1975; Graen & Cashman, 1975; Graen, 1976). An advantage of this perspective is that it acknowledges the complexity of leadership and the impact of interpersonal dynamics on a leader's style. A disadvantage of this perspective is that it does not systematically address contextual issues (see Chapter 1) in a way that can help merging or acquiring/acquired organizations develop rules of thumb about what leaders should be doing. The fourth theoretical perspective that we are going to discuss is the informational processing approach to leadership (e.g. Lord & Hall, 2005). Mergers or acquisitions often involve many instances of processing information, making decisions, running consultations, and communicating information. Keeping employees properly informed about an organizational change process can help them cope better with the transformation and buy into the new organizational projects (Bridges, 1991; Appelbaum et al., 2000; Kotter, 1996). A leader who is good at information processing and decision-making could, as part of their leadership capabilities, be someone who helps manage employees' uncertainties or fears by keeping them well informed, consulted, and sufficiently aware about how decisions are made. Such a leader could also help employees understand why the organizational change was necessary, and the advantages of the merger or acquisition in terms of projected financial benefits and job security. This theoretical perspective, therefore, has a number of advantages, such as offering organizations rules of thumb about best practice in mergers or acquisitions. A disadvantage of the perspective is that it does not sufficiently foresee "random" or "noise" variables such as motivation, group processes, leaders' emotions or employees' emotions, or behaviour. Leaders might have excellent information processing abilities but group processes (see Chapter 5), their own emotions (see Chapter 3), or being on the job market and planning to quit (see Chapter 4) could make them feel unmotivated to harness their information processing abilities at an optimum level. Psychological flaws within the organization's knowledge management processes (see Chapter 8) can also limit the realism of the information processing approach to leadership during mergers or acquisitions. After our brief review of the main theoretical approaches to leadership, we will draw conclusions about what constitutes "best practice" in leadership during a merger or acquisition.

Should leaders in mergers and acquisitions be charismatic visionaries?

In Burns' (1978) theory of leadership, a good leader has a vision and inspires other people to help them make that vision a reality. This style of leadership is called transformational leadership, and it involves acknowledging that employees are motivated by their own interests, desires, and goals, and therefore leading them requires harnessing those motivations through an individualised approach, including offering employees the right intellectual stimulation (Burns, 1978, 2007). One leader who embodies the transformational leadership style is Richard Branson (Niphadkar, 2017), who told *Forbes* that "If you love what you do and if you believe in what you do, others will share your enthusiasm." When Branson was asked about his top three leadership principles, he said:

> Too much credit goes to me for what we have achieved at Virgin but the successes happen from working and learning with some of the world's most inspiring and inspired people . . . Laughter: My number one rule in business, and in life, is to enjoy what you do. Running a business involves long hours and hard decisions; if you don't have the passion to keep you going, your business will more than likely fail. If you don't enjoy what you are doing, then you shouldn't be doing it.
>
> (Richard Branson's interview with Forbes; Schawbel, 2014)

Branson's emphasis on having a passion, a creative and energetic spirit, inspiring people, and trusting people to make his vision a reality suggests that he is a transformational leader. Branson was born in 1950 and, with only a secondary school education, he went from living as a squatter to launching a business selling music records, then progressed into growing a business empire by launching a large number of companies in many different industries (e.g. music retail, holidays, airlines, TV cable channel provision, alcohol, trains, space travel) under his brand the Virgin Group. Along the way, as well as starting many companies, Branson's companies also acquired firms such as the Mastertronic Group in 1984 (which manufactures computer games products such as Sega consoles), the bank Northern Rock in 2012, and the airline FlyBe in 2019 (FlyBe, 2019). Branson was knighted, has an estimated net worth of nearly $4.6 billion and is said to be the sixth-richest person in the United Kingdom (Schawbel, 2014). Branson's description of his leadership style in the interview with *Forbes* (Schawbel, 2014) suggests that he is a transformational leader who had the dream of spotting what the market lacked for consumers in terms of valuable products or services.

Branson's emphasis on humour and laughter in leadership suggests that he is charismatic, thus embodying both Burns' (1978, 2007) theory of leadership and other theories that can be called "neo-charismatic" theories of leadership (House, Spangler, & Woycke, 1991; Beyer, 1999). Although charisma appears to be the essential criterion of transformational leadership, there are five sub-components of transformational leadership according to the Multifactor Leadership Questionnaire (Bass & Avolio, 2000; Avolio & Bass, 2004). We present some examples of each sub-type and how they apply to a merger or an acquisition context:

1   **Inspirational motivational leadership:** A leader with this style of transformational leadership talks about, and shows, their vision in a way that employees find inspiring. An example would be a CEO who clearly and positively explains the reasons for a merger that employees and shareholders feel sceptical about. The CEO vividly articulates a future picture of success in profits, the brand's popularity with customers, the respectability of the brand for employees, and the company's share value, thus transforming the scepticism into excitement and anticipation about the positive outcomes of the merger.

2   **Idealized attributed influence leadership:** A leader with this style of transformational leadership is seen by employees as someone who genuinely cares, thus he or she inspires a sense of trust and employees feel emotionally close to him or her. An example would be a leader from an acquiring company who is asked to lead the employees of the acquired company. The leader understands the needs of all the employees and their fears. His or her sympathetic style persuades the employees to respect him or her and they are seen as a role model.

3   **Idealized influence behaviour leadership**: A leader with this style of transformational leadership displays model behaviour; they behave in a way that shows what values they hold. An example is a manager in a company that is about to be acquired. The manager leads a team of employees who are loyal to their professional values, and they are shocked and angry about the acquisition because they are afraid of its impact on their freedom and their deep-rooted value system. The manager defends his or her team when necessary and communicates all necessary information about the acquisition (including information about uncertainty or risk) in a way that inspires employees on the team to feel that the manager is doing his or her best to protect the team's professional values.

4   **Intellectual stimulation leadership:** A leader with this style of transformational leadership interacts and speaks with employees on an intellectual level by debating with them analytically as part of reaching goals. An example is a merger involving a large well-known software company and a less-known,

but reasonably successful, computer games company. The CEO of the soft-ware company is not convinced that the product development costs incurred by the computer games company are necessary or reasonable, but she has a style of leadership that involves being intellectually curious and is receptive to alternative arguments using logic and evidence. The CEO has meetings with managers and staff in the computer games company, asks many techni-cal questions, engages in an intellectually meaningful debate, uses logic or evidence, and through these analytical, intellectually interesting meetings, the CEO concludes that the costs are reasonable and comparable to other companies in that industry. The CEO's style impresses the managers and staff within the company that is about to be acquired, and they start to feel posi-tive and receptive towards the acquisition.

5   **Individualized consideration leadership:** A leader with this style is atten-tive to the things that individual employees find motivating or interesting, and he or she achieves the vision by inspiring employee to make the best use of their talents, motivations, or interests. An example is a supervisor who has been tasked with creating a cross-site team representing two manufacturing companies that are about to merge. Communication between the two sites has been previously difficult because of missed calls, unattended meetings, and unanswered emails caused by a mixture of stress-related staff absence and turnover after the merger was announced. The supervisor starts by hav-ing individual meetings with every employee possible, and he finds out what concerns, interests, and goals each employee has about their work and the merger. The supervisor finds that some employees are worried about being made redundant after the merger. He finds out that employees who are about to retire are worried about a hike in their company pension contributions after the merger. Other employees are worried that an innovative chemical process they have spent a year developing will be shelved after the merger, leading them to feel disappointed and demoralised. Other employees are worried that there will be a pay and promotion freeze after the merger. By finding out about their individual concerns or motives, the supervisor dis-covers what assurances are going to be the right ones for each employee as an individual. This approach inspires the employees to feel less stressed and less likely to look for another job, thus reducing absence and turnover and allowing progress with the cross-site team work.

Rowold (2005) found that all five sub-types of transformational leadership are positively correlated, with coefficients ranging from approximately 0.3 to 0.5 when leaders were rated by colleagues of a similar rank, or ranging from 0.35 to 0.7 when leaders were rated by colleagues of a lower rank. We do not have information about whether Richard Branson conveys all five sub-types of trans-formational leadership, or information about the impact of his style of leadership on the success of acquisitions by Virgin, but it is plausible that such a successful entrepreneur can make an acquisition successful. Aside from his leadership, it plausible that Branson's personal drive, determination, and talent for spotting good business opportunities predict the success of his acquisitions as much as his style of leadership. Rather than delineating the indicators of leadership in the way that Bass and Avolio (2000) and Avolio and Bass (2004) do, some theorists conceptualise charismatic leadership more generally (House et al., 1991; Howell & Frost, 1989; House, 1977) because literature about transformational leadership and literature about charismatic leadership could broadly capture the same types of leaders (House & Podsakoff, 1994; Conger & Kanungo, 1998). Literature suggests that what matters is whether the leader is effective at inspiring employees to identify with and support his or her goals (Judge & Piccolo, 2004; Conger & Kanungo, 1998; DeGroot, Kiker, & Cross, 2000; Lowe, Kroeck, & Sivasubramaniam, 1996).

There are certain factors that can help a transformational leader be effective at motivating employees (Meindl, 1990). In theory, executives, managers, and supervisors with a transformational leadership style should inspire employees to accept and work towards supporting a merger or acquisition even if the employees were initially sceptical of the idea. Theoretically, the inspiration should happen when the leader charms employees into putting their trust in them, modelling positive behaviour such as being collaborative with staff from the partner organization, motivating employees to support the merger or acquisition by showing them how they can personally benefit (e.g. pay, promotion, doing work that harnesses their individual passions), and by leading discussions or activities about the merger or acquisition that the employees find intellectually stimulating. However, employees are unlikely to respond to the same leader in the same way, and therefore some employees are likely to end up more motivated about the merger or acquisition than others. For example, Shamir, House, and Arthur (1993) theorised that charismatic leaders do not produce the same effects or effects to the same extent among all employees because some factors facilitate or inhibit the influence of the leader on employees. It is plausible that the leader's behaviour needs to appeal to the existing values and identities of the employees and be perceived as similar to them in their value and goals. A charismatic leader is unlikely to have the same impact inspiring an employee who perceives work as a means to an end as on an employee who perceives work or tasks as an end in itself (Goldthorpe, Lockwood, Bechhofer, & Platt, 1968). Similarly, transformational leadership might not be equally effective in all situations, states, or industries the organization is in or operates in if there is a clash in social, political, or ethical values.

The debate, however, is whether all leaders (e.g. chief executives, directors, managers, or supervisors) actually *need* to be transformational leaders during a merger or acquisition, and whether transformational leadership has a significant impact on outcomes such as employee performance, turnover, job satisfaction, or team harmony. The study of charisma in leader behaviour has gained a lot of attention (e.g. Dinh et al., 2014) and there is empirical support for the idea that transformational or charismatic leadership has a positive association with a range of organizational and employee performance indicators such as profit, employee absenteeism, and employees' willingness to engage in continuous development

(Rowold & Laukamp, 2009). Research has also found that transformational leaders may be associated with more positive organizational citizenship behaviours among employees and an ethical working climate (Zehir, Müceldili, Altindağ, Şehitoğlu, & Zehir, 2014). Other studies point to the positive relationship between charismatic leadership and positive work attitudes, job involvement, job satisfaction, and turnover intentions (de Hoogh et al., 2005; Cicero, 2007). On the other hand, leaders high on charisma may abuse their power over followers and have them discard any negative information (Conger, 1990). In terms of outcomes for mergers or acquisitions, in a review of 69 empirical studies in leadership in mergers and acquisitions, Junni and Sarala (2014) found that behaviours that fall under the transformational leadership category, such as providing employment security, showing empathy and caring towards employees, as well as having an open communication with them had a positive influence on variety of employee reactions and attitudes that are common in mergers and acquisitions (see Chapters 3, 4, 5 and 6). Employees are much more satisfied with their work and the organization after the merger and feel more positive about the impact of the change event (Covin, Kolenko, Sightler, & Tudor, 1997). They feel more motivated to work and are more committed to the organization and the job (Chipunza, Samuel, & Mariri, 2011). Also, they show increasing willingness to change (Hinduan, Wilson-Evered, Moss, & Scannell, 2009) and are more accepting of the change (Nemanich & Keller, 2007). A more positive approach to the merger or the acquisition reflects on their level of engagement and performance on the job (Nemanich & Vera, 2009). In fact, the organization performs better overall under a transformational leadership (Vasilaki, 2011; Babić, Savović, & Domanović, 2014). Therefore, by communicating the purposes, vision, and expectations to employees, providing challenges and attending to employees' needs, transformational leadership in mergers and acquisitions can minimise the impact of uncertainty on employees' attitudes towards the change. Employees are provided with the necessary resources to cope with the change while leaders ensure a climate of safety and self-expression. This is reflected in employees' dedication and commitment to their work, and ultimately, in the success of the merger or the acquisition.

In short, we can surmise that good leadership during a merger or acquisition should most probably be transformational, especially in cases where employees are resistant to the organizational changes and a leader has the opportunity to directly inspire and motivate employees to support the goals of the merger or acquisition. However, leaders must be aware that transformational leadership will not have a uniform effect on all employees because of variation in employees' work-related goals.

Should leaders in mergers and acquisitions be transactional?

Leaders in mergers or acquisitions might not need to be charismatic and inspirational if they do not have the power or the opportunity to have meaningful influence over employees. For example, a manager of a team in an organization that has formally agreed to axe that team as part of a merger might have little influence over the employees' sense of feeling demoralised, upset, and uncommitted to their jobs. A department director in a company undergoing an acquisition who decided to go on the job market might intrinsically possess transformational leadership traits, but lack the time or incentive to behave like a transformational leader because they are planning on changing jobs. Therefore, the question is whether transformational leadership is always necessary or feasible in circumstances of mergers or acquisitions. Perhaps a leadership style that is focused on checking whether employees have completed their tasks is more realistic or useful. Burns (1978) conceptualised transformational leadership as something different from a style of leadership called transactional leadership, where the leader focuses on the exchange between himself or herself and followers (e.g. employee) based on a reciprocal relationship of the employee completing his or her job and the leader issuing rewards or penalties. Burns argued that a transactional leader strives to offer followers something they want but in exchange for something the leader wants (see also Kuhnert & Lewis, 1987). Burns (2007) argued that transactional leadership is like substituting one thing for another, whereas he conceptualised transformational style as a process that initiates changes in what something is. Transactional leaders are thus defined as people who explain what work needs to be done by an employee or what standards they need to meet, and when the employee meets these requirements, the leader compensates them (Bass, 1985, 1990), such as through praise, rewards (e.g. bonuses, promotion, time off, or a reduced workload). Burns (2007) argued that a leader can be transformational or transactional, but never both. However, evidence by Bass (1985) and others shows that the same leader can display both leadership styles, and that people with transformational leadership traits also tend to have transactional leadership traits. For instance, research asking employees or colleagues to rate a certain leader has shown that their ratings of his or transformational leadership traits tend to correlate with two types of transactional leadership traits (Rowold & Laukamp, 2009). According to the Multifactor Leadership Questionnaire (Bass & Avolio, 2000; Avolio & Bass, 2004), there are the three sub-types of transactional leadership. We present some examples of each sub-type from the merger or acquisition contexts:

1   **Contingent rewards leadership**: A leader with this style of transactional leadership is someone who emphasises the task elements of a job, and he or she rewards employees who complete tasks and/or who complete tasks to the standard required. The leader thus makes an employee's access to rewards such as positive feedback, a pay rise, or a promotion contingent on the employee fulfilling the task requirements. Imagine a manager in an organization that is being acquired, and the manager leads a team of IT staff required to combine the two organizations' data management systems while also completing their regular job responsibilities. The manager sets an overtime pay scheme to reward those IT staff who work extra hours to complete the IT tasks relating to the acquisition.

2   **Active management by exception leadership:** A leader with this style of transactional leadership is proactive in monitoring whether employees are completing the tasks they are required to complete and/or to the standard required. The leader looks to spot employees who are deviating from the task expectations (e.g. completing work on time or completing tasks using procedural rules) and punishes them, such as by negative feedback, a negative appraisal, performance management, or disciplinary processes. An example is a director of a company that is about to merge with another company. The director wants all employees to support the merger and he actively searches for signs of employees whose actions disrupt or obstruct the merger (e.g. being hostile towards, ignoring, or discriminating against staff from the merging partner organization). The director penalises such employees by giving them a formal warning.

3   **Passive management by exception leadership:** A leader with this style of transactional leadership lets employees complete their tasks without monitoring them, then takes action against an employee only when he or she does not fulfil the task requirements. An example is a supervisor of a team of drivers in a logistics company that has just been acquired by another logistics company, and for whom new rules apply about aspects of their job. The supervisor does not actively look for evidence of whether or not drivers are complying with the new rules, but she intervenes when a problem occurs in an instance where a driver did not comply with the new rules set by the acquiring company.

Rowold (2005) found that leaders who use a contingent rewards approach tend to use an approach of active management by exception, with a correlation of 0.21 when rated by colleagues at a lower rank (but no significant correlation when rated by colleagues of a similar rank), whereas active management by exception and passive management by exception tend to be negatively correlated with coefficients between -0.34 and -0.22. The focus of transactional leadership in a merger or acquisition context would thus be on accomplishing the tasks at hand with the leader controlling which employees get rewarded or penalised. In terms of outcomes for mergers or acquisitions, transactional leadership is positively associated with job satisfaction and normative commitment to change (obligation to support change initiatives), and negatively with employees' intentions to quit an organization (Hinduan et al., 2009). Transactional leadership may also help reduce job role ambiguity (Mackenzie, Podsakoff, & Rich, 2001), which can be a significant problem in mergers and acquisitions (Fried et al., 1996). By setting clear objectives and monitoring the performance of the employees, leaders with a transactional style clarify employees' role and task requirements in exchange of rewards (Lo, Ramayah, Min, & Songan, 2010). Thus, in a merger or acquisition context, a transactional style can alleviate the employees' anxiety (Rafferty & Restubog, 2010) and state of confusion (Lundbäck & Hörte, 2005). However, the orientation of transactional leaders towards achieving goals, meeting task requirements, ensuring employee performance and problem-solving can be to the detriment of inspiring emotional engagement among the employees, which can be a barrier to change (Beatty & Lee, 1992). Cultivating a sense of commitment or engagement among employees might thus require more than a task-focused leader (Shamir et al., 1993).

However, this is not to say that transactional leadership is not good leadership – it is. We suggest that leaders in mergers and acquisitions should embody both a transactional and transformational leadership style because they are not antagonistic leadership styles. The evidence that the same leader can be both a transactional leader *and* a transformational leader suggests that managers, supervisors, and other types of leaders during a merger or acquisition could adapt their leadership style to the demands of the situation. Bass (1985), Conger and Kanungo (1988), (Waldman, Bass, & Yammarino, 1988) and others suggest that a leader can complement their transactional leadership style with a transformational leadership style as a way of increasing the extent to which employees or other types of followers boost their effort and performance. This implies that an effective leader should focus on both exchanges of effort and rewards with employees, and also inspiring employees with charm and a vision that boosts their effort and performance (Waldman et al., 1988; Conger & Kanungo, 1988, 1987; Bycio, Hackett, & Allen, 1995). The augmentation effect has been validated in empirical studies, whereby transformational leadership did add beyond the effects of transactional leadership on a range of outcomes, such as follower satisfaction with the leader, follower motivation, leader job performance, and leader effectiveness (Judge & Piccolo, 2004).

Therefore, context is quite important in determining what counts as good leadership. Before we delve into the issue of context in more detail, let us consider an approach to leadership that resonates with the notion of transformational and transaction leadership, but differs in arguing that leaders vary their style from employee to employee, according to the relationships that they have with them. This is an approach that emphasises the importance of interpersonal contextual factors when it comes to deciding what counts as good leadership.

Leader-member exchange theory

Another dominant perspective in leadership research is the leader-member exchange (LMX) paradigm (Dinh et al., 2014). The theory, although identified more than 40 years ago, is still of much interest to researchers, and together with the neo-charismatic, trait, and information processing theories, dominates much of the literature in the field. The main tenet of the leader-member exchange theory is that leaders develop closer exchange relationships with certain followers, while with the rest, the relationship is based on formalized roles of authority and rules (Dansereau et al., 1975; Graen & Cashman, 1975; Graen, 1976). Therefore, leaders vary their interactions with different followers, which determines the nature of the relationship. These relationships tend to develop early during the leader-follower exchange and to remain relatively stable over time (Graen & Cashman, 1975; Liden & Graen, 1980). The quality of these relationships is what determines the attitudes and behaviours of both leaders and followers (Gerstner & Day, 1997; Liden, Sparrowe, & Wayne, 1997).

In the initial theory formulation, the relationships between subordinates and leaders was classified into ingroup, which included relations based on trust and support, and outgroup, which referred to the relations largely based on formal rules and procedures and roles of authority (Dienesch & Liden, 1986; Graen, 1976). Later on, these discrete classification of relations between leaders and followers were eventually discarded and replaced by a continuous measure of quality (Graen & Scandura, 1987). As such, a high LMX relationship is characterized by trust (Brower, Schoorman, & Tan, 2000), interaction, and supportive behaviours that go beyond the confines of the normatively prescribed contract. By contrast, a low LMX relationship is characterized by attitudes and behaviours limited by the working arrangements, job tasks, and formal roles of subordinate and superior (Brower et al., 2000).

The leader-member exchange theory has found strong empirical support in the literature. A high-quality relationship between follower and leader, based on mutual trust and support, has been found to be linked to organizational performance and citizenship behaviours (Ilies, Nahrgang, & Morgeson, 2007). Previous meta-analysis on the outcomes of a high-quality leader-follower relationship (Gerstner & Day, 1997) found significant positive associations with satisfaction with supervision, overall satisfaction, organizational commitment, and role clarity. Authors found significant negative associations with role conflict and turnover intentions. Overall, they concluded that having a high LMX relation with one's supervisor has a positive impact on the entire work experience, including performance and affective outcomes. Later meta-analytic evidence (Dulebohn, Bommer, Liden, Brouer, & Ferris, 2012) on the antecedents and outcomes of leader-member relations suggested that there are a range of factors that influence the quality of the interaction between subordinate and leader. Authors categorised the antecedents into follower characteristics, leader characteristics, and interpersonal relationships. Follower characteristics include affect-related variables such as positive/negative affectivity, trait-related factors (namely those discussed earlier in the Big Five Factor model), locus of control, and skill-related aspects. Leader characteristics include leadership style (transformational/contingent-reward behaviour), personality traits (extraversion and agreeableness), as well as supervisor's expectations of the followers. The relationship characteristics found by Dulebohn et al. (2012) in their meta-analysis included perceived similarity, affect/liking, ingratiation (reported by supervisor and subordinate), self-promotion, assertiveness, and leader trust. The outcomes seem to confirm the previous similar analyses. A high-quality relationship between leader and follower is linked to lower turnover and turnover intentions, role ambiguity and role conflict, higher job performance, OCB, employee commitment, job satisfaction, justice perceptions, and empowerment.

Various issues arise in a merger process and the leaders may find themselves engulfed in problems and situations that need to be taken care of. Furthermore, most of the time, information is sterilized by the middle management when passed to the top management. It is thus important that leaders become aware and avoid the false sense of security (Vaara, 2001) and remain vigilant to any potential source of conflict or event that might require his or her intervention (Fulop et al., 2002). The management needs to establish a high-quality leader member exchange with the employees so that the working climate becomes one where employees trust each other and the management. Otherwise, a disinterested behaviour from the leader may easily backfire and crystallize into fiercer forms of resistance to change (e.g. voicing complaints in the media).

Building a high-quality exchange relationship with the employees is crucial in mergers and acquisitions. Employees fearful about the change may become disengaged and lose commitment or withdraw psychologically from their job (Fried et al., 1996). A relationship between the employee and the supervisor characterized by mutual support and trust helps maximize the employee's resources to cope with the distressing work situation, thus reducing risk of employee turnover and turnover intentions, role job performance, satisfaction, and empowerment (Dulebohn et al., 2012). The leaders will thus be able to prevent the development of divisive relationships between groups and a working climate characterized by conflict (Barratt-Pugh et al., 2013). The relational skills are thus crucial for the success of post-merger integration, which may sometimes outweigh the managerial skills.

This perspective resonates with the idea of transactional and transformational leadership to some extent, but the main difference is that the latter perspective views leadership style as something that is fixed across different employees, whereas the leader-member-exchange approach views leadership style as something that can vary from one employee to another. Our view of the evidence is that there is not enough empirical evidence comparing these theoretical perspectives and providing a definitive conclusion about which theory of leadership is supported by real data across different organizations and contexts. Many studies tend to focus on one theory rather than test competing theories. What this leaves us with is the conclusion that different leadership styles exist, but we now ask when certain leadership styles are more appropriate than others. How can leaders in mergers or acquisitions who want to adapt their leadership style know what style is most appropriate?

Why leaders should adapt their style to the demands of the situation

Fiedler's contingency theory of leadership posits that the effectiveness of a leader is a function of not just their style of leadership, but also the demands of the situation that they are leading (Fiedler, 1971). Although Fielder conceptualised leadership style in terms of whether someone is task-oriented (focused on getting employees to get the job done) or relationship-oriented (focused on having amiable interpersonal connections and rapport with employees) (Fiedler, 1967; Miner, 2005), his theory offers a vital emphasis on contextual factors. Leaders with one style or another perform differently in particular situations the organization is experiencing (Fiedler, 1971). Fielder defined the favourableness or unfavourableness of a situation in three ways. The first is the extent to which a leader has power or authority over employees, such as having a say in what happens, being able to reward or punish employees, and being able to have a meaningful influence. The second is the structure of the task, such as having clear rules, procedures, job designs, and defined end goals (e.g. revenue or profit rises) versus ambiguous processes or end goals. The third is the quality of the relationship between the leader and the employees, such as a situation where the latter are loyal, respectful, and receptive on one hand or rebellious, rejecting, and combative on the other. For instance, Fielder suggested that situations with high levels of authority accorded to leaders, strict rules and policies, and employees who are respectful and loyal to the leader can benefit from task-oriented leadership more than relationship-oriented leadership in terms of employees' task performance (Fiedler, 1965). In contrast, in work situations where leaders have low authority, the rules or procedures are ambiguous, and the relationships between leaders and employees are poor, a leader who is relationship-oriented will produce higher group performance (see Fiedler, 1965 for a detailed description of the different categories). These types proposed by Fiedler are also called "octants," as a depiction of author's graphical representation of the taxonomy as a cube (Fiedler, 1965, 1971).

Contextual factors are important in mergers and acquisitions because they are not all the same. Sitkin and Pablo (2004) suggested that in mergers and acquisitions, a leadership style that encompasses personal, relational, contextual, and charismatic attributes can stimulate commitment, confidence, and comfort for employees, but this suggests a mixture of the different leadership styles that we have discussed. Sitkin and Pablo (2004, 2005) argue that mergers and acquisitions require a sense of personal leadership or the ability to convey a personal vision, emotions, and beliefs, which ultimately helps in building credibility among employees. This implies that leader-member exchange theory is applicable in organizations that have experienced mergers or acquisitions in the sense that individual relationships with employees matter, but it also suggests that transformational leadership is the most appropriate leadership style because it involves inspiring employees to support a vision. A review by Junni and Sarala (2014) suggested that different leadership styles have a variety of psychological effects on employees. Transformational leadership is associated employee reactions, integration, and the performance of a merger or acquisition (Chipunza et al., 2011; Schweizer & Patzelt, 2012; Nemanich & Vera, 2009). In contrast, a high-quality leader-member exchange relationship appears to encourage supportive rather than resistant employee behaviours given that relational, contextual, supportive, and stewardship leadership had a positive impact on the success that organizations have at achieving integration after a merger or acquisition (Schweizer & Patzelt, 2012)

Likewise, transactional leadership might be the best style in certain circumstances after a merger or acquisition, or you might even want to conceptualise a leadership style in the way that Fiedler did, which is in terms of how focused a leader is on relationships with employees and how focused they are on getting employees to do their jobs. Many of these leadership styles are unlikely to be mutually exclusive, which means that managers and other types of leaders are capable of adapting their style to suit the demands of a particular employee or group of employees. Other contextual factors include those within the wider global or national context in cross-border mergers and acquisitions (Aguilera & Dencker, 2004; Krug & Nigh, 2001; Goulet & Schweiger, 2006), as well as the broader organizational context (Stahl, Chua, & Pablo, 2012). National culture can determine norms about leaders' power and employees' tolerance for dominant leadership or leadership promulgating uncertainty (Hofstede, 1991) and their responses to mergers or acquisitions (Goulet & Schweiger, 2006; Stahl et al., 2012, and Chapter 6). National culture can also determine norms, laws, or regulations about employee relations, such as the presence or power of unions, and therefore a tailored approach is needed by leaders in cross-border mergers or acquisitions (Angwin, 2001). (Goulet & Schweiger, 2006).

It seems to be common in mergers and acquisitions for the management to be enthusiastic about combining the partner organizations (Choi et al., 2011), therefore leaders can play an important role in helping employees support the organization's goals. Nonetheless, a word of caution is needed in viewing leadership as a panacea for the problems likely to face organizations after a merger or acquisition Choi et al.'s (2011). Evidence suggests that as time goes by after the merger or acquisition, leaders can lose their initial enthusiasm and remain passive and fairly invisible. The study suggested that they withdrew from work and the organization, and were waiting out the changes to be enacted at a middle-management level or leaving the employees on their own to cope with the organizational changes without providing any form of support. This raises the question of whether transformational and transactional leadership relating to a merger or acquisition's goals is at risk of ebbing away after the organizational change, and fizzling into laissez-faire leadership. According to the Multifactor Leadership Questionnaire (Bass & Avolio, 2000; Avolio & Bass, 2004), laissez-faire leadership is a third possible type of leadership that is comprised of avoiding telling employees what to do, making decisions about their work, not getting involved in setting their goals, and not punishing or rewarding them for their performance. An example is a chief financial officer in an acquired organization who does not get involved when his or her team comes for guidance regarding the implementation of new accounting systems following the acquisition, and does not offer support in mediating conflicts or relationships between employees in the two partner organizations.

To summarise, good leadership during or after a merger or acquisition can be one or more of several leadership styles, such as transactional versus transformational leadership, and good leadership can also involve personalising the style to individual employees or depending on the demands of the situation. Good leadership can also be conceptualised in terms of how focused leaders are on getting employees to complete tasks that they need to complete versus focusing on having rapport with employees which, again, should be tailored towards the demands of the situation. Each leadership style can be good, depending on the context. Next, having discussed perspectives about leadership that consider a leader's style, we will discuss perspectives on leadership that consider a leader's personality.

Is a leader's personality important in mergers and acquisitions?

Some theoretical perspectives emphasise a leader's personality traits as an important correlate of his or her success in emerging as a leader and leading effectively (Judge & Bono, 2000; Judge et al., 2002; Derue et al., 2011; Bono & Judge, 2004). One of the major theories about personality, the Big Five theory, postulates that people have some level of five personality traits – extraversion, conscientiousness, agreeableness, openness to experience, and neuroticism (Costa & McCrae, 1992; McCrae & Costa, 1994). Extroversion involves being sociable and preferring to spend time with other people. Conscientiousness involves being honest, well-organised, disciplined, and fulfilling one's duties or responsibilities to a high standard. Agreeableness involves avoiding conflict or debates with other people. Openness to experience involves being adventurous, inventive, and curious, such as seeking exciting new activities and being creative. Neuroticism involves being anxious about a lot of things, having a tendency to easily experience negative emotions, and being emotional unstable. Judge, Ilies, et al. (2002) found that extraversion is a personality trait that correlates positively with the likelihood of someone emerging as a leader and in being an effective leader. Extraversion helps the quality of behaviour and interactions in group settings, and it helps people be successful at persuading or motivating other people. Another personality trait that the study found to correlate positively with both leadership emergence and effectiveness was openness to experience, whereas conscientiousness was only positively related to leadership emergence, and agreeableness was negatively associated with leadership emergence.

However, Hogan and Kaiser (2005) argue that the Big Five model of personality only captures positive human personality traits which, in work settings, could be manifest during circumstances where people want to make a positive impression, such as in a job interview, whereas there may be personality traits that people have when they are not impression managing their behaviour. In their review of the trait leadership perspective, Judge, Piccolo, and Kosalka (2009) suggested that there is a "bright" and a "dark" side of each personality trait. They suggested that the following are bright personality traits because they represent socially desirable attitudes or behaviours with positive social consequences: conscientiousness, extraversion, agreeableness, emotional stability, openness to experience, and traits represented by other personality perspectives such as core self-evaluations. This trait captures the fundamental evaluations people hold of themselves. The dispositional traits encompassed by the core self-evaluations construct are self-esteem, internal locus of control, generalized self-efficacy, and neuroticism (Judge & Bono, 2000; Resick, Whitman, Weingarden, & Hiller, 2009). Leaders high on core self-evaluations may cultivate a climate of fair and just exchanges between effort and rewards, and are more willing to consider the individual needs of the employees. On the other hand, a very high core self-evaluation is equivalent to very positive self-appraisals, and consequently to narcissism and hubris. In certain situations, they may optimistically pursue projects based on the generalized conviction of enhanced management capabilities. Although the personality traits that we have discussed so far could be generally positive in organizations and for leaders (Judge et al., 2009), it is plausible that they require certain contexts. For example, a highly conscientious leader could be very effective in an organization that values procedures, conventions, and prescribed norms. The same leader in an organization that is volatile might be less effective than another type of leader in being indecisive or resisting change (LePine, Colquitt, & Erez, 2000), even when urgent decisions are needed (Hogan & Hogan, 2001). In a merger or acquisition, a conscientious leader might remain effective only within the confines of prescribed rules and regulations, but less so if there is chaos or uncertainty about rules. Likewise, extraversion is a common trait among leaders (Judge, Ilies, et al., 2002; Stogdill, 1948) and it is associated with positive employee outcomes (Judge et al., 2002; Judge, Erez, et al., 2002). However, leaders high on extraversion are also prone to hold inflated views of themselves and of their capabilities (Hogan & Hogan, 2001). As such, they may be motivated to engage in large-scale projects (Beauducel, Brocke, & Leue, 2006) including mergers or acquisitions, but with a sense of overconfidence that lacks due consideration to all aspects (Oancea & Kamau, 2015). This implies that each personality trait has a "good" and "bad" side. Table 7.1 provides a summary that helps you understand what this means.

Therefore, no single personality trait is entirely good or entirely bad. The impact of a leader's personality trait on employees within organizations experiencing a merger or acquisition will thus depend on a variety of factors, including a leader's overall personality. Furthermore, we caution against placing leaders on a pedestal because, in reality, the impact of one given manager or executive within an organization can be limited, especially in large organizations where they rely on the people they manage, or on the people managed by the people they manage. We thus conclude that a leader's personality is important, but only one of many factors relevant to effective leadership in mergers and acquisitions. We also highlight the fact that perspectives about personality (Table 7.1) do not capture everything that can be said about a leader's personality. We will look at additional perspectives next.

More about "dark" personality traits

Dispositional traits that are socially undesirable and have negative implications in social circumstances are commonly referred to as dark traits (Judge, Ilies, et al., 2002; Judge et al., 2009). These include: narcissism, hubris, social dominance, and Machiavellianism. The bright and dark sides of dark traits are summarized in Table 7.2. Narcissism is a relatively stable dispositional trait which is characterized by perception of grandiosity, inflated self-appraisals, and self-love (Campbell, Brunell, & Finkel, 2006; Campbell, Hoffman, Campbell, & Marchisio,

Table 7.1 The "bright" and "dark" sides of different personality traits

Personality traits and their characteristics	"Bright" side of the trait	"Dark" side of the trait
Conscientiousness Conscientious people pay a high amount of attention to detail, they are self-disciplined, organized, and dependable.	Conscientious people tend to be ethical leaders (Walumbwa & Schaubroeck, 2009); they motivate employees to perform better at work (Barrick & Mount, 1991); they inspire employees to engage in organizational citizenship behaviour (Organ & Ryan, 1995); they encourage voice behaviour, a type of extra-role behaviour that involves speaking out and offering suggestions with the aim of improving the situation (Walumbwa, Morrison, & Christensen, 2012); and they foster work cultures that are regarded as just and fair (Mayer, Nishii, Schneider, & Goldstein, 2007).	Highly conscientious leaders may resist innovation and change (Hogan & Hogan, 2001). They could spend too long making decisions because they feel the need to gather as much information as possible, which might explain why highly conscientious people may find moments of crisis highly distressing. They may be less adaptable to change (LePine et al., 2000).
Extraversion Extraverted people tend to be assertive, socially active, gregarious, talkative, and not shy in group situations.	Extraverted people tend to establish authority and direction (Hogan, Curphy, & Hogan, 1994), closer relationships with employees (Avery, 2003; Nahrgang, Morgeson, & Ilies, 2009), and are assertive and oriented towards action (Marinova, Peng, Lorinkova, Van Dyne, & Chiaburu, 2015).	Highly extraverted individuals may engage in over-confidence in their own capabilities (Hogan & Hogan, 2001). They may be aggressive and seek moments where they are the centre of attention (Hogan & Hogan, 2001). They may make hasty decisions and engage in large-scale projects (such as mergers or acquisitions) (Beaducel et al., 2006). Their interest in projects may be short-lived, and they may not be able to lead projects through to completion (Beaducel et al., 2006).

(*Continued*)

Table 7.1 (Continued)

Personality traits and their characteristics	"Bright" side of the trait	"Dark" side of the trait
Agreeableness Agreeable people tend to avoid conflict. They tend to be cooperative and compliant.	Agreeable people can tend to inspire trust among employees (Costa & McCrae, 1992), promote cooperation, and avoid conflict (Gelfand, Leslie, Keller, & de Dreu, 2012). They can also be empathetic towards employees and promote employee wellbeing, satisfaction, and professional development (Templer, 2012).	Agreeable people tend to not be assertive and they can avoid making decisions that will harm relationships with the employees (Graziano & Eisenberg, 1997). They tend to not be confrontational and they may not give accurate feedback in order to avoid conflict with employees (Bernardin, Cooke, & Villanova, 2000).
Emotional stability Emotionally stable people tend to have a state of calm. They are low on neuroticism and tend to not display dramatic behaviour or attitudes, such as making rash decisions or having emotional outbursts.	Emotionally stable people tend to be considerate to employees' needs and are patient about their development (DeNeve & Cooper, 1998). They can tend to be systematic in decision-making and not exhibit stress or anxiety in negative situations (Judge & LePine, 2007). They may recover quickly from situations and not ruminate on past failures (Northouse, 1997).	Emotionally stable people may be perceived as disinterested in employees (Goldberg, 1999). When interacting with employees or giving them feedback, their low emotional expressiveness may come across to employees as a lack of authenticity (Kouzes & Posner, 2003).
Openness to experience People who are open to experience tend to be curious and eager to learn and try new things, and are adventurous in seeking new experiences. In some personality theories, this trait is described as being comprised of intelligence, creativity, and/or being able to gather, integrate, and interpret large amounts of information (Judge, Colbert, & Ilies, 2004).	People with this trait can provide intellectual simulation to employees (Bono & Judge, 2004), support in helping them cope with organizational change (Judge, Thoresen, Pucik, & Welbourne, 1999). They tend to be good at solving problems and finding solutions to complex problems (Williams, 2004), stimulating creativity among followers (Williams, 2004; Tierney, Farmer, & Graen, 1999).	People with this trait may engage in risky ventures or pursue ideas that are against organizational traditions (Judge et al., 2009). They may challenge the stability of an organization by pursuing ideas or experiences that are risky (Mayfield, Perdue, & Wooten, 2008), and their fantasy thinking and behaving might alienate employees who prefer clearer, rigid work instructions (Judge et al., 2009).

Personality traits and their characteristics	"Bright" side of the trait	"Dark" side of the trait
		They may also discard any information or not attend to matters they consider mundane or simple (Heinström, 2003). High intelligence might mean taking too long to make decisions because of needing information about all possible alternatives (Heinström, 2003).
Core self-evaluations People with high core self-evaluations have a positive outlook, confidence, and a sense of control over the outcomes of their actions (Judge & Bono, 2001).	People with this trait can provide vision and motivate employees to pursue that vision (Resick et al., 2009), and are able to personalise their treatment of employees (Resick et al., 2009).	People with this trait might have extremely positive views about themselves that correspond to narcissism and hubris (Hiller & Hambrick, 2005). They may engage optimistically in risky projects or decisions, convinced that they have highly positive personal capabilities (Cheung, Wu, & Tao, 2016). They may pursue mergers and acquisitions in a way that involves overpricing entities within the deal or inflating the positive prospects they expect (Hayward & Hambrick, 1997).

2011). People with a narcissistic trait, exhibit a strong desire for power and high self-esteem. They tend to engage in actions meant to attract others' attention and admiration. They do not display empathy towards others and display manipulative or exploitative tendencies. However, there are situations where a narcissistic leader (in being charismatic) may be beneficial for leadership and group effectiveness (Rosenthal & Pittinsky, 2006). Motivated by the desire to attract attention and be looked upon by followers, narcissistic leaders are likely to engage in more innovative endeavours, such as corporate acquisitions (Chatterjee & Hambrick, 2007).

Table 7.2 The "bright" and "dark" sides of "dark" personality traits

Dark traits	Characteristics	Bright sides	Dark sides
Narcissism	People with narcissism tend to be arrogant and self-absorbed, and have a high sense of entitlement. (Deluga, 1997). They can also have a high sense of positivity, uniqueness, vanity, and a desire for power (Campbell et al., 2011).	People with narcissism tend to engage in innovative actions in order to attract attention to their leadership capabilities and vision (Chatterjee & Hambrick, 2007), suggesting that they may initiate or support grand ventures such as mergers or acquisitions.	People with narcissism tend to think of themselves in mainly positive terms and therefore overlook actions or attitudes that are socially harmful (Morf & Rhodewait, 2001). They may lack empathy and only think in terms of how particular events or decisions might reflect on their reputations (Jonason & Krause, 2013).
Hubris	Hubris leaders have an inflated view of themselves and of their abilities (Hayward, Rindova, & Pollock, 2004).	They can inspire confidence (Baumeister et al., 2003) and make fast decisions (Hayward et al., 2006).	They may engage in irrational decision-making (Singh, 2012), and discard any information that conflicts with their self-views (Kernis & Sun, 1994). They may be prone to paying higher premiums in acquisitions (Hayward & Hambrick, 1997).
Social dominance orientation	People with social dominance orientation tend to have a strong belief in stable hierarchical systems. They have a tendency to	They may appear attractive to followers because they portray behaviours or attitudes that allude to a sense of things in control (Foti & Hauenstein, 1993).	They may instil fear among employees and make them feel under intense pressure to perform (Altemeyer, 2004).

Dark traits	Characteristics	Bright sides	Dark sides
	engage and support actions meant to sustain a particular hierarchical arrangement (Pratto et al., 1994).	In leadership positions, dominance is stereotyped as a useful skill and is sometimes seen as corresponding to competence as a leader (Anderson & Kilduff, 2009).	They may be regarded as manipulative and power-hungry (Driskell, Olmstead, & Salas, 1993).
Machiavellianism	This personality trait is comprised of cunningness and manipulation (Paulhus & Williams, 2002). People with this trait use power or status to persuade followers towards self-serving purposes (Goldberg, 1999).	Machiavellian people may be extremely flexible in the way they manage various organizational situations (Deluga, 2001), they may be strategic thinkers (Mael, Waldman, & Mulqueen, 2001), and are charismatic (Deluga, 2001).	They may abuse power to persuade followers to engage in actions for their benefit (Goldberg, 1999). They may disobey rules and procedures in pursuit of their own benefits (Richmond, 2001).

Hubris refers to an individual's excessive self-esteem based on overly positive evaluations of themselves and inflated self-appraisals of their capabilities (Blais et al., 2008). Hubristic leaders grossly overestimate their abilities and competences, and underestimate the resources needed for organizational success. They tend to be dismissive of others' opinions, as they are convinced no one has a better understanding of the problem than he or she does (Hotchkiss, 2002). The hubris hypothesis posits that in mergers or acquisitions, CEOs are overconfident in their abilities to capture value from the merger, and thus engage in combinations that actually destroy value (Roll, 1986; Hayward & Hambrick, 1997). Hubris-infected managers, acting on fabricated compatibility between the two organizations and inflated evaluations of their capabilities, systematically pursue the objectives of the merger which may contribute to short-term gain but not necessarily sizable gains over the long run. On the other hand, hubristic leaders are likely to maintain their perceptions of self-worth even in challenging situations. They manage to inspire confidence and provide a sense of security for the followers. They are quick to make decisions and engage in innovative ventures (Baumeister, Campbell, Krueger, & Vohs, 2003; Hayward, Shepherd, & Griffin, 2006; Haynes, Hitt, & Campbell, 2015).

One of the most common types of personality that is studied in research about mergers and acquisitions is managerial hubris (Roll, 1986; Hayward & Hambrick, 1997; Alexandridis, Fuller, Terhaar, & Travlos, 2013). Hubristic leaders might be overconfident in their abilities to capture value from a merger or acquisition, they might have inflated expectations about what can be gained, and they may help short-term gains but not necessarily sizable gains for the organizations in the long term (Hodgkinson & Partington, 2008). There are several hypotheses about what causes and correlates with hubristic personalities. Some suggest that past success encourages leaders to formulate higher goals for themselves, and thus hubris (Oancea & Kamau, 2015; Bandura, 1977). In other words, past success can help leaders learn to be overconfident (Billet & Qian, 2008; Zollo, 2009; Doukas & Petmezas, 2007). It is also possible that hubristic leaders can behave in a risky manner because they are anxious to succeed and they may therefore respond to signs that their plans are failing by engaging in risky corrective measures (Campion & Lord, 1982; Hollenbeck, Williams, & Klein, 1989; Oancea & Kamau, 2015; Nadolska & Barkema, 2014; Choi et al., 2011). Thirdly, they may perceive an otherwise unstable environment as highly controllable (Bandura & Wood, 1989; Vaara et al., 2014) and they might fail to engage in effective self-regulation by pursuing certain goals, even when evidence suggests that the goals are not going to succeed (Zimmerman, 2013; Oancea & Kamau, 2015). Aside from hubris, there is a lack of sufficient research about the impact of many other "dark" personality traits on employees within organizations experiencing mergers and acquisitions. Therefore, we encourage further research about narcissism, Machiavellianism, and social dominance orientation within organizations that are about to merge or acquire/be acquired.

You will notice that the previous theories about leadership style and leaders' personality traits focus on what we can call general dispositional trends, but what about a leader's competence with job-related knowledge and tasks such as processing information or making decisions? We will discuss this next.

Information processing theories about leadership

There is scepticism about the deterministic view of perspectives that focus on fixed traits (Mumford, Zaccaro, Harding, Jacobs, & Fleishman, 2000), such as a leader's style or their personality. Leadership is a function of unique characteristics, such as feelings, thought patterns, and behaviour (Funder, 2001; Allport, 1961; Feist & Feist, 2009), but these might be characteristics that leaders could learn even if they do not have the "natural" disposition towards them. The information processing approach to leadership argues that good leadership is a complex mix of behavioural, cognitive, and social skills that can be developed over time (Zaccaro & Klimoski, 2001). These skills, according to the information processing paradigm, can be learned with experience or through observations and integration of what is learnt into cognitive systems that govern a person's behaviour, thoughts, and social experiences (Lord & Hall, 2005). Good leadership is, in this perspective, a matter of how competent a leader is at knowing the work (e.g. knowing about engineering while leading an engineering company), how competent the leader is at accessing and using their knowledge, and how much a leader can be considered an expert within the field. In order for leaders to progress from being novices to experts, Lord and Hall (2005) proposed that they need to rely less on processing knowledge from working-memory (a type of short-term memory within the brain that focuses on the immediate tasks at hand) and more on processing knowledge in a way that taps into broader memory, thus allowing more complex problem-solving and collaborative work with employees. In other words, the perspective suggests that leaders who are novices use a system of knowledge that focuses on surface-level or immediately apparent problems, whereas leaders who are experts have achieved a sense of connecting patterns among the different problems that they have ever encountered (or pattern learning with time), and this helps them better lead a variety of situations and employees. Expert leaders are thus quicker in identifying solutions to various problems without resorting to general heuristics or rules of thumb about superficially similar situations (Patel & Groen, 1991). They can tend to store and retrieve knowledge unconsciously (Hanges, Lord, & Dickson, 2000; Smith, 1996; Newell, 1990).

The information processing approach includes the dual-system processing perspective proposed by Smith and deCoster (2000), which implies that novice leaders engage in rule-based processing by using knowledge that is case-based, and thus it is a slow and effortful process for such leaders to use new information and process unfamiliar problems. On the other hand, there is the associative processing mode, which is based on connectionist memories (Smith and deCoster 2000) and this tallies with previous conceptualisations about expert leadership. In simplistic terms, over years of experience, individuals develop associations between information or stimuli, and this can explain why expert leaders may be better at solving problems in a wide variety of situations. Some authors suggest that such leaders develop automatic thinking in the sense that, even in the presence of one stimulus or a few stimulus, they are able to access other relevant information and use it based on intuition that the association most probably holds true in the new context (Smith & deCoster, 1998). This suggests that expert leaders have information processing networks within their brain that help them interpret new or unfamiliar stimuli, determine the causes or solutions to problems, and develop new goals because they are able to generalise knowledge from previous experiences (Martinko, Harvey, & Douglas, 2007). Think, for example, of a taxi driver. At first, he or she may not be familiar with all the routes or streets in a big city, or how house numbering works in some areas. He or she might not use shortcuts and lack familiarity with alternative routes, therefore they may prefer to take routes they know well. But as he or she begins to drive the streets frequently, consciously choosing landmarks for guidance in the city like buildings or other such points of interests, he or she becomes proficient at manoeuvring around. The driver may become so adept at it that he or she may not ultimately need any GPS assistance to complete a ride. They automatically build on the knowledge they have accumulated, make connections between landmarks and destinations, know when to avoid particularly congested areas, and take different routes in certain time intervals. This allows them to perform their jobs faster and with less effort than novices. The same goes for leaders. They build knowledge, associations, and connections between various facts and events, and then, as they are exposed to various situations, they put this knowledge to use by searching for similar situations and contingencies they have already experienced and managed in the past. As know-how reaches some form of maturity, leaders can develop the necessary skills to perform their jobs.

Therefore, good leaders in mergers in acquisitions could be those who are competent experts within the domain concerned (e.g. a manager within an oil services company that is competent at oil service analytics). They may also be leaders who are able to develop across time in identity terms, such that their identity as a leader becomes a part of their sense of self (Lord & Hall, 2005). Lord and Brown (2004) distinguish between individual and collective identities and, building on Chapter 5, it is plausible that leaders who are more experienced in leadership become more oriented towards the employees they lead (Hogg, 2001; see Chapter 4). In mergers and acquisition, leaders may, with time, learn how to manage effectively, and there is thus scope for leaders to change from being novices to experts. Poor prior experience with a merger or acquisition can correspond with low organizational performance after the merger or the acquisition (Ellis, Reus, Lamont, & Ranft, 2011). Prior experience can also increase the likelihood that a prospective merger or acquisition will actually complete its intended transactions (Muehlfeld, Sahib, & Van Witteloostuijn, 2012). In terms of pricing and target valuation during the bidding process, leaders seem to learn as experience accumulates, and gradually converge to a more accurate assessment of the real value of the target firm (Aktas, de Bodt, & Roll, 2009, 2011). Similarly, after a merger or acquisition, during the integration stage, more experience can help intercultural learning and performance (Dikova & Rao Sahib, 2013).

In summary, the idea that leaders have fixed styles or personalities is not set in stone, and nor is it the case that what matters is only what a leader's style or personality is. It is also important to consider a leader's competence within the domain of knowledge or expertise that is the focus of the employees they manage, as well as a leader's accumulation of experience at leading. This section shows that leadership can mature with experience.

Conclusions

In this chapter, we have addressed the topic of leadership in mergers and acquisitions. We reviewed dominant theories about the psychology of leadership and we discussed how to apply these theories in understanding what counts as good leadership in mergers and acquisitions. We discussed transformational and transactional leadership styles, and their implications for employees and organizations that are experiencing mergers and acquisitions. We discussed related approaches that conceptualise leadership in terms of style, while also conceptualising leadership in terms of context, such as the leader-member exchange theory and contingency theory of leadership. We then discussed theories about how the personality of a leader is relevant to their work as a leader, and we evaluated the so-called dark and bright sides of various personality traits, including considering how they can help or be a hindrance in mergers or acquisitions. We discussed personality in terms of standard perspectives such as the Big Five theory (e.g. extraversion, agreeableness, openness to experience) and also in terms of perspectives focusing on "pathological" personality traits such as narcissism, hubris, and Machiavellianism. We discussed evidence that even these "bad" traits can have advantages as well as disadvantages. We then discussed information processing approaches comparing novice and expert leaders, and discussing why experience helps leaders transition from using knowledge or expertise in a simple, case-by-case way, to using it in a more generalizable manner that allows more complex problem-solving with employees. This raises the question of how relevant expertise among all employees (not just managers) is to the success of mergers and acquisitions, and therefore how important organizational learning among employees is, which Chapter 8 will discuss.

8 Organizational learning is a common goal in mergers and acquisitions, but what psychological processes help or hinder it?

In Chapter 1, we discussed different types of mergers and acquisitions, and the different types of deals between organizations based on how similar or different they are in their products or geographical markets. We explored five types of mergers (horizontal mergers, market extension mergers, vertical mergers, product extension mergers, and conglomerate mergers) and 15 ways of classifying acquisitions. There are a number of challenges facing organizations involved in different types of deals from the point of view of integrating the knowledge, skills, and experience of employees from each partner organization, and making the best out of the new combined knowledge for the purpose of "adding value" or innovating the organization formed from the merger or acquisition. We can broadly call this process "organizational learning." For instance, horizontal mergers take place between organizations operating within the same line of business (e.g. similar products or services), therefore, they may face fewer challenges to organizational learning than conglomerate mergers, which involve organizations in unrelated lines of business, and therefore the need for the organization to invest a lot of time or resources to facilitate the process of organizational learning is lower. In some types of acquisitions, such as a type 1 or 2 conglomerate acquisition, the changes within the organization can seem drastic to employees, and thus require them to develop new knowledge or skills about navigating the structure of the acquired organization. Aside from the type of merger or acquisition posing many challenges to organizational learning, the motives behind the deal can determine what sorts of learning goals the organization has. Whilst some types of mergers or acquisitions are said to prioritise knowledge acquisition or organizational learning as a goal, others will prioritise other types of goals, e.g. achieving higher profits through economies of scale or expanding to a new type of product or geographical market (Roller, Stennek, & Verboven, 2006). Even then, the *type* of organizational learning goal can vary and not necessarily be appropriate from the point of view of employees. For example, an organization involved in a market extension merger might concentrate training efforts on helping employees learn about a new geographical market's trading laws, consumer profiles, marketing channels, and export options, but employees who are not directly involved with trading could benefit more from other types of training. This chapter will discuss the benefits of mergers and acquisitions for organizational learning, because merging partners or acquired firms can provide the missing ingredients (relating to employees' knowledge, skills, or experience) that help organizations achieve their business goals of new products, markets, or better profits (Brealey & Myers, 2006). It can be more expensive for organizations to build employees' expertise in the field from scratch, therefore organizations could pursue mergers or acquisitions with organizations whose employees have knowledge, skills, or experience they can capitalize on.

This chapter will start by discussing different approaches that organizations have towards organizational learning after a merger or acquisition. Some knowledge management processes can capture the innovation potential embedded within the two sets of employees better than others, and in different ways. This chapter will discuss the "exploitation" approach, which is where an organization seeks to improve productivity and efficiency by using existing resources; and the "exploration" approach, which is where organizations seek innovation or experimentation by exploring new opportunities (March, 1991). We will examine literature about the intricate complexities of knowledge management processes after a merger or acquisition from the point of view of the exploration versus exploitation paradigm (March, 2001; Benner & Tushman, 2002; Rothaermel & Deeds, 2004). This chapter will then discuss why some theorists suggest that a balance between exploitation and exploration (or ambidexterity) is crucial for the survival and performance of an organization (Ghemawat & Costa, 1993; March, 1991). We will then follow with a discussion evaluating the question of whether or not organizations fail to realise their potential for innovation by failing to engage in effective organizational learning, and thus failing to use the expertise of employees to their full potential. We will then explore psychological challenges that can hinder optimum knowledge sharing among employees between different partner organizations involved in a merger or acquisition, such as low motivation or commitment to the organization because of job insecurity, intentions to quit, or attitudes of "us versus them." Finally, we will discuss a case study of the General Electric and Baker Hughes merger that illustrates why achieving optimum organizational learning is only one of the many complex and competing priorities facing organizations involved in mergers and acquisitions.

Approaches to organizational learning – exploration, exploitation, and ambidexterity

Organization theorists suggest that for an organization to survive and be able to compete over time, it needs to build on its expertise and knowledge to allow small incremental innovations and to develop new types of expertise and knowledge that allow discovery and innovations that are more radical (Teece, Pisano, & Shuen, 1997). Some theorists suggest that organizations can approach organizational learning in two ways: exploration and exploitation (March, 1991). An organizational learning approach of exploration involves experimentation, flexibility, and innovation, whereas an approach of exploitation involves focusing on utilising existing knowledge, skills, and expertise to meet organizational goals such as production and efficiency. March (1991) suggested that exploration and exploitation are mutually exclusive approaches in that an organization cannot pursue innovative endeavours and develop new knowledge while simultaneously focusing on exploiting the existing knowledge, skills, and the expertise of staff (March, 1996). Organizations are thought to make decisions about how best to allocate resources and to make a rational choice between investing in advancements *or* investing in current resources (March, 1991, 2006). That results in decisions that put organizations in semi-permanent states of exploration *or* exploitation (not both) because of the establishment of organizational structures, processes, and routines that cement the organization's learning approach (March, 1996; Lazer & Friedman, 2007; Ancona, Goodman, Lawrence, & Tushman, 2001). For example, exploitation is said to be associated with rigid organizational structures in relatively stable markets, whereas exploration is associated with loose organizational structures with high levels of autonomy for employees and is associated with emerging industries (Eisenhardt & Brown, 1998; Lewin, Long, & Carroll, 1999). Whereas March proposed that the two are fundamentally in opposition, Gupta and colleagues (2006) suggested that the two may be both orthogonal to each other but also two ends of a continuum, depending on whether one's focus is on a single or multiple domains. For example, exploration and exploitation might simply represent different stages of an organization, such that exploration is necessary in the early life of an organization when it is establishing a unique selling point or filling a gap in the market, whereas exploitation may be the default approach necessary in maintaining the status quo after an organization has finished establishing itself.

On the other hand, exploration and exploitation might not be mutually exclusive approaches to organizational learning. Literature suggests that, for an organization to survive and be competitive, it needs to achieve equilibrium between exploration and exploitation (Ghemawat & Costa, 1993; Teece et al., 1997; Tushman & O'Reilly, 1996; He & Wong, 2004). If an organization's tilts too heavily towards exploration at the cost of exploitation, it might suffer stalling in existing projects, whereas an overly exploitative approach at the cost of exploration might make an organization not as cutting-edge as competitors in discovering new ways of making money or cutting costs (March, 2001). Therefore, an organization that wants to simultaneously pursue exploitation of existing knowledge, skills, and expertise, and exploration of new ideas and opportunities, needs to allocate its resources effectively, making trade-offs where necessary. These are trade-offs in the way that the organization allocates resources to short-term versus long-term projects, the present versus the future, and stability versus adaptability (Lavie, Stettner, & Tushman, 2010). This suggests that when resources are scarce, an organization may be either oriented towards exploration or exploitation, but not both. Alternatively, if resources are plentiful, exploration and exploitation could coexist (Koza & Lewin, 1998; Rothaermel, 2001; Rothaermel & Leeds, 2004; Beckman, Haunschild, & Phillips, 2004). This supports the idea that an organization's approach of exploration or exploitation does not represent a choice between two discrete options, but rather a matter of necessity based on the resources available (Lavie et al., 2010; Mehlhorn et al., 2015; Sidhu, Commandeur, & Volberda, 2007). Organizations with a high amount of resources (e.g. very high net profits after costs) are more likely to engage in exploration (Voss, Sirdeshmukh, & Voss, 2008; Greve, 2007). The idea of achieving optimal balance between exploration and exploitation is thought of as organizational ambidexterity (Tushman & O'Reilly, 1996; Duncan, 1976; O'Reilly & Tushman, 2013; Benner & Tushman, 2002) or punctuated equilibrium (Burgelman, 1991).

Aside from the resources available, certain factors can help organizations pursue exploration, exploitation, or ambidexterity. Lavie et al. (2010) categorised the antecedents in terms of whether they are environmental factors, organizational factors or management factors. For example, environmental factors include the dynamic nature of the market in which the organization operates, with a dynamic industry defined in terms of rapid changes in what consumers prefer or fast advancements in technology that force an organization to remain competitive by investing in the time or other resources that help their employees engage in experimentation (Butler & Grahovac, 2012; Sidhu et al., 2007; Kim & Rhee, 2009; Jansen, Vera, & Crossan, 2009). Environmental factors may also include shocks within an economic market, such as changes in the prices or availability of raw foodstuffs because of weather events, compelling an organization to maintain a certain level of flexibility so that it can respond to such shocks (Xia & Dimov, 2019; Mudambi & Swift, 2011). An intensely competitive market can also lead an organization to lean towards exploration rather than exploitation, because it wants to attract customers in its competitive differentiation (Auh & Menguc, 2005; Saemundsson & Candi, 2014; Abebe & Angriawan, 2014; Anand, Mesquita, & Vassolo, 2009). However, environmental factors might not determine the organizational learning approaches of those organizations that have a dominant share of the market. In Chapter 2, you learned about the history of mergers and acquisitions, and the sorts of factors that inspire them, including market dominance. Perversely, a merger or acquisition that achieves market dominance could dis-incentivise an organizational learning approach of exploration because of fewer competitors with less power in the market.

Organizational antecedents of exploration, exploitation, or ambidextrous learning activities include the organization's "absorptive capacity," which is the ability to recognize the benefits of new knowledge and to apply it internally (Cohen & Levinthal, 1990). Organizations with greater exposure to outside knowledge and which internalise that knowledge are more likely to engage in exploration rather than exploitation (Lavie & Rosenkopf, 2006) or achieve ambidexterity (Solís-Molina, Hernández-Espallardo, & Rodríguez-Orejuela, 2018). Other factors that determine whether organizations have an approach of exploration, exploitation, or both is their structure (Csaszar, 2013; Fang, Lee, & Schilling, 2010), culture or identity (Sorensen, 2002; Andriopoulos & Lewis, 2009), age, and size (Jain, 2016; Le Mens, Hannan, & Pólos, 2015; Rothaermel &

Deeds, 2004). The problem with defining organizational antecedents is that they can depend on many factors, and the results from previous research might not be generalizable. For example, the age or size of an organization might matter, but only relative to other organization within the same sector. For organizations embarking on a merger or acquisition, factors such as culture, size, or structure are open to change and may continue changing for several years, raising the question of *when* to define the organizational antecedents. It might be the case that organizational factors are correlates rather than predictors of an organization's learning approach. For example, an organization structured in such a way that there is a research and development department or officer with significant power might engage in more exploration than organizations without the infrastructure to support experimentation.

Managerial antecedents of exploration, exploitation, and ambidexterity in learning include the way that managers think about new ideas versus maintaining the status quo, and the personality traits or behaviours of managers when leading staff or making decisions. In Chapter 7 on leadership, we discussed how leaders with a transformative approach to leadership tend to have a vision and they inspire employees to support new ideas, which suggests that transformational leadership is a correlate of an exploration approach to organizational learning. On the other hand, one manager alone is unlikely to define the approach of an entire organization, therefore, what matters is whether transformational leadership is the most frequently observed leadership style within the organization. Furthermore, transformational leadership is not necessarily synonymous with an exploratory approach to learning – it may depend on whether or not the leader is autocratic about being the source of new ideas and the gatekeeper to innovation within his or her team. Leaders with certain personality traits, such as being open to experience and seeking intellectual stimulation, might be more open to exploration in organizational learning because they want to pursue new ideas even if they are against the tradition of the organization (Luo, Zheng, Ji, & Liang, 2018; Keller & Weibler, 2015). This suggests that leaders with low levels of these personality traits will be more inclined towards exploitation in organizational learning because it offers more stability and less risk than exploration.

Moreover, although organizational learning might be a key reason for many mergers or acquisitions, organizations might experience crises that make achieving the learning goals less of a priority. When organizations face competing demands such as falling revenues or changing market conditions, achieving optimal organizational learning might take a back seat.

Merged or acquired organizations deal with competing demands

There is a difference between what organizations should or could do in achieving optimum organizational learning, and what organizations that have undergone a merger or acquisition actually do. This is because mergers or acquisitions happen in organizational climates that can be considered to be unusual in many ways, such as in closing sites, restructuring the organization, replacing an entire senior management team, introducing new products, procedures, or policies, and so on. Organizations also often face competing demands from the market, shareholders, investors, competitors, and national or international events that can precipitate the failure of a merger or acquisition (see Chapter 2). You therefore need to balance the notion of optimum organizational learning, including the idea of equilibrium between exploration and exploitation approaches, against the competing demands facing organizations that have been through a merger or acquisition. As an example, let us look at the many complex factors within the following case study about the merger between General Electric Oil and Gas and Baker Hughes. When the merger was announced, an analyst from JP Morgan said:

> [The merger] enables the sharing of research and engineering, so materials developed in one business, for example, become accessible to others . . . [The merger offers] potential for more sophisticated product development by tapping into the shared technology . . . [This is the] most compelling rationale for the deal.
>
> (Sean Meakim, a JP Morgan analyst quoted
> in www.thestreet.com)

Portfolio managers likewise said that certain expertise (specifically technological knowledge) was an important motive for the merger:

> We believe the true underlining motivation for the deal alights with [General Electric Oil and Gas's] efforts in big data via its Predix platform . . . Importantly, [General Electric Oil and Gas] has the scale and technological expertise to succeed in this space and has only added to its offerings through ownership of a new Baker Hughes, which will bring forth a larger client base for Predix, allowing for additional learning capabilities and a large stage to prove its worth.
>
> (Jim Cramer and Jack Mohr, portfolio managers
> quoted in www.thestreet.com)

Therefore, knowledge exchange between the two organizations was thought to be a good reason for the merger. Despite this, because of the many complex factors affecting General Electric Oil and Gas, Baker Hughes, and the oil industry, it is difficult for a researcher or consultant to extrapolate whether or not the two organizations actually engaged in optimum learning, whether they took an approach of exploitation, exploration, or ambidexterity, and whether this matters in explaining the fate of the merger.

The case of General Electric Oil and Gas's merger with Baker Hughes

General Electric is an international organization with headquarters in the United States that owned a subsidiary organization called General Electric Oil and Gas which engaging in drilling, refining, storing, and transporting petroleum as well as other activities within the oil and gas industry. The parent company, General Electric, was founded in 1889 by Thomas Edison, the well-known American inventor, and others through a series of mergers and acquisitions of several companies within the industry. General Electric has engaged in a large number of acquisitions. General Electric Oil and Gas was a subsidiary of General Electric, and it, too, had engaged in a number of acquisitions before deciding to merge with Baker Hughes.

Whereas General Electric Oil and Gas's operations involved finding, storing, and processing petroleum and other products within the industry, Baker Hughes' operations involved providing equipment or services that companies within the oil industry can use in drilling, processing, or sourcing oil and evaluating where to locate oil. Baker Hughes was an international company with clients in many countries and was headquartered in Houston, Texas, United States. Baker Hughes had a history of a number of acquisitions. Before the merger, Baker Hughes was one of the world's largest providers of oilfield services.

The oil market experienced a crash in 2014/2015 because the price of crude oil fell substantially. One contributing factor was that demand for oil from countries such as China and India, which had rapidly risen for a few years, had slowed down. Another contributing factor was that Saudi Arabia, which is one of the biggest sources of oil, continued to supply the market with oil even as demand fell. The Organization of the Petroleum Exporting Countries (OPEC), which coordinates petroleum policies, decided not to reduce the rates of oil production. At the same time, the demand was decreasing further because of milder winters in some countries (Mănescu & Nuño, 2015). The imbalance between supply and relatively lower demand contributed to the price crashes. Before the oil crash of 2014/15 (Behar & Ritz, 2016), the rising price of oil had encouraged many companies to embark on large investments and technological innovations such as oil extraction techniques (e.g. relating to drilling techniques and hydraulics) and technological innovations (e.g. computer models that helped companies find large volumes of oil through mathematical algorithms). These opened up new opportunities in accessing previously unreachable oil reservoirs and in discovering new reservoirs by targeting searches within certain geographic locations. Innovation within the oil industry was therefore something that many organizations and investors viewed positively. However, the technological improvements inadvertently led to an influx of new quantities of oil continuing to enter the market in a period when global demand for oil had fallen. By autumn 2015, oil production was at a record high of nearly 500 million barrels, as reported by the U.S. Energy Information Administration, but prices had fallen from $115 per barrel to below $35 per barrel.

The unfavourable conditions within the oil market around that time made many organizations think about ways of retaining their previous profit levels, such as through layoffs, scaling down, or mergers/acquisitions that offered them the opportunity to reduce costs by bringing together organizations within the oil mining and oil services sectors. General Electric Oil and Gas and Baker Hughes, decided to embark on a merger on October 31, 2016. The name of the merged company changed from "Baker Hughes" to "Baker Hughes, a General Electric company," or BHGE (General Electric, 2016b; Mattioli, Linebaugh, & Lublin, 2016), and it became the second-largest listed oilfield services group (Crooks, 2016). The executive board of the new organization consisted of five directors from General Electric Oil and Gas and four from Baker Hughes (Cimilluca, Mattioli, & Benoit, 2016). After the merger, the two organizations had a workforce numbering approximately 70,000 (Mann, 2017). Among the motivations for the merger were:

- The two organizations had business interests that complemented each other.
- The oil and gas production operations were able to utilise knowledge and expertise from Baker Hughes, such as evaluating the oil potential of reservoirs and making decisions about which oil exploration ventures were worth the effort.
- The merger allowed the two organizations to reduce costs that were common to both of them, in some cases eliminating duplicate jobs, improving buying costs, sales, and combining some administrative operations where necessary (General Electric, 2016a).

A major part of the integration plan was for the merged organization BHGE to adopt General Electric Oil and Gas's expertise in digital technology practices (Ward, 2017). The integration plan was coordinated by a team of 30 senior leaders from both organizations, and they developed a new strategy and operating model for the new organization, as well as other plans about achieving synergies. Cloud computing, artificial intelligence, innovative scanning technologies, and advances in robotics opened up new opportunities to explore remote and inaccessible areas for oil. Expertise in such technology also opened up the possibility of automating processes for optimality. Although automation, artificial intelligence, and some other technologies were already a part of Baker Hughes before the merger (Crooks, 2018), General Electric Oil and Gas was at a much more advanced stage of adopting the technology and it also had a history in big data analytics.

Therefore, organizational learning about adopting such technology across all of BHGE was an important purpose of the merger. However, achieving this goal was difficult at the time because of a number of internal and external factors. Tension between the United States and Iran and lower demand for oil, severely affected BHGE's revenues, as well as those of many others within the oil industry. In the first quarter of 2017, there was a 9% drop in revenue compared to the previous year (General Electric, 2017), and by the fourth quarter of 2017, the year-on-year revenue drop increased further to 70% (General Electric, 2018), with the revenue drop blamed primarily on lower demand for oil or oil services (Crooks, 2017). However, BHGE's revenue performance is said to have been far worse than that of other competitors, amounting to a $175 billion loss since the beginning of 2016 (Spencer, 2018). The pressure of coping with lost revenue was more urgent for BHGE than implementing the organizational learning goals of the merger. For instance, efforts to improve profits included raising charges to customers, cutting costs by making the way that employees did business with customers less time or resource consuming, cutting jobs, and other measures. A study by Thomson Reuters suggested that there were cultural problems within BHGE and problems integrating the management teams which affected employees and led to deteriorating relationships with customers and suppliers (Hampton, 2018). The study found that BHGE's management imposed strict cost-cutting measures, increased prices to customers, and imposed demanding sales targets on employees. Some long-term customers are said to have switched from BHGE to other suppliers because of the price increases and because of changes in the customer-supplier relationship. BHGE's urgent cost-reduction measures had included changing the way that Baker Hughes employees managed employees (which was previously more personalised), making it less personal and rigid in a way that was more common with General Electric Oil and Gas before the merger (Hampton, 2018). This affected Baker Hughes' relationships with its existing customers. BHGE's management also initiated cost-cutting measures that included renegotiating contracts with suppliers by pushing for discounts in prices and lengthier bill payment arrangements. This was said to have made relationships with suppliers difficult to the extent that one long-time supplier of Baker Hughes, a company called Markall Inc, filed a lawsuit (Hampton, 2018) and the difficulties with suppliers persisted (Motley Fool Transcribers, 2019). Baker Hughes employees are said to have complained about

General Electric's urge for quick profits, and about the cultural differences between the two organizations. The pressure of job cuts, job insecurity, and the impact of higher sales targets on the work-life balance of employees caused many employees from Baker Hughes to quit. There were also leadership changes, which might have exacerbated the sense of upheaval within BHGE.

From 2018, General Electric sold its majority stake in Baker Hughes (Clough & Serafino, 2018; Platt & Crooks, 2018a, June 26, 2018b, June 27; Ennes, 2018; Platt & Crooks, 2018a, June 26) from 62% to 50% then 38.% (Rivas, 2018; Crooks & Wigglesworth, 2018; Baker Hughes, a GE Company, 2019). The divestment was followed by Baker Hughes' decision to revert from a merged identity back to an independent identity in 2019, changing its name to the Baker Hughes Company. The merger could be said to have been a failure because it ended. The speed with which the integration process happened might have meant that there was not enough time for BHGE to achieve the organizational learning goals, because the speed of integration has a negative effect on the success of a merger or acquisition (Homburg & Bucerius, 2006). The organizational learning goals of the merger are unlikely to have been achieved because of competing priorities such as BHGE needing to cope with drops in revenue. Therefore, we can see that organizational learning as a goal of the merger was competing against a number of other factors that BHGE may have placed higher on its list of priorities for time, resources, and management strategies. Examples are:

- Coping with external market conditions such as lower demand for oil.
- Coping with falls in revenue such as finding ways of cutting costs.
- Coping with the effects of pushing for cost-cutting costs, such as harming relationships with suppliers.
- Coping with the effects of raising prices and reducing service levels, such as losing customers.
- Coping with changes in leadership and discontinuity in strategic priorities.
- Coping with cultural differences between the two organizations, such as the extent to which relationships with suppliers and clients are personalised.

A thread running through many of these points is that the priority for BHGE was to urgently increase revenue and reduce costs. Although achieving optimal organizational learning might have been useful in the long run, we can see why it was unlikely to be BHGE's biggest priority and, in fact, it is likely to have suffered because of the overall cost-cutting and profit-making goals that drove BHGE's activities at the time.

What we can conclude from this case study is that organizational learning can be a goal of a merger or acquisition in theory, but, in reality, organizations could prioritise more urgent demands such as coping with falls in revenue due to external market factors.

When is organizational learning a priority after a merger or acquisition?

Organizational learning could be a priority among organizations that engage in a merger or acquisition specifically because research and development is a necessary ingredient for commercial success. Some informal collaborations between organizations in research and development can result in a merger or acquisition (Porrini, 2004; Zollo & Reuer, 2010). Organizations that join together so that research and development will result in making and selling a product can tend to focus on an exploitation approach, whereas those without specific commercialisation plans can tend to deploy an exploration approach (Lavie & Rosenkopf, 2006; Koza & Lewin, 1998; Hoang & Rothaermel, 2010). The type of approach that an organization has to exploration matters. Organizations with a poor history in research and development might not have the infrastructure or culture necessary to absorb knowledge from a merger or acquisition (Hitt, Hoskisson, Ireland, & Harrison, 1991b), and this can limit the extent to which the commercialisation goals associated with acquiring new knowledge or expertise are reached (Henderson & Cockburn, 1996). The practicalities facing the organizations also matter. For instance, geographic distance between the two organizations can make exploitation more or less feasible than exploration (Yang, Lin, & Peng, 2011; Beckman et al., 2004; Phene et al., 2012). Also, mergers or acquisitions involving organizations with a similar domain of expertise might make exploitation more probable (Lavie, Kang, & Rosenkopf, 2011; Sabidussi, Lokshin, & Duysters, 2018; Jin, Zhou, & Wang, 2016). Even then, cooperation, time, long-term stability, and good governance are important for success in achieving the desired learning goals (Das & Teng, 2000; Amesse, Latour, Rebolledo, & Séguin-Dulude, 2004). Exploration alliances are said to be more likely to end in acquisitions in comparison to exploitation alliances (Yang et al., 2011), whereas organizations that view their combined expertise as a valuable attribute are said to be more likely to result in a merger (Burt, 1992; Yang et al., 2011; Phelps, 2010). Mergers or acquisitions create diversification that could also be associated with an exploratory approach to organizational learning (Lin, 2014). Additionally, the similarity or complementarity of the knowledge base within the two organizations matters. For instance, organizations that use similar technologies (Hagedoorn & Duysters, 2002) or have similar expertise or knowledge (Prabhu, Chandy, & Ellis, 2005) are said to be quite conducive to innovation. Some literature suggests that similarity helps organizations have a comparable approach to absorbing and using new knowledge (Ahuja & Katila, 2001; Cohen & Levinthal, 1990; Hitt, Hoskisson, Ireland, & Harrison, 1991a). Organizations with different but complementary types of expertise are said to benefit from radical innovations (Makri, Hitt, & Lane, 2010; Ahuja & Katila, 2001; Cloodt, Hagedoorn, & Kranenburg, 2006). However, there is a lack of international evidence showing whether the results from these studies provide generalizable rules of thumb for all mergers or acquisitions. It is possible that there is too much variation in what motivates organizations to enter into a merger or acquisition, and the factors that motivate organizations to prioritise organizational learning (and to focus on certain approaches to learning) vary too widely to allow generalizable rules of thumb.

It is important to note that making organizational learning a priority after a merger or acquisition is not necessarily a recipe for success in profit-making, therefore organizations that think of organizational learning as something that will not improve profits might not prioritise it. Although the lack of exploration of new ideas is said to have negative consequences for organizations in general (John, Weiss, & Dutta, 1999; Wind & Mahajan, 1997), some studies suggest that research and development outputs actually decline after mergers and acquisitions (Hitt et al., 1991a; Ernst & Vitt, 2000; Hitt et al., 1991b; Stiebale & Reize, 2011). This might be because the pro rata expenditure on research and development falls after a merger or acquisition, comparing average investments in innovation before and after (Hitt et al., 1991a, 1991b). Some studies suggest that acquisitions result in better investments in innovations than mergers (de Man & Duysters, 2005), but such assumptions need to be corroborated with an analysis of international data.

There is also the question of what happens to organizational learning in the long term, beyond the initial months or years after a merger or acquisition. Managers might become more risk-averse and less supportive of innovations (Hitt, Hoskisson, & Ireland, 1990). Also, an organization that engages in frequent acquisitions might not fully utilise the expertise of existing employees, and it might not sufficiently internalise the expertise of employees from organizations it acquires (Hitt et al., 1990; Hitt, Hoskisson, Johnson, & Moesel, 1996). Mergers and acquisitions often lead to high rates of staff turnover (Kiessling, Harvey, & Moeller, 2012; Walsh, 1989), and the long-term fate of organizational learning might be reduced by the departure of employees who are central to research and development (Ernst & Vitt, 2000; Hitt et al., 1991b).

In short, different factors can determine whether or not an organization will make organizational learning the goal of a merger or acquisition, and different factors also determine whether organizations are successful in being innovative. Even when organizations *do* make it a priority, a number of psychological processes can reduce the extent to which employees engage in effective organizational learning, such as their attitudes about the expertise of the partner organization, and their motivation to remain working with the organization.

Psychological processes among employees and organizational learning

In Chapter 5 we discussed group processes in mergers and acquisitions or, in other words, "us versus them" attitudes and behaviours among employees. These psychological processes can reduce the extent to which employees feel motivated to learn from employees in partner organizations, or think that the latter have worthwhile knowledge to learn from. Since a context in which trust exists helps certain types of learning (Gibson & Birkinshaw, 2004), it may thus follow that a context of mistrust or attitudes of "us versus them" could hamper organizational learning (Haspeslagh & Jemison, 1991; Vaara et al., 2012). Successful knowledge transfer requires that employees in one organization can access the partner organization's knowledge (Zollo & Reuer, 2010). The transfer happens through many interactions among employees that should ideally involve them conveying their own knowledge and absorbing new knowledge from employees in the partner organization (Haspeslagh & Jemison, 1991). However, attitudes of "us versus them" can mean that some employees do not feel like they have anything to learn from one another and avoid contact, such as in the case of Chrysler Corporation and Daimler-Benz discussed earlier in this book (Apfelthaler et al., 2002).

Psychological processes that can hinder optimum organizational learning after a merger or acquisition can also include employees fearing that they will be exploited or contaminated (Empson, 2001; Junni, 2011; Mirc, 2012), such as when they perceive a disparity in the status or power of the two organizations (see Chapters 4 and 5). The fear of exploitation could lead to employees withholding valuable information, thinking that their organization's knowledge is more valuable and guarding it as a valuable asset that maintains the status differences. Fear of contamination could include employees fearing that the partner organization has a poor reputation and therefore that copying what they do will lead to a dilution of their own "better" practices or skills. Studies suggest that some employees make no attempt to learn from the partner organization (Chua & Goh, 2009), and this hampers knowledge transfer between the organizations (Vaara et al., 2012). Some employees can also limit who they relay their expertise to, giving their knowledge to employees within their organization but refusing to give it to employees in the partner organization (Empson, 2001). "Us versus them" psychological processes among employees can thus hinder an organization from fulfilling the learning goals of a merger or acquisition. Organizations could mitigate these processes by encouraging a cooperative organizational climate rather than a competitive one (Nemanich & Vera, 2009).

Conclusions

What we call "organizational learning" in a merger or acquisition involves integrating the knowledge, skills, and experience of employees from each partner organization, and making the best out of the new combined knowledge for the purpose of "adding value" or innovating the organization formed from the merger or acquisition. This chapter discussed the different approaches to organizational learning and ways such as exploitation, exploration, and ambidexterity approaches. The exploitation approach is where an organization seeks to improve productivity and efficiency by using existing resources, and the exploration approach is where organizations seek innovation or experimentation by exploring new opportunities. This chapter examined literature about the intricate complexities of knowledge management processes after a merger or acquisition by extending perspectives suggesting that a balance between exploitation and exploration (or ambidexterity) is crucial for the survival and performance of an organization. We then considered the question of whether or not organizations fail to realise their potential for innovation by failing to engage in effective organizational learning, thus failing to use the expertise of employees to their full potential. We explored psychological challenges that can hinder optimum knowledge sharing among employees between different partner organizations involved in a merger or acquisition, such as low motivation to share knowledge because of attitudes of "us versus them" as well as economic pressures to cope with falling revenues or profits, such as in the case study of the merger between General Electric and Baker Hughes. We conclude that achieving optimum organizational learning is only one of the many complex and competing priorities facing organizations involved in mergers and acquisitions. This leads to the question of broader issues facing organizations that are relevant to psychology but are under-represented within the literature, such as the occupational health and safety of employees which we will discuss in Chapter 9, next.

9 Considering occupational health and safety in due diligence for mergers and acquisitions – learning from lawsuits about cancer mortality

This book has discussed psychological implications of mergers and acquisitions in a myriad of different ways. Our extensive review of the field shows that one area that is neglected within the literature is the issue of employees' health and safety, and this will therefore be the focus of this chapter. Organizations in what we can call "traditional" sectors such as mining, manufacturing, transport, and construction might consider mergers or acquisitions within the same sector, and deals in these sectors might seem financially attractive because investing in an established industry with a long history of profits and stock market value could offer a more predictable or stable investment than merging or acquiring an organization in a newer industry (e.g. new technology). Organizations outside the sector can also consider mergers or acquisitions with organizations in traditional sectors as a way of improving the security of their profits if their other operations are within sectors that offer less certainty about costs, competitors, or profits. The problem is that sectors such as mining, producing metals, manufacturing automobiles, tyres, leather or pharmaceuticals, or constructing buildings present a number of occupational health risks for workers. For example, within these (and other industries), workers are sometimes or often exposed to substances that increase their risk of developing cancer. A merger or acquisition in such an industry can lead to something called "inherited liability," which is the legal responsibility to answer lawsuits from workers who developed cancer or any illness (or families of workers who died from the illness) because of being exposed to a hazardous substance at work, even if the exposure happened before the merger or acquisition. This chapter will focus on cancer-inducing substances (these are known as carcinogens) because cancer is one of the biggest causes of mortality in many countries, and because of the abundance of high-quality evidence (e.g. meta-analyses) about how exposure to certain substances raises the risk of cancer. This chapter will examine a number of case studies showing that the cost of inheriting liability after a merger or acquisition can be as much as millions or billions of dollars. Other costs include harm to the organization's reputation on the stock market, dips in share prices, and, in some cases, upheaval within the organization (e.g. shareholders voting out the CEO who instigated the merger or acquisition). This chapter encourages organizations to include occupational health risk management as a mandatory component of their due diligence about a prospective merger or acquisition. We encourage organizations to consult scientific experts or practitioners (e.g. medical doctors specialising in occupational medicine) about the types of occupational health risks that are prevalent in an organization with which they want to merge or acquire based on their expert summation of the up-to-date peer-reviewed published evidence, including meta-analyses of risk ratios. We specifically encourage organizations to consult scientific experts rather than relying on standard guidance (e.g. a government's classification of hazardous substances) because the standard guidance can be out-of-date with the published scientific evidence. This chapter looks at examples of substances from many different industries that increase the risk of workers developing cancer and meta-analytic evidence about the average relative risk of different types of cancer. This chapter will also discuss some case studies of mergers or acquisitions that have resulted in inherited liability for cancer or cancer-related mortality, such as Bayer's acquisition of Monsanto, which was sued by people who developed cancers such as non-Hodgkin's lymphoma from Monsanto's product Roundup, and Pfizer's acquisition of Quigley, which was sued by workers who developed lung cancer after being exposed to asbestos while working at Quigley. Both led to acquirers Bayer and Pfizer losing the lawsuits and paying millions or billions of dollar in compensation as well as, in Bayer's case, reportedly losing 44% of its share value after the acquisition. This chapter will start by introducing occupational health to help you discover the complexities of establishing what elements of physical or mental health can be attributed to work-related factors. The next section will help you explore the statistical principles behind predicting the different causes of health issues in order to understand how, why, and when work-related factors can be said to have contributed significantly to a specific illness. This chapter offers a new perspective that will hopefully encourage further research and literature about the occupational health and safety implications of mergers and acquisitions.

Understanding statistical principles behind predicting occupational health and safety

First, let us understand how a large number of factors predict workers' health and how work-related factors (such as exposure to harm) are only one of many potential consequences of occupational health and safety problems. The possible causes include personal variables (e.g. genetics, smoking, diet, or exercise) to work-related variables (e.g. hazardous substances that cause illness, a bullying manager that causes a mental disorder, or faulty equipment that causes an accident and injury). In order to understand the definition of occupational health, we need to understand the statistics about how different variables significantly predict health or illness, significantly raise the risk of a certain symptom or condition (e.g. cancer). By "significantly predict" or "significantly raises," we mean in the statistical sense of probability theory. Many statistical analysis techniques in health research use something called a regression model. As an analogy, imagine that you are a researcher tasked with analysing the variables that predict an outcome – a cake. A regression model is an equation that defines the variables that predict an outcome. In the case of cake as an outcome, a regression equation can include butter, sugar, eggs, flour, fruit, and vanilla essence as predictors. Regression analysis tells us what proportion of the outcome is explained by each predictor uniquely, and also what proportion of the outcome is explained by all the predictors jointly. A regression equation in which butter, sugar, eggs, flour, fruit, and vanilla essence are the predictors could find that the regression model explains 80% of the outcome (with the remaining 20% being predictors that were not tested, such as oven temperature, time, and method). Imagine we now want to understand what proportion of cake is explained by each predictor, and we find that the regression model tells us that the flour explains 50% of the variance in cake, butter explains 15%, sugar explains 13%, and vanilla essence and fruit each explain 1%. What this means, in practice, is that flour is the biggest contributing factor when understanding what properties make a cake, followed by butter, then sugar. If we look at the probability (p) values, we may find that flour is a statistically significant unique predictor of cake, but that none of the other predictors by themselves can explain a cake because the p values are greater than 0.05, which means that there is a 5% probability or more that it is inaccurate to define cake using butter or sugar alone. However, we may find that the overall regression model is significant (at $p < 0.05$) which means that, when put together, all of the predictors accurately define the outcome of cake. This would make sense because butter by itself, or sugar by itself, cannot sufficiently define a cake, and we can see that vanilla essence or fruit are nice, but non-mandatory components of cake.

Returning from this metaphor, let us consider illness as an outcome that researchers are trying to predict. Illness has several predictors, from personal variables such as genetics, substance abuse or diet, social or environmental variables such as homelessness or poverty, to work-related variables such as toxins encountered at work. We can define any given illness under the umbrella of occupational health *if* evidence shows that incidences of the illness are significantly predicted by job-related factors such as exposure to certain toxins in the workplace. That is if the evidence is based on regression models showing that the job-related factors are significant unique predictors, or if the evidence is based on the risk of that illness among workers in that job compared to a control group of people (where the difference between the workers and the control group is e.g. exposure to a certain substance). Therefore, a regression model might find that many different variables predict variance in incidences of cancer, with genetics, diet, exercise, and toxins encountered at work as unique, significant predictors of a specific type of cancer. In this case, the type of cancer is one which we believe should be noted as an occupational health risk because a worker employed in a place where the toxin exists faces a significant risk of developing that type of cancer. In another type of regression model comparing workers inside and outside that profession, we believe that the type of cancer is relevant as an occupational health consideration if meta-analytic evidence shows that the odds of that cancer are significantly higher among workers in that profession. Not all workers who are exposed to the toxin will develop cancer, perhaps because the carcinogenic effects of that toxin rely on some non-work-related factors (e.g. genetics or lifestyle).

However, because the risk is present and significant for the average employee, we believe that organizations and practitioners need to be aware of it. Therefore, our definition of occupational health is any aspect of physical or mental health that is significantly predicted by work-related factors, or in which the risk of illness is significantly raised by work-related factors, with a 5% probability or lower that the result is inaccurate. In terms of weighing the published evidence about a certain illness, we recommend that organizations consult scientists or scientific practitioners because they are in the best position to interpret the quality of published evidence and statistics such as odds ratios. This approach fits with recent research which has defined workers' symptoms of ill health under the umbrella of occupational distress because the odds of those symptoms are significantly raised by work-related factors, such as burnout (Medisauskaite & Kamau, 2019a, 2019b).

What is occupational health?

Following on from previous section, we offer a definition of occupational health that emphasises the fact that it is a new branch of science and that whether or not a specific illness is significantly caused by work-related factors should be determined by evidence. Evidence about each illness should be assessed on a case-by-case basis or, in other words, there is no "rule of thumb" about which groups of illnesses are significantly related to work factors and which are not. For example, one cannot say that respiratory illness or cancer tends to be related to work-related factors, because one needs to specify what type of cancer is in question, and what work-related factors are in question. This chapter offers a "taster" of the evidence, but it is not designed as a manual for organizations to use when determining the likelihood of work-related cancer within a certain industry or sector. We recommend that organizations contemplating a merger or acquisition consult occupational health practitioners such as medical doctors who specialise in occupational medicine. They are involved in diagnosing, treating, and giving advice about work-related injuries and illnesses, and their professional training also gives them the expertise needed to interpret the results of peer-reviewed published evidence about specific injuries or illnesses. This recommendation does not negate the expertise of staff with certificates or diplomas about occupational health and safety policies, practices, and the legal obligations of organizations. However, we believe that due diligence should include not just organizations being aware of current occupational health and safety rules, but also current published evidence. It could be years or decades before published evidence is used by governments or health and safety bodies to set rules or laws, but this does not necessarily mean that organizations cannot be sued about work-related illnesses, even when they complied with the rules or laws of the time.

Occupational health, as a profession, thus includes medical doctors specialising in occupational medicine, and a variety of other practitioners with certificates, diplomas, or degrees in occupational health and safety theory, policies, and practices. Many organizations also offer workers training or information about occupational health to improve their awareness and practices about it. The problem within the current field is that non-medical training about occupational health tends to focus on broader concepts such as "wellbeing" and less on specific diseases such as cancer and the impact of industrial toxins. We emphasise the issue of cancer and cancer-related mortality as an important topic within occupational health because of the prevalence of cancer among working-age adults, because exposure to hazards that raise the risk of cancer is quite common in certain types of manufacturing, and because of the cancer risk of workers in these types of manufacturing is known to be significantly high. Gaining this knowledge is vital not just because organizations should protect the welfare of workers, but also because of the practical and financial implications for organizations planning a merger or acquisition.

In conclusion, the field of occupational health is a new branch of science. One area where there is some conclusive evidence concerns how the risks of some specific illnesses or injuries are raised in industrial settings that expose workers to certain toxins. The next section will introduce the concept of industrial toxins with examples of methods of classifying toxins according to the level of danger that they pose to humans.

What are industrial toxins?

We can define an industrial toxin as a physical substance (e.g. a chemical or biological organism) that is hazardous to the health of workers, immediately or eventually, by causing illness or injury, or by significantly increasing the risk of illness or injury. An industrial toxin can, strictly speaking, be thought of in terms of its physical capacity to infect or injure but (e.g. chemical or biological agents) but we can also extend the definition of industrial toxins to include "invisible" agents, such as certain types of radiation. We can go further and define any chemical, biological, or radiological hazard as an industrial toxin if workers are routinely at risk of being exposed to it during the normal course of their work there. Chemical toxins include combustible dusts, flammable or oxidizing solids, liquids or gases, pressurized gases, asphyxiates, pyrophorics, self-heating or reactive substances, carcinogens, and germ cell mutagens (CCOHS, 2015). Biological toxins include infectious or toxic organisms ranked on a gradient of severity from 1 (very low risk to humans), 2 (low risk, but treatment or prophylaxis is available), 3 (high risk, but treatment or prophylaxis is available) to 4 (high risk and no treatment or prophylaxis is available) (Health & Safety Executive, 2019). Class 4 biological toxins are typically banned or very highly restricted, although class 1–3 biological agents still pose a considerable risk of infection or toxicity. Examples of bacteria rated 3 by the Health & Safety Executive for being highly biologically hazardous are *bacillus anthracis, burkholderia mallei, coxiella burnetti, escherichia coli, verocytotoxigenic strains, mycobacterium microti, type-1 shigella dysenteriae, histoplasma capsulatum* and *var farcinimosum*. Examples of helminths or parasitic worms rated 3 for being highly biologically hazardous are *taenia solium, leishmania brasiliensis, naegleria fowleri, plasmodium falciparum,* and trypanosoma *brucei rhodesiense*. Examples of prions rated 3 are sporadic, genetic, or acquired agents linked with human transmissible spongiform encephalopathies such as (respectively) variably protease-resistant prionopathy agent, Gerstmann-Sträussler-Scheinker syndrome agent, and iatrogenic Creutzfeldt-Jakob disease agent, all of which are high-risk biological hazards. Examples of viruses rated 3 by the Health & Safety Executive for being highly biologically hazardous but with treatment or prophylaxis available are duvenhage virus, MERS-related coronavirus, flexal virus, bunyavirus Germiston, and absettarov virus. Not all of these chemical or biological toxins are classifiable as industrial toxins because their occurrence in manufacturing or other workplace contexts may be rare. However, some types of toxins are quite common in manufacturing contexts, e.g. carcinogens.

Workers exposed to toxins can experience blood or organ toxicity (e.g. poisoning, septicaemia, organ failure), asphyxiation or suffocation, skin burns or corrosion, injury, respiratory problems, eye damage or irritation, cancer, gem cell mutation, reproductive problems, and other health problems (Centers for Disease Control and Prevention, 2020; Health & Safety Executive, 2019). Organizations are compelled by the national regulations in many countries to ensure that workers are not exposed to health hazards without a suitable risk assessment, regular health surveillance, and suitable methods of controlling risk (Centers for Disease Control and Prevention, 2020; Health & Safety Executive, 2019). For example, the United Kingdom and Great Britain's government legislation (2002) about occupational health and safety informs organizations about health hazards within the section on "Control of Substances Hazardous to Health" (COSHH). COSHH regulations are used by many other countries, and some countries have alternative or additional regulations, such as about hazard classifications. COSHH defines a workplace as any place in which employees work or use to access work, including stairways, corridors, and where work-related facilities are provided, such as a site car park. That means that the legislation covers workers who are on-site and it could also cover workers who are off-site, including remote workers. Organizations planning mergers and acquisitions must assess whether any hazardous or banned substances (see COSHH, 2002) exist within products or by-products manufactured by or handled by employees in the intended partner organizations. Examples of substances banned by COSHH (2002) are 2-naphthylamine, benzidine, 4-nitrodiphenyl, benzene, pentachloroethane, carbon tetrachloride, or substances containing these chemicals at a volume of 0.1% or more, as well as free silica, carbon disulphide, white phosphorus, hydrogen cyanide, and others. It is thus important to ensure that an intended partner in a merger or acquisition has observed COSHH regulations or their equivalent, depending on the country. It is also useful, when weighing the costs and benefits of a planned merger or acquisition, to assess the supply chain for product components that could contain the banned substances – noting that these substances might be undeclared and therefore it may be vital to invest in expert testing. In cross-border mergers or acquisitions, or situations where a partner organization or supply chain involves a country without regulations similar to COSHH, it is important to use COSHH regulations (or more stringent regulations, where available) for the benefit of employees' health. Where employees from one country will travel to work in a partner organization from another country, it is important to note that "home" health and safety regulations could remain applicable to that employee.

Let us now explore the concept of industrial toxins in more detail by focusing on carcinogens, which are a commonly occurring type of toxin within the literature. A carcinogen is a substance that raises the risk of humans developing cancer, and they are often classified among substances that are defined as health hazards in government legislation or public guidance documents.

Common industrial toxins such as carcinogens

This chapter will discuss types of manufacturing that are high-risk because they expose workers to carcinogenic substances or processes that raise the risk of workers developing cancer. It is important for organizations to consider the impact of the safety costs and insurance liabilities on the profitability of such a merger or acquisition. Later on in this chapter, we will examine case studies of mergers or acquisitions that have led to organizations inheriting liability for workers developing cancer as a result of being exposed to certain substances during their job, and the organizations having to pay compensation in the millions or billions of dollars to workers or their relatives. This chapter focuses on cancer and cancer-related mortality because cancer is one of the most common causes of death among working-age adults and because there is an abundance of evidence about work-related cancer incidences and mortality in the literature. It is important for organizations to be aware of the current list of known carcinogens and to be aware that, although they might not be legally bound to control employees' exposure to listed carcinogens *now*, they could become legally culpable in the future. For example, the next section will provide examples of how employees who developed cancer from working with asbestos when asbestos had not yet been banned have successfully sued their employers and been compensated. The International Agency for Research on Cancer (IARC, 2019) provides a list of carcinogens. We will discuss the IARC list rather than COSHH's (2002) list of carcinogens because the COSHH list is more limited and less up-to-date than the IARC's list. Timing is important in cancer research because there have been many studies published about the connection between certain toxins and certain types of cancer since the COSHH 2002 list was published. In this discussion, we'll review substances that are classified by the IARC as having sufficient evidence of being causes of cancer, and that are relevant to workplaces (thus excluding causes such as genetics, alcohol use, tobacco use, or bacterial/viral infections unconnected with work).

The IARC (2019) list is based on comprehensive reviews of empirical studies about cancer-related incidences, including cancer-related mortalities. It is important to understand the concept of risk statistically speaking, which means that neither the IARC nor this chapter suggest that everyone who is exposed to a listed carcinogen will develop cancer. What "risk" means is that, based on known evidence from empirical studies reviewed the IARC, the named carcinogen increases the probability that people will develop the type(s) of cancer stated. We report only those substances that the IARC has categorised as having sufficient evidence of causing the type of cancer stipulated. Organizations considering merging with or acquiring an organization involved with products, production processes, or environments that contain known carcinogens should carefully weigh the potential costs of such a venture, and conduct a thorough occupational health risk assessment. The potential human costs of entering such ventures include cancer incidences among employees, cancer-related deaths, treatment-related health problems (e.g. side effects), employee sickness-related absences from work, and co-morbidities (e.g. depressive or anxiety disorders instigated by cancer diagnosis or prognosis). The potential economic costs include litigation by employees, government fines where the organization is deemed to have been negligent in exposing employees to known carcinogens, the costs of liability insurance, the costs of safety-related products or procedures to protect employees from carcinogens, and the costs of eliminating carcinogens from the workplace if they are subsequently classified as banned substances but are embedded within expensive equipment or the built environment. Organizations can actually get retrospectively sued by employees, depending on applicable laws in the country or region (including legal precedents set by employees elsewhere who sue successfully for the same reason or a similar reason). Organizations can also, depending on the laws of the country or region (e.g. the UK TUPE Regulations, 2006), be sued for exposing employees to carcinogens even in cases where the carcinogens were not banned substances at the time of exposure. This means that organizations that venture into a merger or acquisition involving carcinogenic products should think very carefully about the potential human and economic costs. Although this may seem obvious, the major problem is that many organizations are unfamiliar with current evidence about carcinogens and are at risk of entering into a merger or acquisition by assessing the potential profits to be made rather than the human or economic risks associated with the product or industry that could cancel out profit gains because of litigation-related pay-outs and brand notoriety.

Organizations considering a merger or acquisition in types of manufacturing with known risks of exposing workers to carcinogens should therefore be aware of the occupational health and safety implications so that they can effectively plan policies, practices, and budgets that protect the welfare of workers. Knowing about carcinogens is important not just to protect the health of employees, but also to protect the liability of an organization planning a merger or acquisition.

We will now review examples of risky industries for planned mergers or acquisitions, giving examples of known carcinogens (from the International Agency for Research on Cancer, IARC, 2019), and discussing their presence in types of products, manufacturing, and/or work-related environments. We will do this alongside presenting case studies of mergers or acquisitions involving organizations that have inherited liability for workers developing cancer and/or for cancer-related mortality among workers.

Lessons from organizations that were sued for cancer or cancer-related mortality after a merger or acquisition

1. Bayer's acquisition of Monsanto and Bayer's losses from non-Hodgkin's lymphoma lawsuits

A merger or acquisition of an organization that manufactures or works with substances that have carcinogenic effects can create financial and reputational harm to the merging or acquiring partner, as the recent case of Bayer and Monsanto shows. The harm includes legal costs, paying compensation to claimants who win lawsuits, and suffering drops in the organization's stock market value because the lawsuits reduce investors' confidence in the organization. Monsanto manufactures the weed killer Roundup, a commonly used pesticide, and Monsanto was previously thought of as a very financially successful organization. The pharmaceutical and agricultural science company Bayer then acquired Monsanto in 2016, no doubt buoyed by Monsanto's record of high profit levels. Before Bayer acquired Monsanto, there was some evidence from the scientific literature implicating pesticides as substances that raise the risk of consumers or workers who use them developing cancer, including meta-analyses such as that by Van Maele-Fabry and Willems (2003). A meta-analysis is a study that looks at previous evidence and calculates the average relative risk ratio. Put simply, a risk ratio is a number representing the chances of a group of people (X, exposed to a certain substance or condition) being diagnosed with cancer compared to a control group (Y, of people who were not exposed to the same substance or condition). A relative risk ratio of 1.0 means that X and Y have an equivalent risk of cancer, a relative risk ratio greater than 1 means that X has a greater risk of cancer than Y, and a relative risk ratio less than 1.0 means that Y is at greater risk of cancer than X. A meta-risk ratio is calculated by averaging the risk ratio from several studies. Van Maele-Fabry and Willems (2003) meta-analysed 22 studies and found that workers who were exposed to certain pesticides have a higher risk of prostate cancer, with a risk ratio of 1.13. A subsequent meta-analysis of 25 studies by Lewis-Mikhael et al. (2016) also found a relative risk ratio of 1.3 for prostate cancer. Examples of pesticides listed by IARC (2019) as carcinogens include lindane, an insecticide used to treat plants or animals that raises the risk of lymphoma or leukaemia in humans, and pentachlorophenol, a pesticide that kills insects, fungus, or plants.

Evidence from the scientific literature focusing on glyphosate, an ingredient in the pesticide manufactured by Monsanto (Roundup), has also emerged. A meta-analysis by Chang and Delzell (2016) examined studies of varying numbers (depending on the type of cancer) and found that exposure to glyphosate was associated with an increased risk of certain types of lymphohematopoietic cancer, with a relative risk ratio of 1.3. Chang and Delzell (2016) suggested that their results applied to leukaemia, multiple myeloma and some sub-types of non-Hodgkin's lymphoma but not Hodgkin's lymphoma. A subsequent meta-analysis of five case-controlled studies by Zhang, Rana, Shaffer, Taioli, and Sheppard (2019) confirmed that high exposure to glyphosate exposure does increase the risk of non-Hodgkin's lymphoma with a relative risk ratio of 1.4 or, in other words, a 40% higher chance of this type of cancer. Bayer was ordered by courts to pay compensation to several claimants in the US who filed lawsuits against Monsanto, including $289.2 million to a former groundskeeper, over $2 billion to a couple, and $89 million to an individual who sprayed Roundup on his property, all of whom had non-Hodgkin's lymphoma (Guardian, 2019b; Weyant, 2019). The *Financial Times* (2019b) reported recently that the number of lawsuits filed against Bayer because of Monsanto's product Roundup has grown to 20,000, and claims are being filed in other countries, such as in Australia.

Bayer's acquisition of Monsanto was subsequently deemed to be a "failure" by the *Financial Times* (2019a) because of the financial and reputational costs of the lawsuits filed against Monsanto. An article in *Fortune* claims that Bayer lost 44% of its share value after acquiring Monsanto (Meyer, 2019) and the *Financial Times* (2019a) reported that Bayer's shareholders cast no-confidence votes against the Bayer CEO who oversaw the Monsanto acquisition. Bayer should reflect on whether it conducted enough due diligence about the financial and reputational risks of acquiring a pesticide manufacturer, and whether a risk analysis of the available evidence from the scientific, peer-reviewed literature would have changed its decision to embark on the merger. The Bayer-Monsanto acquisition demonstrates the need for any organization considering a similar merger or acquisition to commission a scientifically rigorous report written by an independent academic expert (e.g. an epidemiologist or other scientist whose research examines cancer risk) or a qualified practitioner (e.g. an oncologist or a doctor of occupational medicine). Using advice based on readily available published, peer-reviewed evidence – particularly meta-analyses of relative risk ratios – can help organizations foresee highly risky mergers or acquisitions. Bayer should consider whether, in hindsight, the advice it sought about the cancer risks of Roundup was independent advice from people qualified to comment on cancer risk and how to interpret relative risk. A relative risk ratio of 1.3/1.4 might sound "small" if one imagines that relative risk can range from >1 to infinity. However, interpreting the seriousness of a relative risk ratio requires some knowledge about the size of the population affected, therefore a ratio of 1.3/1.4 is actually not a small risk when it concerns a relatively common substance exposed to hundreds, thousands, or millions of people. Scientists helping organizations understand relative risk also need to make them aware that the actual risk might be higher among workers who have prolonged and sustained exposure to the substance over many years. It is possible that Bayer was aware of the actual published evidence, but chose to proceed with its acquisition of Monsanto after surmising that the profit risks were relatively low given, that not many people had sued Monsanto yet or on the assumption that Monsanto was financially successful enough to buffer any losses from lawsuits. Either way, Bayer's acquisition of Monsanto should serve as a cautionary tale to any organization considering a merger or acquisition involving a substance known within published scientific literature to raise the risk of workers or consumers developing cancer, that is, a carcinogen.

2. Michelin's acquisition of BF Goodrich and liability for BF Goodrich's benzene leaks

Another example that we will discuss is cancer risk within the rubber industry and an example of an organization (Michelin) inheriting liability for lawsuits filed against an organization that it acquired (in Michelin's case, BF Goodrich). The IARC list shows that workers in rubber manufacturing have a higher risk of stomach cancer, lung cancer, urinary bladder cancer, lymphoid cancer, and cancer of the hematopoietic or related tissues. Although a meta-analysis by Alder et al. (2006) of 31 studies found that rubber workers had similar or better mortality and cancer risk ratios than the general population (0.82–0.94), the meta-analysis found a 1.21 higher risk of leukaemia and the risk of leukaemia was higher among rubber workers whose exposure was not in the tyre industries (1.7). As well as tyre production, workers can be exposed to rubber production during the manufacturing of waterproof sealants in building materials, electrical cables, and shoes. A more recent meta-analysis of 59 case-controlled studies by Boniol, Koechlin, and Boyle (2017) found that rubber workers had a higher risk of cancer of the larynx (1.46), bladder cancer (1.36), leukaemia (1.29), and lymphatic/haematopoietic cancers (1.16). When Boniol et al. stratified the samples of data, they found that these risks existed only among rubber workers who started working before 1960. The evidence about cancer risk for rubber workers thus suggests that there is a liability risk facing organizations that were in existence before 1960, and those using rubber production methods common at the time. IARC reports that some of the substances used in rubber production (e.g. 3-butadiene used in synthetic rubber production) raise the risk of lymphoma or leukaemia, therefore organizations considering mergers or acquisitions in the rubber industry need to consider not just evidence about rubber as a carcinogen, but also evidence about the carcinogenic effects of 3-butadiene and other substances used in the industry. An example of a merger or acquisition in the sector with liability implications is the international tyre manufacturer Michelin's acquisition of BF Goodrich in 1990. Mercer (2019) reported that, as early as 1980, BF Goodrich was made aware by a scientific report that some of the substances its workers were exposed to increased the risk of cancer and other health problems such as genetic mutations. BF Goodrich took some steps to protect workers, such as improving ventilation and banning eating in areas with the substances, but the risk to workers who had already been exposed remained, with Mercer reporting that workers had been handling the substances without gloves for years (Mercer, 2019). Some regions in Canada have laws preventing workers from suing rubber companies and compelling them to claim compensation from Canada's Workplace Safety and Insurance Board (WSIB), but Mercer (2019) reports that many workers' claims were rejected. However, the international basis of Michelin and BF Goodrich means that they have been sued in the US. In 2017, 112 people from Oklahoma filed a lawsuit against Michelin because they said that BF Goodrich's rubber plant exposed them to benzene, a known carcinogen, through leaks into groundwater. IARC (2019) lists benzene as a carcinogen that increases the risk of lymphoma or leukaemia. BF Goodrich's plant in Oklahoma closed in 1986, four years before Michelin acquired BF Goodrich, but Michelin could be made liable for these exposures and it will be forced to pay compensation if the claimants win the lawsuit.

As well as in rubber production, benzene is implicated within the transportation sector as a potential carcinogen. Organizations like Michelin could consider lawsuits by workers in other sectors who were exposed to substances that are common in both sectors. In the transportation sector, a railroad worker filed a lawsuit against the Norfolk Southern Railway Company and the Consolidated Rail Corporation, a portion of the latter company having been acquired by the former in 1999. The railroad worker claimed to have suffered ill health after being exposed to benzene and other substances released from diesel exhaust fumes. A meta-analysis by Lipsett and Campleman (1999) examined 30 studies about truck drivers, bus drivers, equipment operators, mechanics, and other transportation workers exposed to diesel exhaust fumes. The meta-analysis showed that most studies find that such workers have a higher risk of lung cancer. Although the study found heterogeneity (that is, wide variation) in risk ratios ranging from 0.6 to 3.32, most studies showed pooled estimates of relative risk ranging from 0.97 to 1.85.

Organizations like Michelin should commission scientists or qualified practitioners to assess the evidence about *all* occupational health risks in the industry, including risks from substances such as benzene that were commonly used in the industry. We thus encourage organizations to consider all examples of liability for a given carcinogen, inside and outside their immediate industry.

3. Metals, mining, and tales of Pfizer's liability for asbestos lawsuits against bankrupt Quigley

Another cautionary tale about a merger or acquisition that led to being liable for lawsuits filed by people who developed cancer comes from the metals sector. The risk of litigation can stretch back to decades before the merger and therefore the financial risks (from paying court-ordered compensation) could be high and difficult to quantify. One of the world's largest aluminium companies, Alcoa Aluminum, merged with Reynolds Metals in 2000, the world's third-largest aluminium company, in a $4.4 billion deal with a reported 120,000 employees in three-dozen countries (Alcoa, 2020; US Department of Justice, 2000). The merger was so significant that the United States government's Antitrust Division tried to block it by filing an antitrust complaint because of the market dominance and reduced competition that would result from the merger (US Department of Justice, 2000). The merger did go ahead. Alcoa has since faced lawsuits from the families of workers who died from conditions such as cancer whose risks rose because the workers were exposed to substances that increase the risk of cancer (Top Class Actions, 2018). IARC (2019 reports that workers in aluminium production are also at risk of urinary bladder cancer. A meta-analysis by Gaertner and Theriault (2002) examined 24 studies about workers involved in melting, moulding, alloying, and welding metal, and workers who were exposed to silica, mineral dust, metal fumes, and other substances. The meta-analysis found that workers with 20 years of experience or more had a higher risk of bladder cancer (with ratios of 1.6 to 1.7) and, among workers with any experience level, the summary risk estimate was 1.16. Reynolds Metals, now subsumed under Alcoa, has also recently experienced a lawsuit filed by the family of an employee who died from lung cancer after being exposed to asbestos while working in the company between 1968 to 1972 (Top Class Actions, 2018). Eyeballing the Alcoa share price data in the month before and after the lawsuit was announced on 23 July 2018 suggests that there was a dip in share value around that time (New York Stock Exchange, 2018), although not all investors might have heard of the lawsuit and other factors might have contributed to the dip. Alcoa and Reynolds Metals have also been ordered to pay a number of large fines to communities for polluting the natural environment. For example, in 2013, Alco and the former Reynolds Metals company were ordered to pay $19.4 million for environmental damages caused by harmful chemicals released into rivers because of nearby aluminium factories (Office of Response and Restoration, 2013). Therefore, the merger between Alcoa Aluminum and Reynolds Metals represents a multiplying of the risk of litigation from workers or families of deceased workers. Although Alcoa and Reynolds Metals do not have as many lost lawsuits as some organizations, the risk of lawsuits is not just from having to pay compensation. The dips in Alcoa share prices (e.g. New York Stock Exchange, 2018) following the announcement of a lawsuit suggests that lawsuits harm the reputation of organizations, at least in the short term.

As well as aluminium production posing a cancer risk, IARC (2019) reports that iron and steel production puts workers at risk of lung cancer. The mining of certain metals can also expose workers to carcinogens, such as nickel compounds that workers are exposed to during nickel mining and increase their risk of cancers of the nasal cavity or sinus (IARC, 2019). The risk of cancer of the nasal cavity or sinus is also high among workers in industries such as shoe manufacturing because of the carcinogenic properties of leather dust. Other types of metal mining can also expose workers to carcinogenic combustion fumes such as soot and fumes from burning fossil fuels, which increase the risk of lung cancer, as does the mining of hematite and chromium (IARC, 2019). Gamma rays can also increase workers' cancer risk. They are commonly used in mining to detect certain precious stones in enclaves that are physically inaccessible (e.g. deep caves) to mining workers, and in irradiating precious stones to change their colour or enhance their attractiveness. Gamma rays increase the risk of cancers of the salivary gland, oesophagus, stomach, colon, rectum, lung, bone, skin, breast, kidney, urinary bladder, brain, central nervous system, thyroid gland, and cancers of the lymphoid or related tissues. The cancer risks of gamma rays exist not just in mining, but also in the food industry, where gamma rays are commonly used to kill bacteria or other organisms during the process of sterilising food and food-related equipment. Gamma rays are also commonly used to kill bacteria or sterilising equipment in pharmaceutical companies. Gamma rays increase the risk of cancers of the salivary gland, oesophagus, stomach, colon, rectum, lung, bone, skin, breast, kidney, urinary bladder, brain, central nervous system, thyroid gland, and cancers of the lymphoid or related tissues (IARC, 2019).

As well as the techniques used during mining being potentially hazardous (e.g. use of gamma rays), the type of substances mined can sometimes be carcinogenic. One of the most commonly known carcinogens is asbestos and it is still mined in some countries, despite research showing that it increases the risk of cancers of the larynx, lung, cancers of mesothelioma (a type of tissue around the chest or stomach), and ovarian cancer (IARC, 2019). Although over 50 countries have banned asbestos, it is still legally mined in Russia, China, and other countries with about 1 million tonnes of asbestos mined in Russia alone. There are 38,500 workers employed in the asbestos industry in Russia, with 17% of workers employed in the asbestos industries in the Russian town of Asbest (Povtak, 2013). As well as mining, another sector that exposes workers to asbestos is the construction and building materials industry, where asbestos was commonly used in building materials, thus exposing workers in manufacturing and workers in building construction. Asbestos remains legal in several countries and is used in building materials such as tiles, pipes, and coatings. Asbestos is also found in many buildings built in the past, therefore workers involved in demolishing or refurbishing buildings can also be exposed to asbestos. IARC (2019) shows that workers handling building materials containing asbestos, including imported materials containing undeclared asbestos, can have a higher risk of cancers of the larynx, lung, cancers of mesothelioma (a type of tissue that surrounds organs) around the chest or stomach, and ovarian cancer. Workers in the building industry also face cancer risks from other substances, such crystalline silica (released in concrete or brick dust) or inhaled water droplets contaminated with arsenic (e.g. during excavation or building sites with contaminated rainwater), which can increase the risk of lung cancer. Arsenic also raises the risk of urinary bladder cancer. Workers in brick manufacturing and workers exposed to certain welding fumes during parts manufacturing or construction can also have an increased risk of lung cancer (IARC, 2019). Manufacturers of graphite that use the "Acheson process" could be increasing the risk of lung cancer.

Many workers in building and other industries where they developed illnesses relating to certain substances have filed lawsuits and won, such as in the case of asbestos-related illnesses where Stiglitz, Orszag, and Orszag (2002) estimate that asbestos-related liabilities have led to 61 companies filing for bankruptcy, with direct costs of between $325 and $650 million. One of the many examples of asbestos lawsuits involves the Quigley Company, a manufacturing company that used to use asbestos in some products. Quigley was acquired by Pfizer in 1968 and, despite reportedly knowing about the risks of asbestos since the late 1950s, Quigley continued using asbestos until the late 1970s, just before the first asbestos lawsuit they faced (Povtak, 2012; Strand, 2019). The number of lawsuits from workers about asbestos grew to 160,000, even though Quigley stopped operating in 1991/1992, and by the time Pfizer filed for Quigley's bankruptcy, Pfizer is said to have paid between $430 million and $1.25 billion in lawsuit settlements (Povtak, 2012; Strand, 2019). Quigley was declared bankrupt in 2004, but workers can still claim asbestos-related illnesses from an asbestos trust fund. In 2011, the asbestos litigation reportedly cost Pfizer $701 million, with a judge ruling that Pfizer is still liable to pay workers compensation because, although Pfizer did not itself manufacture products with asbestos, the Pfizer logo appeared on those products (Povtak, 2012). Considering the commonly known risks of cancer and considering the quantity of asbestos-related lawsuits that led to many companies going bankrupt, it is paradoxical that asbestos mining and asbestos use in building is still legal in many countries, including the US (albeit tightly regulated), and that there are organizations still willing to mine asbestos or manufacture products containing asbestos. The fact that asbestos is legal to mine and use in some countries can perversely incentivise some organizations to consider mergers or acquisitions in those countries as a way of circumventing liability, raising questions about their organizational ethics. Aguilar-Madrid et al. (2003) conducted a study whose findings suggested that multinational companies were exporting the manufacturing of asbestos to Mexico because of less strict, up-to-date occupational health and safety laws. However, the legality of asbestos in these countries might not preclude organizations that are multinational from future lawsuits filed by workers who develop cancer and for whom courts might decide that the organizations were aware of the cancer risks (because of laws prohibiting asbestos in their own country). Organizations that are aware of carcinogens such as asbestos have the moral responsibility to protect workers from the cancer and mortality risks.

Asbestos has also featured as a carcinogen within the automobile industry because it used to be used in clutch and brake linings, as well as several other parts of vehicles. The Genuine Parts Company acquired the National Automotive Parts Association (NAPA) and faced a number of lawsuits, including from the family of a worker who died from mesothelioma, a type of cancer, where the court ordered NAPA to pay a settlement of $81.5 million. The automobile industry, one of the largest employing industries in United Kingdom, with approximately 856,000 workers, of which approximately a fifth work in manufacturing, is notable not just because of its size, but also because of the frequency with which substances common within it appear within the IARC (2019) list of carcinogens. One example is formaldehyde, a by-product of motor-vehicle exhaust fumes or oxidation of certain compounds, that when inhaled or ingested can increase the risk of cancers of the nasopharynx and lymphoid, hematopoietic, or related tissues (IARC, 2019). Formaldehyde is also harmful in other industries, such as the food industry, where it is used as a food preservative in countries where it is not banned. Another example of a carcinogen common within the automobile industry is isopropyl alcohol, which is can be used in various ways, such as to clean vehicle braking systems. Isopropyl alcohol increases the risk of cancers of the nasal cavity or sinus, and its dangers are notable not just in the automobile industry, but also in industries where it is used as solvent or cleaning fluid, in healthcare settings where it is used as a sanitizer, and in the manufacturing of some pharmaceuticals. Welding fumes or fumes from diesel or engine exhausts raise the risk of lung cancer. Mineral oil also raises the risk of skin cancer, and workers in the automobile industry can be exposed to it because it is commonly used as a lubricant for machine parts and a coolant. Unrefined mineral oils raise the risk of skin cancer, therefore workers in several industries are at risk, including those involved in manufacturing petroleum, electronics where mineral oil is used in processing, and in cosmetics containing unrefined mineral oil. Vehicle manufacturers that use trichloroethylene to clean metal equipment could also increase the risk of kidney cancer among workers. Trichloroethylene is also used by workers in dry cleaning companies or companies that use cleaning products containing it, and they too have an increased risk of kidney cancer. Trichloroethylene is also found in refrigeration fluids, therefore workers in companies that manufacture refrigerators, or use refrigerators with leaks, could also be at risk of kidney cancer. Strong mists from inorganic acids that contain sulphuric acid can be used in the automobile industry (and others) to treat metals and in the manufacturing of some types of batteries. These mists increase the risk of cancers of the larynx. The carcinogenic properties of some acids are also notable in other industries, for example in cases where companies manufacture inorganic acids containing sulphuric acid. Workers close to the strong mists have a higher risk of developing cancer of the larynx. Additionally, automobile manufacturers or companies that expose workers to nickel compounds (e.g. in welding metal alloys that contain nickel compounds), can also increase the risk of cancers of the nasal cavity or sinus.

In short, the metals, minerals, building, and automobile industries expose workers to substances that raise risk of developing several types of cancer. Despite evidence of the cancer risks, and the risk of being sued, some organizations continue to work with substances that are carcinogenic even in the case of a substance like asbestos where litigation by workers with cancer (or their families) has led to many companies going bankrupt. Organizations must realise that substances that might be legal now, or merely regulated now, might one day become the "next" asbestos. Organizations considering a merger or acquisition in sectors exposing workers to carcinogens should consider the ethics of doing so, from the point of view of protecting workers' health, because they have a moral responsibility towards workers. Organizations should consider it unethical to merge or acquire organizations that deal with substances that the organization knows to be carcinogenic, even if the substances are legal. Organizations may also wish to avoid mergers or acquisitions within sectors that multiply their liability risk, as the case of Pfizer's inherited liability for workers exposed to asbestos at Quigley shows.

4. Sector "inbreeding" in acquisitions can multiply liability – the case of British Airways

There is some literature encouraging due diligence in mergers and acquisitions more generally, including acknowledgement about the issue of successor liability (e.g. Harroch, Lipkin, Smith, & Cook, 2019), but there is very little literature encouraging organizations that embark on a large number of acquisitions to be aware of the consequences of inheriting liability for exposing workers to carcinogens at any point in their acquiree's past. In the UK, for example, the "Transfer of Undertakings (Protection of Employment)" regulations (2006) mean that employees retain their terms of employment after a merger or acquisition, and they can therefore sue the acquiring organization the same as if they could have sued the organization before it was acquired (and likewise for cases of mergers). An example of inherited liability after a merger or acquisition comes from the aviation sector where British Airways, having acquired several airlines in the past, is facing 41 out of 51 lawsuits filed with the backing of the workers' union, the Unite Union (2019). The 51 lawsuits were filed by pilots and flight staff against various airlines. A meta-analysis of six studies by Ballard, Lagorio, De Angelis, and Verdecchia (2000) found that flight attendants and pilots who are exposed to hazards such as ionising radiation and contaminated air have a higher risk of several types of cancer. Among male pilots, mortality risk ratios from skin cancer, prostate cancer, and brain cancer ranged from 1.49 to 1.97. Among female flight attendants, relative risk ratios for mortality from melanoma and breast cancer were 1.35 to 1.54. Losing the 41 lawsuits could be very costly to British Airways (BBC, 2019) and potentially inspire subsequent lawsuits. Details of the claimants' workplaces are not yet available but it is plausible that, because British Airways acquired several airlines and therefore has a large share of the market, the lawsuit claimants could include workers who are employed by airlines that British Airways acquired. If British Airways loses the lawsuit, the case could serve as a cautionary tale against acquisitions carried without a proper scrutiny of workers' health risks. Although the UK Employers' Liability (Compulsory Insurance) Act of 1969 obliges UK organizations to buy insurance against liability for, for example, health problems or injuries suffered by employees, this might not protect organizations that are sued by employees in acquired organizations. Although insurers are required to pay compensation to claimants, as ordered by courts, some insurers' terms and conditions could ask organizations to pay back some of the compensation that was awarded to claimants. Insurers can also refuse to pay out in cases where they determine that organizations failed to meet their legal responsibilities to protect employees. Therefore, if British Airways acquired airlines that broke rules about cabin air purification (e.g. by having faulty equipment), it is British Airways that could end up paying the compensation to the employees. What is more, employers' liability insurance is not compulsory in all countries and, even in the UK, organizations do not have to cover employees who work abroad unless they spend a certain amount of time in the UK each year. This means that, theoretically, organizations like British Airways that acquire overseas organizations could be forced to pay claimants compensation from their own budget. International mergers and acquisitions involving countries without compulsory liability insurance might thus be quite financially vulnerable to litigation from employees or families of employees.

Conclusions

We encourage organizations in industries where workers are exposed to health hazards to budget for the costs of being sued when estimating the profitability of a potential merger or acquisition. This aspect of "due diligence" in mergers and acquisitions is a new advance within literature about mergers or acquisitions, and this is the first book to examine workers' cancer risks in different industries, and examples of mergers or acquisitions marred by litigation by workers who developed cancer (or families of workers who died from cancer). In previous literature, a few authors have encouraged organizations to be aware about managing environmental health risks when planning a merger or acquisition (International Management Group, 2016), but ours is (to our knowledge) the first book to give organizations and practitioners involved in mergers or acquisitions information about workers' cancer risks, examples of legal culpability, and the cost or reputational consequences of losing a lawsuit, paying compensation, and losing investors' confidence on the stock market, leading to dips in share prices around the time that lawsuits against the organization are publicised. This chapter examined examples of organizations inheriting liability after a merger or acquisition because of workers developing cancer or dying as a result of exposure to hazardous substances in the workplace. This chapter examined examples of such organizations losing lawsuits, paying millions or billions in compensation, facing dips in share prices, and facing unknown future costs from future litigation from workers employed by the acquired or merged organization at any point in the past. This chapter thus encourages organizations in sectors that are already at risk of litigation for cancer or cancer-related mortality to avoid entering into mergers or acquisitions with organizations that face a similar level of liability. Of course, more important than cost or reputational considerations is the moral responsibility that organizations have to protect employees from known harm, to safeguard their health, and to prioritise workers' safety above profits. We therefore encourage all organizations, including those involved in mergers or acquisitions, to develop an ethos of terminating operations that raise workers' risk of cancer as soon as they become aware of the evidence. This chapter has examined harm relating to carcinogenic substances because cancer is one of the leading causes of mortality, but organizations must consider *all* types of occupational health hazards when understanding the risks of a prospective merger or acquisition. We also encourage researchers to place the occupational health and safety of employees on their research agenda when they are planning new studies about mergers and acquisitions.

References

Abebe, M. A., & Angriawan, A. (2014). Organizational and competitive influences of exploration and exploitation activities in small firms. *Journal of Business Research, 67*(3), 339–345.

Abrams, D., & Hogg, M. A. (1988). Comments on the motivational status of self-esteem in social identity and intergroup discrimination. *European Journal of Social Psychology, 18*(4), 317–334. doi:10.1002/ejsp.2420180403

Aguilar-Madrid, G., Juárez-Pérez, C. A., Markowitz, S., Hernández-Avila, M., Sanchez Roman, F. R., & Vázquez Grameix, J. H. (2003). Globalization and the transfer of hazardous industry: Asbestos in Mexico, 1979–2000. *International Journal of Occupational and Environmental Health, 9*(3), 272–279.

Aguilera, R. V., & Dencker, J. C. (2004). The role of human resource management in cross-border mergers and acquisitions. *International Journal of Human Resource Management, 15*(8), 1355–1370.

Ahuja, G., & Katila, R. (2001). Technological acquisitions and the innovation performance of acquiring firms: A longitudinal study. *Strategic Management Journal (John Wiley & Sons, Inc.), 22*(3), 197.

Ailon-Souday, G., & Kunda, G. (2003). The local selves of global workers: The social construction of national identity in the face of organizational globalization. *Organization Studies, 24*(7), 1073–1096.

Aktas, N., de Bodt, E., & Roll, R. (2009). Learning, hubris and corporate serial acquisitions. *Journal of Corporate Finance, 15*, 543–561.

Aktas, N., de Bodt, E., & Roll, R. (2011). Serial acquirer bidding: An empirical test of the learning hypothesis. *Journal of Corporate Finance, 17*(1), 18–32.

Alcoa (2020). *Our history.* Retrieved from https://www.alcoa.com/global/en/who-we-are/history/default.asp

Aldao, A., Nolen-Hoeksema, S., & Schweizer, S. (2010). Emotion-regulation strategies across psychopathology: A meta-analytic review. *Clinical Psychology Review, 30*(2), 217–237.

Alder, N., Fenty, J., Warren, F., Sutton, A. J., Rushton, L., Jones, D. R., & Abrams, K. R. (2006). Meta-analysis of mortality and cancer incidence among workers in the synthetic rubber-producing industry. *American Journal of Epidemiology, 164*(5), 405–420.

Alexandridis, G., Fuller, K. P., Terhaar, L., & Travlos, N. G. (2013). Deal size, acquisition premia and shareholder gains. *Journal of Corporate Finance, 20*, 1–13.

Alexandridis, G., Mavrovitis, C. F., & Travlos, N. G. (2012). How have M&As changed? Evidence from the sixth merger wave. *The European Journal of Finance, 18*(8), 663–688.

Allen, D. G., Bryant, P. C., & Vardaman, J. M. (2010). Retaining talent: Replacing misconceptions with evidence-based strategies. *Academy of Management Perspectives, 24*(2), 48–64.

Allen, F., Thorsten, B., Carletti, E., Lane, P., Schoenmaker, D., & Wagner, W. (2011). *Cross-border banking in Europe: Implications for Financial stability and macroeconomic policies.* London, UK: Centre for Economic Policy Research.

Allport, G. W. (1961). *Pattern and growth in personality.* Oxford, England: Holt, Reinhart & Winston.

Almeder, R., & Carey, D. (1991). In defense of sharks moral issues in hostile liquidating takeovers. *Journal of Business Ethics, 10*(7), 471–484.

Altemeyer, B. (2004). Highly dominating, highly authoritarian personalities. *Journal of Social Psychology, 144*, 421–447.

Alter, A., & Schuler, Y. S. (2012). Credit spread interdependencies of European states and banks during the financial crisis. *Journal of Banking and Finance, 36*(12), 3444–3468.

Amesse, F., Latour, R., Rebolledo, C., & Séguin-Dulude, L. (2004). The telecommunications equipment industry in the 1990s: From alliances to mergers and acquisitions. *Technovation, 24*(11), 885–897.

Amiot, C. E., Terry, D. J., & Callan, V. J. (2007). Status, equity and social identification during an intergroup merger: A longitudinal study. *The British Journal of Social Psychology, 46*(Pt 3), 557–577.

Amiot, C. E., Terry, D. J., Jimmieson, N. L., & Callan, V. J. (2006). A longitudinal investigation of coping processes during a merger: Implications for job satisfaction and organizational identification. *Journal of Management, 32*(4), 552–574.

Anand, J., Mesquita, L. F., & Vassolo, R. S. (2009). The dynamics of multimarket competition in exploration and exploitation activities. *Academy of Management Journal, 52*(4), 802–821.

Ancona, D. G., Goodman, P. S., Lawrence, B. S., & Tushman, M. L. (2001). Time: A new research lens. *Academy of Management Review, 26*(4), 645–563.

Anderson, C., & Kilduff, G. J. (2009). Why do dominant personalities attain influence in face-to-face groups? The competence-signaling effects of trait dominance. *Journal of Personality and Social Psychology, 96*, 491–503.

Andriopoulos, C., & Lewis, M. W. (2009). Exploitation-exploration tensions and organizational ambidexterity: Managing paradoxes of innovation. *Organization Science, 20*(4), 696–717.

Angwin, D. (2001). Mergers and acquisitions across European borders: National perspectives on preacquisition due diligence and the use of professional advisers. *Journal of World Business, 36*(1), 32–57.

Apfelthaler, G., Muller, H. J., & Rehder, R. R. (2002). Corporate global culture as competitive advantage: Learning from Germany and Japan in Alabama and Austria? *Journal of World Business, 37*(2), 108–118.

Appelbaum, S. H., Gandell, J., Yortis, H., Proper, S., & Jobin, F. (2000). Anatomy of a merger: Behavior of organizational factors and processes throughout the pre-during- post-stages (Pt 1). *Management Decision, 38*(9), 649.

Armstrong-Stassen, M., & Cameron, S. J. (2003). The influence of prior coping resources and constraints on nurses' coping responses to hospital amalgamation in Canada. *International Journal of Stress Management, 10*(2), 158–172.

Arthur, C. (2014, June 24). *Google acquisition spree takes in Dropcam and Alpental.* Retrieved from www.theguardian.com/technology/2014/jun/24/google-dropcam-alpental

Ashforth, B. E., & Mael, F. (1989). Social identity theory and the organization. *The Academy of Management Review, 14*(1), 20–39.

Astrachan, J. H. (2004). Organizational departures: The impact of separation anxiety as studied in a mergers and acquisitions simulation. *Journal of Applied Behavioral Science, 40*(1), 91–110.

Auh, S., & Menguc, B. (2005). Balancing exploration and exploitation: The moderating role of competitive intensity. *Journal of Business Research, 58*(12), 1652–1661.

Avery, D. R. (2003). Personality as a predictor of the value of voice. *The Journal of Psychology, 137*, 435–446.

Avolio, B. J., & Bass, B. M. (2004). *Multifactor leadership questionnaire. Manual and sampler set* (3rd ed.). Redwood City, CA: Mind Garden.

Babić, V. M., Savović, S. D., & Domanović, V. M. (2014). Transformational leadership and post-acquisition performance in transitional economies. *Journal of Organizational Change Management, 27*(6), 856–876.

Badrtalei, J., & Bates, D. L. (2007). Effect of organizational cultures on mergers and acquisitions: The case of DaimlerChrysler. *International Journal of Management, 24*(2), 303–317.

Baker Hughes, a GE Company (2019, September 16). Baker hughes, a GE company announces closing of secondary offering by GE and its share repurchase. [Press release].

Bakker, A. B., & Oerlemans, W. M. (2012). Subjective well-being. In K. S. Cameron, G. M. Spreitzer, K. S. Cameron, & G. M. Spreitzer (Eds.), *The Oxford handbook of positive organizational scholarship* (pp. 178–187). New York, NY: Oxford University Press.

Ballard, T., Lagorio, S., De Angelis, G., & Verdecchia, A. (2000). Cancer incidence and mortality among flight personnel: A Meta-analysis. *Aviation, Space, and Environmental Medicine, 71*(3), 216–224.

Bandura, A. (1977). Self-efficacy: Toward a unifying theory of behavioral change. *Psychological Review, 84*(2), 191–215.

Bandura, A., & Wood, R. (1989). Effect of perceived controllability and performance standards on self-regulation of complex decision-making. *Journal of Personality and Social Psychology, 56*, 805–814.

Barratt-Pugh, L., Bahn, S., & Gakere, E. (2013). Managers as change agents: Implications for human resource managers engaging with culture change. *Journal of Organizational Change Management, 26*(4), 748–764.

Barrick, M. R., & Mount, M. K. (1991). The big five personality dimensions and job performance: A meta-analysis. *Personnel Psychology, 44*(1), 1–26.

Barros-Loscertales, A., Meseguer, V., Sanjuan, A., et al. (2006). Behavioral inhibition system activity is associated with increased amygdala and hippocampal gray matter volume: A voxel-based morphometry study. *Neuroimage, 33*(3), 1011–1015.

Bartel-Radic, A. (2006). Intercultural learning in global teams. *Management International Review (MIR), 46*(6), 647–677.

Bartels, J., Douwes, R., de Jong, M., & Pruyn, A. (2006). Organizational identification during a merger: Determinants of employees' expected identification with the new organization. *British Journal of Management, 17*(Suppl. 1), S49–S67.

Bartunek, J. M., & Franzak, F. J. (1988). The effects of organizational restructuring on frames of reference and cooperation. *Journal of Management, 14*(4), 579–592.

Basinger, N. W., & Peterson, J. R. (2008). Where you stand depends on where you sit: Participation and reactions to change. *Nonprofit Management And Leadership, 19*(2), 243–257.

Bass, B. M. (1985). *Leadership and performance beyond expectations*. New York, NY: Free Press.

Bass, B. M. (1990). From transactional to transformational leadership: Learning to share the vision. *Organizational Dynamics, 18*(3), 19–31.

Bass, B. M., & Avolio, B. J. (2000). *MLQ multifactor leadership questionnaire*. Redwood City: Mind Garden.

Bastien, D. T. (1987). Common patterns of behavior and communication in corporate mergers and acquisitions. *Human Resource Management, 26*(1), 17–33.

Baumeister, R. F., Campbell, J. D., Krueger, J. I., & Vohs, K. D. (2003). Does high self-esteem cause better performance, interpersonal success, happiness, or healthier lifestyles? *Psychological Science in the Public Interest, 4*, 1–44.

BBC (2019, March 28). *Airlines face lawsuits over 'toxic' cabin air*. Retrieved from www.bbc.co.uk/news/business-47740523

Beatty, C. A., & Lee, G. L. (1992). Leadership among middle managers: An exploration in the context of technological change. *Human Relations, 45*(9), 957–989.

Beauducel, A., Brocke, B., & Leue, A. (2006). Energetical bases of extraversion: Effort, arousal, EEG, and performance. *International Journal of Psychophysiology, 85*, 232–236.

Bechara, A., Damasio, A. R., Damasio, H., & Anderson, S. W. (1994). Insensitivity to future consequences following damage to human prefrontal cortex. *Cognition, 50*(1–3), 7–15.

Beckman, C. M., Haunschild, P. R., & Phillips, D. J. (2004). Friends or strangers? Firm-specific uncertainty, market uncertainty, and network partner selection. *Organization Science, 15*(3), 259–275.

Beer, M., & Nohria, N. (2000). Breaking the code of change. *Harvard Business School Press Books, 1.*

Behar, A., & Ritz, R. (2016). *An analysis of OPEC's strategic actions, US shale growth and the 2014 oil price crash*. IMF Working Paper.

Beirne, J., & Fratzcher, M. (2013). The pricing of sovereign risk and contagion during the European sovereign debt crisis. *Journal of International Money and Finance, 34*, 60–82.

Bellou, V. (2007). Psychological contract assessment after a major organizational change: The case of mergers and acquisitions. *Employee Relations, 29*(1), 68–88.

Bellou, V. (2008). Exploring civic virtue and turnover intention during organizational changes. *Journal of Business Research, 61*(7), 778–789.

Benner, M. J., & Tushman, M. L. (2002). Process management and technological innovation: A longitudinal study of the photography and paint industries. *Administrative Science Quarterly, 47*, 676–706.

Berkovitch, E., & Narayanan, M. (1993). Motives for takeovers: An empirical investigation. *Journal of Financial and Quantitative Analysis, 28*(3), 347–362.

Bernardin, H. J., Cooke, D. K., & Villanova, P. (2000). Conscientiousness and agreeableness as predictors of rating leniency. *Journal of Applied Psychology, 85*, 232–236.

Berry, D., & Kamau, C. (2013). *Public policy and media organizations*. London: Routledge.

Beyer, J. M. (1999). Taming and promoting charisma to change organizations. *Leadership Quarterly, 10*(2), 307.

Bhal, K. T., Bhaskar, A. U., & Ratnam, C. V. (2009). Employee reactions to M&A: Role of LMX and leader communication. *Leadership & Organization Development Journal, 30*(7).

Bhide, A. (1989). In praise of corporate raiders. *Policy Review, 47*, 21–23.

Billet, M. T., & Qian, Y. (2008). Are overconfident CEOs born or made? Evidence of self-attribution bias from frequent acquirers. *Management Science, 54*(6), 1037–1051.

Bittlingmayer, G. (1985). Did antitrust policy cause the great merger wave? *The Journal of Law & Economics, 28*(1), 77–118.

Bittlingmayer, G. (2001). The use and abuse of antitrust from Cleveland to Clinton: Causes and consequences. In J. Denson (Ed.), *Reassesing the presidence. The rise of the executive state and the decline of freedom* (pp. 363–384). Auburn, AL: Mises Institute.

Blais, M. A., Smallwood, P., Groves, J. E., & Rivas-Vazquez, R. A. (2008). Personality and personality disorders. In T. A. Stern, J. F. Rosenbaum, M. Fava, & J. Biederman (Eds.), *Massachusetts general hospital comprehensive clinical psychiatry.* Philadelphia, PA: Elsevier.

Blake, R. R., & Mouton, J. S. (1985). How to achieve integration on the human side of the merger. *Organizational Dynamics, 13*(3), 41–56.

Blanchard, D. C., Hynd, A. L., Minke, K. A., Minemoto, T., & Blanchard, R. J. (2001). Human defensive behaviors to threat scenarios show parallels to fear- and anxiety-related defense patterns of non-human mammals. *Neuroscience and Biobehavioral Reviews, 25*(7–8), 761–770.

Block, B. A. (1970). *Levers of power : The Northern Pacific panic and the Northern securities case.* MA Thesis, Ohio: Ohio State University.

Bloomberg (2016). *Global M&A market review. Financial rankings 2015.* Retrieved January 30, from www.bloomberg.com/professional/content/uploads/sites/4/global-ma-financial-2015.pdf

Boateng, A., Qian, W., & Tianle, Y. (2008). Cross-border M&As by Chinese firms: An analysis of strategic motives and performance. *Thunderbird International Business Review, 50*, 259–270.

Boen, F., Vanbeselaere, N., Brebels, L., Huybens, W., & Millet, K. (2007). Postmerger identification as a function of pre-merger identification, relative representation, and pre-merger status. *European Journal of Social Psychology, 37*(2), 380–389.

Bolino, C. M., & Turnley, H. M. (2003). Counternormative impression management, likeability, and performance ratings: The use of intimidation in an organizational setting, *Journal of Organizational Behavior, 24*(2), 237–250.

Boniol, M., Koechlin, A., & Boyle, P. (2017). Meta-analysis of occupational exposures in the rubber manufacturing industry and risk of cancer. *International Journal of Epidemiology, 46*(6), 1940–1947.

Bono, J. E., & Judge, T. A. (2004). Personality and transformational and transactional leadership: A meta-analysis. *The Journal of Applied Psychology, 89*(5), 901–910.

Borghetti, C., Beaven, A., & Pugliese, R. (2015). Interactions among future study abroad students: Exploring potential intercultural learning sequences. *Intercultural Education, 26*(1), 31–48.

Boswell, W. R., Boudreau, J. W., & Tichy, J. (2005). The relationship between employee job change and job satisfaction: The honeymoon-hangover effect. *Journal of Applied Psychology, 90*(5), 882–892.

Botvinik, M., Nystrom, L. E., Fissell, K., Carter, C. S., & Cohen, J. D. (1999). Conflict monitoring versus selection-for-action in anterior cingulate cortex. *Nature, 402*(6758), 179–181.

Bourdieu, P. (1984). *Distinction: A social critique of the judgment of taste.* English manuscript. Oxon, OX: Routledge.

Bourdieu, P. (1986). The forms of capital. In J. Richardson (Ed.), *Handbook of theory and research for the sociology of education* (pp. 241–258). New York, NY: Greenwood.

Bourdieu, P. (1989). Social space and symbolic power. *Sociological Theory, 7*(1), 14–25.

Brannen, M. Y., & Salk, J. E. (2000). Partnering across borders: Negotiating organizational culture in a German-Japanese joint venture. *Human Relations, 53*(4), 451–487.

Brealey, R. A., & Meyers, S. C. (2006). *Principles of corporate finance.* New York, NY: McGraw-Hill/Irwin.

Bridges, W. M. (1991). *Managing transitions: Making the most of change.* Reading, MA: Addison-Wesley.

Brower, H. H., Schoorman, F. D., & Tan, H. H. (2000). A model of relational leadership: The integration of trust and leader – member exchange. *Leadership Quarterly, 11*(2), 227–250.

Brown, A. D., & Humphreys, M. (2003). Epic and tragic tales: Making sense of change. *Journal of Applied Behavioral Science, 39*(2), 121–144.

Brown, R. (2000). Social identity theory: Past achievements, current problems and future challenges. *European Journal of Social Psychology, 30*(6), 745–778.

Brown, R. (2001). *Group processes* (2nd ed.). Oxford: Wiley-Blackwell.

Buono, A. F., & Bowditch, J. L. (1989). *The Jossey-Bass management series. The human side of mergers and acquisitions: Managing collisions between people, cultures, and organizations.* San Francisco, CA: Jossey-Bass.

Buono, A. F., Bowditch, J. L., & Lewis, J. W. (1985). When cultures collide: The anatomy of a merger. *Human Relations, 38*(5), 477–500.

Buono, A. F., Bowditch, J. L., & Lewis, J. W. (1988). The cultural dynamics of transformation: The case of a bank merger. In R. Kilmann & T. Covin (Eds.), *Corporate transformation: Revitalising organisations for a competitive world* (pp. 497–522). San Francisco, CA: Jossey-Bass.

Burgelman, R. A. (1991). Intraorganizational ecology of strategy making and organizational adaptation: Theory and filed research. *Organization Science, 2*(3), 239–262.

Burgelman, R. A. (2002). Strategy as vector and the inertia of coevolutionary lock-in. *Administrative Science Quarterly, 47*(2), 325–357.

Burklund, L. J., Eisenberger, N. I., & Lieberman, M. D. (2007). The face of rejection: Rejection sensitivity moderates dorsal anterior cingulate activity to disapproving facial expressions. *Social Neuroscience, 2*(3–4), 238–253.

Burlew, L. D., Pederson, J. E., & Bradley, B. (1994). The reaction of managers to the pre-acquisition stage of a corporate merger: A qualitative study. *Journal of Career Development (Springer Science & Business Media B.V.), 21*(1), 11–22.

Burns, J. M. (1978). *Leadership.* New York, NY: Harper & Row.

Burns, J. M. (2007). *Transforming leadership: A new pursuit of happiness.* New York, NY: Grove/Atlantic.

Burt, R. S. (1992). *Structural holes: The social structure of competition.* Cambridge, MA: Harvard University Press.

Bush, V. D., Rose, G. M., Gilbert, F., & Ingram, T. N. (2001). Managing culturally diverse buyer-seller relationships: The role of intercultural disposition and adaptive selling in developing intercultural communication competence. *Journal of the Academy of Marketing Science, 29*(4), 391–404.

Butler, F. C., Perryman, A. A., & Ranft, A. L. (2012). Examining the effects of acquired top management team turnover on firm performance post-acquisition: A meta-analysis. *Journal of Managerial Issues, 24*(1), 47–60.

Butler, J. C., & Grahovac, J. (2012). Learning, imitation, and the use of knowledge: A comparison of markets, hierarchies, and teams. *Organization Science, 23*(5), 1249–1263.

Bycio, P., Hackett, R. D., & Allen, J. S. (1995). Further assessments of Bass's (1985). conceptualization of transactional and transformational leadership. *Journal of Applied Psychology, 80*, 468–478.

Campbell, W. K., Brunell, A. B., & Finkel, E. J. (2006). Narcissism, interpersonal self-regulation, and romantic relationships: An agency model approach. In E. J. Finkel & K. D. Vohs (Eds.), *Self and relationships: Connecting intrapersonal and interpersonal processes* (pp. 57–83). New York, NY: Guilford.

Campbell, W. K., Hoffman, B. J., Campbell, S. M., & Marchisio, G. (2011). Narcissism in organizational contexts. *Human Resource Management Review, 21*(4), 268–284.

Campion, M. A., & Lord, R. G. (1982). A control system conceptualization of goal setting process. *Organizational Behavior and Human Performance, 30*, 265–287.

Carlson, H. J. (1991). The role of the shopping center in US retailing. *International Journal of Retail & Distribution Management, 19*(6).

Carter, M. E., & Pavur, E. J. (2003). Management psychology during mergers and acquisitions. *The Psychologist-Manager Journal, 6*(2), 31–46.

Cartwright, S., & Cooper, C. L. (1993). The psychological impact of merger and acquisition on the individual: A study of building society managers. *Human Relations, 46*(3), 327–347.

Cartwright, S., & Cooper, C. L. (1996). *Managing mergers, acquisitions and strategic alliances* (2nd ed.). Oxford, UK: Butterworth-Heinemann.

Cartwright, S., Tytherleigh, M., & Robertson, S. (2007). Are mergers always stressful? Some evidence from the higher education sector. *European Journal of Work and Organizational Psychology, 16*(4), 456–478.

Carver, C. S. (2006). Approach, avoidance, and the self-regulation of affect and action. *Motivation & Emotion, 30*(2), 105–110. doi:10.1007/s11031-006-9044-7

Carver, C. S., & Harmon-Jones, E. (2009). Anger is an approach-related affect: Evidence and implications. *Psychological Bulletin, 135*(2).

Carver, S. C., & White, T. L. (1994). Behavioral inhibition, behavioral activation, and affective responses to impending reward and punishment: The BIS/BAS scales. *Journal of Personality and Social Psychology, 67*(2), 319–333.

CBInsights (2017, September 20). *Research briefing: Regtech trends.* Retrieved from www.cbinsights.com/research/regtech-startup-acquisitions-ipo/

CCOHS. WHMIS (2015). *Hazard classes and categories. Canadian Centre for Occupational Health and Safety.* Retrieved from http://www.ccohs.ca/oshanswers/chemicals/whmis_ghs/hazard_classes.html

Centers for Disease Control and Prevention (2020). *The National Institute for Occupational Safety and Health (NIOSH).* Retrieved from https://www.cdc.gov/niosh/

Chambon, M. (2005). How to look modest in an organization: Supervisors' perceptions of subordinates' account for success. *Psychologie Du Travail Et Des Organisations, 11*(3), 151–164.

Chang, E. T., & Delzell, E. (2016). Systematic review and meta-analysis of glyphosate exposure and risk of lymphohematopoietic cancers. *Journal of Environmental Science & Health, Part B – Pesticides, Food Contaminants, & Agricultural Wastes, 51*(6), 402–434.

Chang, H.-C., & Holt, R. (1994). A Chinese perspective on face as inter-relational concern. In S. Ting-Toomey (Ed.), *The challenge of facework: Cross-cultural and interpersonal issues*. Albany, NY: State University of New York.

Chan-Olmsted, S. M. (1998). Mergers, acquisitions, and convergence: The strategic alliances of broadcasting, cable television, and telephone services. *Journal of Media Economics, 11*(3), 33–46.

Chatterjee, A., & Hambrick, D. C. (2007). It's all about me: Narcissistic Chief executive officers and their effects on company strategy and performance. *Administrative Science Quarterly, 52*(3), 351–386.

Chatterjee, S. (1986). Types of synergy and economic value: The impact of acquisitions on merging and rival firms. *Strategic Management Journal, 7*, 119–139.

Cheung, H. Y., Wu, J., & Tao, J. (2016). Predicting domain-specific risk-taking attitudes of mainland China university students: A hyper core self-evaluation approach. *Journal of Risk Research, 19*(1), 79–100.

Chipunza, C., Samuel, M. O., & Mariri, T. (2011). Leadership style, employee motivation and commitment: Empirical evidence from a consolidated retail bank operating in a depressed economy. *African Journal of Business Management, 5*(20).

Choi, S., Holmberg, I., Löwstedt, J., & Brommels, M. (2011). Executive management in radical change – The case of the Karolinska University Hospital merger. *Scandinavian Journal of Management, 27*(1), 11–23. doi:10.1016/j.scaman.2010.08.002

Chua, A. Y., & Goh, D. H. (2009). Why the whole is less than the sum of its parts: Examining knowledge management in acquisitions. *International Journal of Information Management, 29*(1), 78–86.

Chun, R., & Davies, G. (2010). The effect of merger on employee views of corporate reputation: Time and space dependent theory. *Industrial Marketing Management, 39*(5), 721–727.

Chung, G. H., Du, J., & Choi, J. N. (2014). How do employees adapt to organizational change driven by cross-border M&As? A case in China. *Journal of World Business, 49*(1), 78–86.

Cicero, L., & Pierro, A. (2007). Charismatic leadership and organizational outcomes: The mediating role of employees' work-group identification. *International Journal of Psychology, 42*(5), 297–306.

Cimilluca, D., Mattioli, D., & Benoit, D. (2016, October 31). GE to combine oil and gas business with baker hughes; Combination creates a company with more than $32 billion in revenue. *Wall Street Journal*. Retrieved from https://www.wsj.com/articles/ge-to-combine-oil-and-gas-business-with-baker-hughes-1477908407

Citera, M., & Stuhlmacher, A. F. (2001). A policy-modeling approach to examining fairness judgments in organizational acquisitions. *Journal of Behavioral Decision Making, 14*(4), 309–327.

Citron, F. M., Gray, M. A., Critchley, H. D., Weekes, B. S., & Ferstl, E. C. (2014). Emotional valence and arousal affect reading in an interactive way: Neuroimaging evidence for an approach-withdrawal framework. *Neuropsychologia, 5679*–5689.

Clark, S. M., Gioia, D. A., Ketchen, J. J., & Thomas, J. B. (2010). Transitional identity as a facilitator of organizational identity change during a merger. *Administrative Science Quarterly, 55*(3), 397–438.

Clarke, C., & Hammer, M. R. (1995). Predictors of Japanese and American managers job success, personal adjustment, and intercultural interaction effectiveness. *Management International Review (MIR)*, *35*(2), 153–170.

Clarke, N., & Salleh, N. M. (2011). Emotions and their management during a merger in Brunei. *Human Resource Development International*, *14*(3), 291–304.

Clegg, S. R. (1989). *Frameworks of power*. London: Sage.

Cloodt, M., Hagedoorn, J., & Van Kranenburg, H. (2006). Mergers and acquisitions: Their effect on the innovative performance of companies in high-tech industries. *Research Policy*, *35*(5), 642–654.

Clough, R., & Serafino, P. (2018, June 26). GE exiting health, oil as CEO races to shrink struggling titan. *Industry Week*.

Coffee, J. C., Lowenstein, L., & Rose-Ackerman, S. (1988). *Knights, raiders, and targets: The impact of the hostile takeover*. New York, NY: Oxford University Press.

Cohen, A., & Freund, A. (2005). A longitudinal analysis of the relationship between multiple commitments and withdrawal cognitions. *Scandinavian Journal of Management*, *21*(3), 329–351.

Cohen, W. M., & Levinthal, D. A. (1990). Absorptive capacity: A new perspective on learning and innovation. *Administrative Science Quarterly*, *35*(1), 128–152.

Collins, G., & Wickham, J. (2002). Experiencing mergers: A woman's eye view. *Women's Studies International Forum*, *25*(5), 573.

Colman, H. L., & Lunnan, R. (2011). Organizational identification and serendipitous value creation in post-acquisition integration. *Journal of Management*, *37*(3), 839–860.

Conger, J. A. (1990). The dark side of leadership. *Organizational Dynamics*, *19*, 44–55.

Conger, J. A., & Kanungo, R. N. (1987). Toward a behavioral theory of charismatic leadership in organizational settings. *Academy of Management Review*, *12*(4), 637–647.

Conger, J. A., & Kanungo, R. N. (1988). *Charismatic leadership: The elusive factor in organizational effectiveness*. San Francisco, CA: Jossey-Bass.

Conger, J. A., & Kanungo, R. N. (1998). *Leadership in organizations*. London: Sage.

Conlon, S. (2018, September 25). *Versace takeover makes business sense and fashion sense*. Retrieved from www.theguardian.com/business/2018/sep/25/versace-takeover-makes-business-sense-and-fashion-sense

Cordeiro, M. (2014). *The seventh M&A wave*. Retrieved from https://camayapartners.com/wp-content/uploads/2016/06/Theseventh-MA-wave.pdf

Cording, M., Harrison, J. S., Hoskisson, R. E., & Jonsen, K. (2014). Walking the talk: A multistakeholder exploration of organizational authenticity, employee productivity, and post-merger performance. *The Academy of Management Perspectives*, *28*(1), 38–56.

Corrigan, T. (1999, November 30). Esser fights for company and country: German group's chief battles nationalist bias and Vodafone. *Financial Times*, p. 35.

COSHH (2002). *Royal society of chemistry. Control of hazardous chemicals in the laboratory: COSHH*. Retrieved October 10, 2017, from www.rsc.org/learn-chemistry/resource/res00001116/coshh-resource?cmpid=CMP00002777

Costa, P. T., & McCrae, R. R. (1992). The five-factor model of personality and its relevance to personality disorders. *Journal of Personality Disorders*, *6*(4), 343–359. Retrieved from https://doi-org.ezproxy.lib.bbk.ac.uk/10.1521/pedi.1992.6.4.343

Covin, T. J., Kolenko, T. A., Sightler, K. W., & Tudor, R. K. (1997). Leadership style and post-merger satisfaction. *Journal of Management Development*, *16*(1), 22–33.

Covin, T. J., Sightler, K. W., Kolenko, T. A., & Tudor, K. R. (1996). An investigation of post-acquisition satisfaction with the merger. *Journal of Applied Behavioral Science, 32*(2), 125–142.

Crooks, E. (2016, October 31). General electric to combine oil and gas unit with baker hughes. *Financial Times.* Retrieved from https://www.ft.com/content/dffedabe-9f73-11e6-86d5-4e36b35c3550

Crooks, E. (2017, November 13). GE boss unveils dividend cut and $20bn asset sales. *Financial Times.*

Crooks, E. (2018, February 12). Drillers turn to big data in the hunt for more, cheaper oil. *Financial Times.* Retrieved from https://www.ft.com/content/19234982-0cbb-11e8-8eb7-42f857ea9f09

Crooks, E., & Wigglesworth, R. (2018, November 13). GE to raise $4bn from selling down baker hughes stake. *Financial Times.* Retrieved from https://www.ft.com/content/14755b0a-e749-11e8-8a85-04b8afea6ea3

Csaszar, F. A. (2013). An efficient frontier in organization design: Organizational structure as a determinant of exploration and exploitation. *Organization Science, 24*(4), 1083–1101.

Dansereau, F. Jr., Graen, G., & Haga, W. J. (1975). A vertical dyad linkage approach to leadership within formal organizations – A longitudinal investigation of the role making process. *Organizational Behavior and Human Performance, 13,* 46–78.

Darley, J. M., & Pittman, T. S. (2003). The psychology of compensatory and retributive justice. *Personality and Social Psychology Review, 7,* 324–336.

Das, T. K., & Teng, B.-S. (2000). Instabilities of strategic alliances: An internal tensions perspective. *Organization Science, 11*(1), 77–101.

Davidson, R. J., & Irwin, W. (1999). The functional neuroanatomy of emotion and affective style. *Trends In Cognitive Sciences, 3*(1), 11–21.

de Hoogh, A. H. B., den Hartog, D. N., Koopman, P. L., Thierry, H., van den Berg, P. T., van der Weide, J. G., & Wilderom, C. P. M. (2005). Leader motives, charismatic leadership, and subordinates' work attitude in the profit and voluntary sector. *Leadership Quarterly, 16*(1), 17–38.

de Man, A.-P., & Duysters, G. (2005). Collaboration and innovation: A review of the effects of mergers, acquisitions and alliances on innovation. *Technovation, 25*(12), 1377–1387.

Dealogic (2007). *Dealogic M&A review, first half, 2007.* Retrieved January 30, 2016, from http://www.theage.com.au/ed_docs/review.pdf

Dealogic (December, 2015). *Dealogic data shows 2015 M&A volume surpasses $5 trillion* [Press release]. Retrieved from www.dealogic.com/press-release/dealogic-data-shows-2015-ma-volume-surpasses-5-trillion/

Deaux, K., & Emswiller, T. (1974). Explanations of successful performance on sex-linked tasks: What is skill for the male is luck for the female. *Journal of Personality and Social Psychology, 29,* 80–85.

DeGroot, T., Kiker, D. S., & Cross, T. C. (2000). A meta-analysis to review organizational outcomes related to charismatic leadership. *Canadian Journal of Administrative Sciences, 17,* 356–371.

Deluga, R. J. (1997). Relationship among American Presidential charismatic.... *Leadership Quarterly, 8,* 49–65.

Deluga, R. J. (2001). American presidential Machiavellianism: Implications for charismatic leadership and rated performance. *Leadership Quarterly, 12,* 339–363.

Demoulin, S., Leyens, J.-P., Paladino, M.-P., Rodriguez-Torres, R., Rodriguez-Perez, A., & Dovidio, J. F. (2004). Dimensions of "uniquely" and "non-uniquely" human emotions. *Cognition and Emotion, 18*(1), 71–96.

DeNeve, K. M., & Cooper, H. (1998). The happy personality: A meta-analysis of 137 personality traits and subjective well-being. *Psychological Bulletin, 124*, 197–229.

DePaulo, B. M. (1992). Nonverbal behavior and self-presentation. *Psychological Bulletin, 111*(2), 203–243.

Derenberg, W. (1955). The influence of the French code civil on the modern law of unfair competition. *The American Journal of Comparative Law, 4*(1), 1–34.

Derue, D. S., Nahrgang, J. D., Wellman, N., & Humphrey, S. E. (2011). Trait and behavioral theories of leadership: An integration and meta-analytic test of their relative validity. *Personnel Psychology, 64*(1), 7–52.

Deschamps, J. C., & Clémence, A. (1987). *L'explication quotidienne. Perspectives psychosociologiques.* Cousset: DelVal.

Dess, G. G., & Shaw, J. D. (2001). Voluntary turnover, social capital, and organizational performance. *Academy of Management Review, 26*(3), 446–456.

DeYoung, R., Evanoff, D. D., & Molyneux, P. (2009). Mergers and acquisitions of financial institutions: A review of the post-2000 literature. *Journal of Financial Services Research, 36*, 87–110.

di Norcia, V. (1988). Mergers, takeovers and a property ethic. *Journal of Business Ethics, 7*(1/2), 109–116.

Dienesch, R. M., & Liden, R. C. (1986). Leader-member exchange model of leadership: A critique and further development. *Academy of Management Review, 11*(3), 618–634.

Dikova, D., & Rao Sahib, P. (2013). Is cultural distance a bane or a boon for cross-border acquisition performance? *Journal of World Business, 48*(1), 77–86.

Dimberg, U., Thunberg, M., & Elmehed, K. (2000). Unconscious facial reactions to emotional facial expressions. *Psychological Science, 11*(1), 86–89.

Dinh, J. E., Lord, R. G., Gardner, W. L., Meuser, J. D., Liden, R. C., & Hu, J. (2014). Leadership theory and research in the new millennium: Current theoretical trends and changing perspectives. *The Leadership Quarterly, 25*(1), 36–62.

Dirks, K. T., & Ferrin, D. L. (2001). The role of trust in organizational settings. *Organization Science, 12*(4), 450–467.

Doukas, J. A., & Petmezas, D. (2007). Acquisitions, overconfident managers and self-attribution bias. *European Financial Management, 13*(3), 531–577.

Driskell, J. E., Olmstead, B., & Salas, E. (1993). Task cues, dominance cues, and influence in task groups. *Journal of Applied Psychology, 93*, 51–60.

Drori, I., Wrzesniewski, A., & Ellis, S. (2013). One out of many? Boundary negotiation and identity formation in postmerger integration. *Organization Science, 24*(6), 1717–1741.

Drory, A., & Zaidman, N. (2007). Impression management behaviour: Effects of the organizational system. *Journal of Managerial Psychology, 22*(3), 290–308.

Dulebohn, J. H., Bommer, W. H., Liden, R. C., Brouer, R. L., & Ferris, G. R. (2012). A meta-analysis of antecedents and consequences of leader-member exchange: Integrating the past with an eye toward the future. *Journal of Management, 38*(6), 1715–1759.

Dumond, J. (2005). Sans licenciements, pourquoi les restructurations sont-elles encore brutales? = Why are mergers without layoffs still rough? *Psychologie Du Travail Et Des Organisations, 11*(4), 241–255.

Duncan, R. B. (1976). The ambidextrous organization: Designing dual structures for innovation. In R. H. Kilmann, L. R. Pondy, & D. P. Slevin (Eds.), *The management of organization design, Strategies and implementation* (Vol. 1, pp. 167–188). New York, NY: North-Holland.

Dutton, J. E., Dukerich, J. M., & Harquail, C. V. (1994). Organizational images and member identification. *Administrative Science Quarterly*, *39*(2), 239–263.

Eddey, P. H. (1991). Corporate raiders and takeover targets. *Journal of Business Finance & Accounting*, *18*(2), 151–171.

Edwards, M. R., & Edwards, T. (2012). Procedural justice and identification with the acquirer: The moderating effects of job continuity, organisational identity strength and organisational similarity. *Human Resource Management Journal*, *22*(2), 109–128.

Eisenberg, N. I., Lieberman, M. D., & Williams, K. D. (2003). Does rejection hurt? An fMRI study of social exclusion. *Science*, *302*(5643), 290–292.

Eisenhardt, K. M., & Brown, S. L. (1998). Competing on the edge: Strategy as structured chaos. *Long Range Planning: International Journal of Strategic Management*, *31*(5), 786–789.

Ekman, P. (1984). Expression and the nature of emotion. In K. Scherer & P. Ekman (Eds.), *Approaches to emotion* (pp. 319–344). Hillsdale, NJ: Erlbaum.

Ekman, P. (1999). Basic emotions. In T. Dalgleish & M. J. Power (Eds.), *Handbook of cognition and emotion* (pp. 45–60). Chichester, UK: John Wiley & Sons Ltd.

Ekman, P., & Davidson, J. (Eds.). (1994). *The nature of emotion: Fundamental questions (Series in Affective Science)*. New York, NY: Oxford University Press.

Ekman, P., & Friesen, W. V. (1971). Constants across cultures in the face and emotion. *Journal of Personality and Social Psychology*, *17*(2), 124–129.

Ekman, P., & Friesen, W. V. (1978). *Facial action coding system*. Palo Alto, CA: Consulting Psychologist.

Elfenbein, H. A., Beaupré, M., Lévesque, M., & Hess, U. (2007). Toward a dialect theory: Cultural differences in the expression and recognition of posed facial expressions. *Emotion*, *7*(1), 131.

Ellemers, N., Doosje, B. J., Van Knippenberg, A., & Wilke, H. (1992). Status protection in high status minority groups. *European Journal of Social Psychology*, *22*(2), 123–140.

Ellis, K. M., Reus, T. H., & Lamont, B. T. (2009). The effects of procedural and informational justice in the integration of related acquisitions. *Strategic Management Journal*, *30*(2), 137–161.

Ellis, K. M., Reus, T. H., Lamont, B. T., & Ranft, A. L. (2011). Transfer effects in large acquisitions: How size-specific experience matters. *Academy of Management Journal*, *54*(6), 1261–1276.

Empson, L. (2001). Fear of exploitation and fear of contamination: Impediments to knowledge transfer in mergers between professional service firms. *Human Relations*, *54*(7), 839–862.

English, S. (2003, August 3). Chrysler settles lawsuit for $300m. *The Telegraph*. Retrieved from www.telegraph.co.uk/finance/2861163/Chrysler-settles-lawsuit-for-300m.html

Ennes, J. (2018, June 27). GE to sell stake in Baker Hughes, spin off healthcare unit. *Project Finance*.

Eriksson, M., & Sundgren, M. (2005). Managing change: Strategy or serendipity – reflections from the merger of Astra and Zeneca. *Journal of Change Management*, *5*(1), 15–28.

Ernst, H., & Vitt, J. (2000). The influence of corporate acquisitions on the behavior of key inventors. *R&D Management, 30*(2), 105.

Fama, E. F. (1980). Agency problems and the theory of the firm. *Journal of Political Economy, 88*(2), 288–307.

Fama, E. F., & Jensen, M. C. (1983). Agency problems and residual claims. *The Journal of Law and Economics, 26*(2), 327–349.

Fama, E. F., & Jensen, M. C. (1986). Separation of ownership and control. In J. B. Barney & W. G. Ouchi (Eds.), *Organizational economics: Toward a new paradigm for understanding and studying organizations* (pp. 276–298). San Francisco, CA: Jossey-Bass.

Fang, C., Lee, J., & Schilling, M. A. (2010). Balancing exploration and exploitation through structural design: The isolation of subgroups and organizational learning. *Organization Science, 21*(3), 625–642.

Farrell, S. (2016, October 17). *Ladbrokes and Coral to sell 359 betting shops in run-up to £2.3bn merger.* Retrieved from www.theguardian.com/business/2016/oct/17/ladbrokes-coral-sell-betting-shops-betfred-stan-james-merger

Feist, J., & Feist, G. J. (2009). *Theories of personality.* Boston: McGraw-Hill.

Felps, W., Mitchell, T. R., Herman, D. R., Lee, T. W., Holtom, B. C., & Harman, W. S. (2009). Turnover contagion: How coworkers' job embeddedness and job search behaviors influence quitting. *Academy of Management Journal, 52*(3), 545–561.

Fiedler, F. E. (1965). Engineer the job to fit the manager. *Harvard Business Review, 43*(5), 115–122.

Fiedler, F. E. (1967). *A theory of leadership effectiveness.* New York, NY: McGraw-Hill.

Fiedler, F. E. (1971). Validation and extension of the contingency model of leadership effectiveness: A review of empirical findings. *Psychological Bulletin, 76*(2), 128–148.

Fiegerman, S. (2016, June 15). *How yahoo derailed tumblr.* Mashable. Retrieved from https://mashable.com/2016/06/15/how-yahoo-derailed-tumblr/?europe=true

Financial Times (2019a). *Bayer's merger failure is a lesson for other buyers.* Retrieved from www.ft.com/content/b5c48f46-6d93-11e9-a9a5-351eeaef6d84

Financial Times (2019b, October 30). *Bayer risks mount as US pesticide lawsuits more than double.* Retrieved from www.ft.com/content/d6649c2e-fae6-11e9-a354-36acbbb0d9b6

Fischer, A. H., & Manstead, A. S. R. (2000). The relation between gender and emotion in different cultures. In A. H. Fischer (Ed.), *Gender and emotion: Social psychological perspectives* (pp. 71–94). New York, NY: Cambridge University Press.

Fischer, P., Greitemeyer, T., Omay, S. I., & Frey, D. (2007). Mergers and group status: The impact of high, low and equal group status on identification and satisfaction with a company merger, experienced controllability, group identity and group cohesion. *Journal of Community & Applied Social Psychology, 17*(3), 203–217.

Fiske, S. T., & Taylor, S. E. (1991). *Social cognition* (2nd ed.). New York and England: Mcgraw-Hill Book Company.

Fligstein, N. (1990). *The transformation of corporate control.* Cambridge, UK: Harvard University Press.

FlyBe (2019, January 11). *Virgin Atlantic, Stobart Group and Cyrus confirm offer for Flybe – delivering enhanced connectivity to UK regions and Ireland under the Virgin Atlantic brand* [press release]. Retrieved from https://corporate.virginatlantic.com/gb/en/media/press-releases/offer-for-Flybe-confirmed.html

Fortune (2018). *Fortune 500 Companies.* Retrieved from https://fortune.com/fortune500/2018/search/

Foti, R. J., & Hauenstein, N. M. (1993). Processing demands and the effects of prior impressions on subsequent judgments: Clarifying the assimilation/contrast debate. *Organizational Behavior and Human Decision Processes, 56*, 167–189.

Frederick, W. R., & de la Fuente Rodriguez, A. (1994). A Spanish acquisition in Eastern Germany: Culture shock. *Journal of Management Development, 13*(2), 42.

Fredrickson, B. L. (2001). The role of positive emotions in positive psychology. The broaden-and-build theory of positive emotions. *The American Psychologist, 56*(3), 218–226.

Freeman, E., Gilbert, D. R., & Jacobson, C. (1987). The ethics of greenmail. *Journal of Business Ethics, 6*(3), 165–178.

Fried, Y., Tiegs, R. B., Naughton, T. J., & Ashforth, B. E. (1996). Managers' reactions to a corporate acquisition: A test of an integrative model. *Journal of Organizational Behavior, 17*(5), 401–427.

Friedman, H. S., Prince, L. M., Riggio, R. E., & DiMatteo, M. R. (1980). Understanding and assessing nonverbal expressiveness: The affective communication test. *Journal of Personality and Social Psychology, 39*, 333–351.

Fugate, M., Kinicki, A. J., & Scheck, C. L. (2002). Coping with an organizational merger over four stages. *Personnel Psychology, 55*(4), 905–928.

Fulop, N., Protopsaltis, G., Hutchings, A., King, A., Allen, P., Normand, C., & Walters, R. (2002). Process and impact of mergers of NHS trusts: Multicentre case study and management cost analysis. *BMJ (Clinical Research Ed.), 325* (7358), 246.

Funder, D. C. (2001). Personality. *Annual Review of Psychology, 52*, 197–221. doi:10.1146/annurev.psych.52.1.197

Gable, P., & Harmon-Jones, E. (2010). The motivational dimensional model of affect: Implications for breadth of attention, memory, and cognitive categorisation. *Cognition and Emotion, 24*(2), 322–337.

Gaertner, R. R. W., & Theriault, G. P. (2002). Risk of bladder cancer in foundry workers: A meta-analysis. *Occupational and Environmental Medicine, 59*(10), 655–663.

Gaertner, S. L., Dovidio, J. F., & Bachman, B. A. (1996). Revisiting the contact hypothesis: The induction of a common ingroup identity. *International Journal of Intercultural Relations, 20*(3–4), 271–290.

Garside, J., & Farrell, S. (2014, May 15). *Carphone warehouse and Dixons agree £3.8bn merger*. Retrieved from www.theguardian.com/business/2014/may/15/carphone-warehouse-dixons-agree-merger

Gaughan, P. (2005). *Mergers: What can go wrong and how to prevent it*. Hoboken, NJ: John Wiley and Sons.

Gaughan, P. (2007). *Mergers, acquisitions and corporate restructurings* (4th ed.). Hoboken, NJ: John Wiley & Sons.

Gelfand, M. J., Leslie, L. M., Keller, K., & de Dreu, C. (2012). Conflict cultures in organizations: How leaders shape conflict cultures and their organizational-level consequences. *Journal of Applied Psychology, 97*(6), 1131–1147.

General Electric (2016a, December 8). *Baker hughes, a GE company investor update* [Investor Release].

General Electric (2016b, October 31). *GE and baker hughes agree to create new fullstream digital industrial services company* [Press release].

General Electric (2017, April 21). *GE Q1 earnings* [Press release].

General Electric (2018, January 24). *GE announces fourth quarter 2017 results* [Press release].

Geroski, P. A., & Vlassopoulos, A. (1990). Recent patterns of European merger activity. *Business Strategy Review, 1*(2), 17–27.

Gerstner, C. R., & Day, D. V. (1997). Meta-analytic review of leader-member exchange theory: Correlates and construct issues. *Journal of Applied Psychology, 82*(6), 827–844.

Ghemawat, P., & Costa, J. E. R. I. (1993). The organizational tension between static and dynamic efficiency. *Strategic Management Journal (John Wiley & Sons, Inc.), 14*, 59–73.

Gibbs, S. (2017, August 31). *Apple joins consortium in revised £14bn bid for Toshiba's chip business.* Retrieved from www.theguardian.com/technology/2017/aug/31/apple-consortium-bid-toshiba-chip-business-bain-capital-iphone-saamsung

Gibson, C. B., & Birkinshaw, J. (2004). The antecedents, consequences, and mediating role of organizational ambidexterity. *Academy of Management Journal, 47*(2), 209–226. Retrieved from https://doi-org.ezproxy.lib.bbk.ac.uk/10.5465/20159573

Giessner, S. R. (2011). Is the merger necessary? The interactive effect of perceived necessity and sense of continuity on post-merger identification. *Human Relations, 64*(8), 1079–1098.

Giessner, S. R., & Mummendey, A. (2008). United we win, divided we fail? Effects of cognitive merger representations and performance feedback on merging groups. *European Journal of Social Psychology, 38*(3), 412–435.

Giessner, S. R., Ullrich, J., & van Dick, R. (2012). A social identity analysis of mergers & acquisitions. In D. Faulkner, S. Teerikangas, & R. J. Joseph (Eds.), *The handbook of mergers and acquisitions.* Oxford: Oxford University Press.

Giessner, S. R., Viki, G. T., Otten, S., Terry, D. J., & Täuber, S. (2006). The challenge of merging: Merger patterns, premerger status, and merger support. *Personality & Social Psychology Bulletin, 32*(3), 339–352.

Giner-Sorolla, R., Kamau, C. W., & Castano, E. (2010). Guilt and shame through recipients' eyes: The moderating effect of blame. *Social Psychology, 41*(2), 88–92.

Gleibs, I. H., Mummendey, A., & Noack, P. (2008). Predictors of change in post-merger identification during a merger process: A longitudinal study. *Journal of Personality and Social Psychology, 95*(5), 1095–1112.

Gleibs, I. H., Noack, P., & Mummendey, A. (2010). We are still better than them: A longitudinal field study of ingroup favouritism during a merger. *European Journal of Social Psychology, 40*(5), 819–836.

Gleibs, I. H., Täuber, S., Viki, G. T., & Giessner, S. R. (2013). When what we get is not what we want: The role of implemented versus desired merger patterns in support for mergers. *Social Psychology, 44*(3), 177–190.

Goddard, S., & Palmer, A. (2010). An evaluation of the effects of a National Health Service Trust merger on the learning and development of staff. *Human Resource Development International, 13*(5), 557–573.

Goldberg, L. R. (1999). A broad-bandwidth, public-domain, personality inventory measuring the lower-level facets of several five-factor models. In I. Mervielde, I. J. Deary, F. De Fruyt, & F. Ostendorf (Eds.), *Personality psychology in Europe* (Vol. 7, pp. 7–28). Tilburg, Netherlands: Tilburg University Press.

Goldthorpe, J. H., Lockwood, D., Bechhofer, F., & Platt, J.(1968). *The affluent worker: Industrial attitudes and behaviour.* Cambridge: Cambridge University Press.

Gordon, R. A. (1996). Impact of ingratiation on judgments and evaluations: A meta-analytic investigation. *Journal of Personality and Social Psychology, 71*(1), 54–70.

Goulet, P., & Schweiger, D. M. (2006). Managing culture and human resources in mergers and acquisitions. In G. K. Stahl & I. Bjorkman (Eds.), *Handbook of research in international human resource management* (pp. 405–426). Cheltenham: Edward Elgar.

Graen, G. B. (1976). Role making process within complex organizations. In M. D. Dunnette (Ed.), *Handbook of industrial organizational psychology* (pp. 1201–1245). Chicago: Rand-McNally.

Graen, G. B., & Cashman, J. (1975). A role-making model of leadership in formal organization: A development approach. In J. G. Hunt & L. L. Larson (Eds.), *Leadership frontiers* (pp. 143–165). Kent, OH: Kent State University Press.

Graen, G. B., & Scandura, T. A. (1987). Toward a psychology of dyadic organizing. *Research in Organizational Behavior, 9*, 175–208.

Grant, A. M., & Pollock, T. G. (2011). Publishing in AMJ-part 3: Setting the hook. *Academy of Management Journal, 54*, 873–879.

Gray, J. A. (1990). Brain systems that mediate both emotion and cognition. *Cognition and Emotion, 4*, 269–288.

Gray, J. A. (1994). Three fundamental emotion systems. In D. Ekman & R. Davidson (Eds.), *The nature of emotion: Fundamental questions* (pp. 243–247). New York, NY: Oxford University Press.

Graziano, W. G., & Eisenberg, N. H. (1997). Agreeableness: A dimension of personality. In R. Hogan, J. A. Johnson, & S. R. Briggs (Eds.), *Handbook of personality psychology* (pp. 767–793). San Diego, CA: Academic Press.

Greenberg, J., Pyszczynski, T., Solomon, S., Rosenblatt, A., Veeder, M., Kirkland, S., & Lyon, D. (1990). Evidence for terror management theory II: The effects of mortality salience on reactions to those who threaten or bolster the cultural worldview. *Journal of Personality And Social Psychology, 58*(2), 308–318.

Greenberg, J., Solomon, S., & Pyszczynski, T. (1997). Terror management theory of self-esteem and cultural worldviews: Empirical assessments and conceptual refinements. In M. P. Zanna (Ed.), *Advances in experimental social psychology* (Vol. 29, pp. 61–139). San Diego, CA: Academic Press.

Greenspan, A. (1996). *The challenge of central banking in a democratic society.* Speech presented at the Annual Dinner and Francis Boyer Lecture of The American Enterprise Institute for Public Policy Research, Federal Reserve, Washington, DC. Retrieved February 14, 2016, from www.federalreserve.gov/

Greenwood, R., Hinings, C., & Brown, J. (1994). Merging professional service firms. *Organization Science, 5*(2), 239–257.

Greve, H. R. (2007). Exploration and exploitation in product innovation. *Industrial and Corporate Change, 16*(5), 945–975.

Guardian, The (2019a). *Google snaps up Fitbit for $2.1bn.* Retrieved from www.theguardian.com/business/2019/nov/01/google-snaps-up-fitbit-for-21bn

Guardian, The (2019b, May 13). *Monsanto must pay couple $2bn in largest verdict yet over cancer claims.* Retrieved from www.theguardian.com/business/2019/may/13/monsanto-cancer-trial-bayer-roundup-couple

Guerrero, S. (2008). Changes in employees' attitudes at work following an acquisition: A comparative study by acquisition type. *Human Resource Management Journal, 18*(3), 216–236.

Gulliver, P., Towell, D., & Peck, E. (2003). Staff morale in the merger of mental health and social care organizations in England. *Journal of Psychiatric and Mental Health Nursing, 10*(1), 101–107.

Gupta, A. K., Smith, K. G., & Shalley, C. E. (2006). The interplay between exploration and exploitation. *Academy of Management Journal, 49*(4), 693–706.

Hagedoorn, J., & Duysters, G. (2002). The effect of mergers and acquisitions on the technological performance of companies in a high-tech environment. *Technology Analysis & Strategic Management, 14*(1), 67–85.

Hals, T., Yamazaki, M., & Kelly, T. (2017, March 29). Huge nuclear cost overruns push Toshiba's Westinghouse into bankruptcy. *Reuters.* Retrieved from www.reuters.com/article/us-toshiba-accounting-board/huge-nuclear-cost-overruns-push-toshibas-westinghouse-into-bankruptcy-idUSKBN17006K

Halsall, R. (2008). Intercultural mergers and acquisitions as "Legitimacy Crises" of models of capitalism: A UK – German case study. *Organization, 15*(6), 787–809.

Hambrick, D. C., & Cannella, J. A. (1993). Relative standing: A framework for understanding departures of acquired executives. *Academy of Management Journal, 36*(4), 733–762.

Hamilton, D. L., & Sherman, S. J. (1996). Perceiving persons and groups. *Psychological Review, 103,* 336–355.

Hamilton, D. L., Sherman, S. J., & Lickel, B. (1998). Perceiving so-cial groups: The importance of the entitativity continuum. In C. Sedikides, J. Schopler, & C. A. Insko (Eds.), *Intergroup cogni-tion and intergroup behavior* (pp. 47–74). Mahwah, NJ: Lawrence Erlbaum Associates, Inc.

Hampton, L. (2018, June 27). The culture clash behind GE's quick exit from Baker Hughes stake. *Thomson Reuters.* Retrieved from https://www.reuters.com/article/us-baker-hughes-ge-future-insight/the-culture-clash-behind-ges-quick-exit-from-baker-hughes-stake-idUSKBN1JM312

Hanges, P. J., Lord, R. G., & Dickson, M. W. (2000). Am information-processing perspective on leadership and culture: A case for connectionist architecture. *Applied Psychology: An International Review, 49*(1), 133–161.

Harbeson, R. W. (1958). The Clayton Act: Sleeping giant of antitrust? *American Economic Review, 48*(1), 92.

Harrington, N. (2005). It's too difficult! Frustration intolerance beliefs and procrastination. *Personality and Individual Differences, 39*(5), 873–883.

Harroch, R. D., Lipkin, D. A., Smith, R. V., & Cook, J. (2019). *A comprehensive guide to due diligence issues in mergers and acquisitions.* Retrieved from www.forbes.com/sites/allbusiness/2019/03/27/comprehensive-guide-due-diligence-issues-mergers-and-acquisitions/

Harwood, I., & Ashleigh, M. (2005). The impact of trust and confidentiality on strategic organizational change programmes: A case study of post-acquisition integration. *Strategic Change, 14*(2), 63–75.

Haspeslagh, P. C., & Jemison, D. B. (1991). *Managing acquisitions: Creating value through corporate renewal.* New York, NY: Free Press.

Haunschild, P. R., Davis-Blake, A., & Fichman, M. (1994). Managerial over-commitment in corporate acquisition processes. *Organization Science, 5*(4), 528–540.

Hawley, E. W. (2015). *The new deal and the problem of monopoly.* Princeton: Princeton University Press.

Haynes, K. T., Hitt, M. A., & Campbell, J. T. (2015). The dark side of leadership: Towards a mid-range theory of hubris and greed in entrepreneurial contexts. *Journal of Management Studies, 52*(4), 479–505.

Hayward, M. L. A., & Hambrick, D. C. (1997). Explaining the premiums paid for large acquisitions: Evidence of CEO hubris. *Administrative Science Quarterly*, 42(1), 103–127.

Hayward, M. L. A., Rindova, V. P., & Pollock, T. G. (2004). Believing one's own press: The causes and consequences of ceo celebrity. *Strategic Management Journal (John Wiley & Sons, Inc.)*, 25(7), 637–653.

Hayward, M. L. A., Shepherd, D. A., & Griffin, D. (2006). A hubris theory of entrepreneurship. *Management Science*, 52, 160–172.

He, Z.-L., & Wong, P.-K. (2004). Exploration vs exploitation: An empirical test of the ambidexterity hypothesis. *Organization Science*, 15(4), 481–494.

Health and Safety Executive (2019). *The approved list of biological agents. Health and safety executive: Advisory committee on dangerous pathogens* (3rd ed.). HSE Books. www.hse.gov.uk/pubns/misc208.pdf

Health and Safety Executive. *Safe working and the prevention of infection in clinical laboratories and similar facilities*. Health and Safety Executive. Retrieved October 10, 2017, from www.hse.gov.uk/pubns/misc208.pdf

Health and Safety Executive Employers' Liability (Compulsory Insurance) Act 1969A brief guide for employers. Retrieved from www.hse.gov.uk/pubns/hse40.pdf

Heinemann, A. (2012). Government control of cross-border M&A: Legitimate regulation or protectionism? *Journal of International Economic Law*, 15(3), 843–870.

Heinström, J. (2003). Five personality dimensions and their influence on information behaviour. *Information Research*, 9(1), 1–24.

Henderson, R., & Cockburn, I. (1996). Scale, scope, and spillovers: The determinants of research productivity in drug discovery. *RAND Journal of Economics (RAND Journal of Economics)*, 27(1), 32–59.

Hern, A. (2014, March 6). *Spotify acquires music data firm The Echo Nest*. Retrieved from www.theguardian.com/technology/2014/mar/06/spotify-echo-nest-streaming-music-deal

Hessen, R. (1975). *Steel titan: The life of Charles M. Schwab*. Pittsburgh, PA: University of Pittsburgh Press.

Hewstone, M., & Jaspars, J. (1982). Explanations for racial discrimination: The effect of group discussion on intergroup attributions. *European Journal of Social Psychology*, 12(1), 1–16.

Hidy, R., Hidy, M., Scott, R., & Hofsommer, D. (1988). *The great northern railway: A history*. Minneapolis and London: University of Minnesota Press.

Hiller, N. J., & Hambrick, D. C. (2005). Conceptualizing executive hubris: The role of (hyper-) core self-evaluations in strategic decision-making. *Strategic Management Journal*, 26, 297–319.

Hinduan, Z. R., Wilson-Evered, E., Moss, S., & Scannell, E. (2009). Leadership, work outcomes and openness to change following an Indonesian bank merger. *Asia Pacific Journal of Human Resources*, 47(1), 59–78.

Hirsch, P. M. (1986). From ambushes to golden parachutes: Corporate takeovers as instances of cultural framing and institutional integration. *American Journal of Sociology*, 91(4), 800–837.

Hitt, M. A., Hoskisson, R. E., & Ireland, R. D. (1990). Mergers and acquisitions and managerial commitment to innovation in M-Form firms. *Strategic Management Journal (John Wiley & Sons, Inc.)*, 11(4), 29–47.

Hitt, M. A., Hoskisson, R. E., Ireland, R. D., & Harrison, J. S. (1991a). Are acquisitions a poison pill for innovation? *Executive (19389779)*, 5(4), 22–34.

Hitt, M. A., Hoskisson, R. E., Ireland, R. D., & Harrison, J. S. (1991b). Effects of acquisitions on R&D inputs and outputs. *Academy of Management Journal, 34*(3), 693–706.

Hitt, M. A., Hoskisson, R. E., Johnson, R. A., & Moesel, D. D. (1996). The market for corporate control and firm innovation. *Academy of Management Journal, 39*(5), 1084–1119.

Hoang, H., & Rothaermel, F. T. (2010). Leveraging internal and external experience: Exploration, exploitation, and R&D project performance. *Strategic Management Journal (John Wiley & Sons, Inc.), 31*(7), 734–758.

Hodgkinson, L., & Partington, G. (2008). The motivation for takeovers in the UK. *Journal of Business Finance & Accounting, 35*(1) & (2), 102–126.

Hofmann, S. G., & Doan, S. N. (2018). Defining emotions. In *The social foundations of emotion: Developmental, cultural, and clinical dimensions* (pp. 11–21). Washington, DC: American Psychological Association.

Hofstede, G. (1991). *Cultures and organizations: Software of the mind*. London: McGraw-Hill.

Hogan, R., Curphy, G. J., & Hogan, J. (1994). What we know about leadership: Effectiveness and personality. American Psychologist, *49*, 493–504.

Hogan, R., & Hogan, J. (2001). Assessing leadership: A view from the dark side. *International Journal of Selection & Assessment, 9*(1/2), 40.

Hogan, R., & Kaiser, R. B. (2005). What we know about leadership. *Review of General Psychology, 9*(2), 169–180.

Hogg, M. A. (2001). A social identity theory of leadership. *Personality and Social Psychology Review, 5*, 184–200.

Hogg, M. A., & Terry, D. J. (2000). Social identity and self-categorization processes in organizational contexts. *The Academy of Management Review, 25*(1), 121–140.

Hollenbeck, J. R., Williams, C. R., & Klein, H. J. 1989. An empirical examination of the antecedents of commitment to difficult goals. *Journal of Applied Psychology, 74*(1), 18–23.

Homburg, C., & Bucerius, M. (2006). Is speed of integration really a success factor in mergers and acquisitions? An analysis of the role of internal and external relatedness. *Strategic Management Journal, 27*, 347–367.

Hotchkiss, S. (2002). *Why is it always about you? The seven deadly sins of narcissism*. New York, NY: Free Press.

House, R. J. (1977). A 1976 theory of charismatic leadership. In J. G. Hunt & L. L. Larson (Eds.), *Leadership: The cutting edge* (pp. 189–207). Carbondale, IL: Southern Illinois University Press.

House, R. J., & Podsakoff, P. M. (1994). Leadership effectiveness: Past perspectives and future directions for research. In J. Greenberg (Ed.), *Organizational behavior* (pp. 45–82). Hillsdale, NJ: Lawrence Erlbaum Associates.

House, R. J., Spangler, D. W., & Woycke, J. (1991). Personality and charisma in the U.S. presidency: A psychological theory of leader effectiveness. *Administrative Science Quarterly, 36*, 364–396.

Howell, J. M., & Frost, P. J. (1989). A laboratory study of charismatic leadership. *Organizational Behavior & Human Decision Processes, 43*(2), 243.

Idel, M., Melamed, S., Merlob, P., Yahav, J., Hendel, T., & Kaplan, B. (2003). Influence of a merger on nurses' emotional well-being: The importance of self-efficacy and emotional reactivity. *Journal of Nursing Management, 11*(1), 59–63.

Ilies, R., Nahrgang, J. D., & Morgeson, F. P. (2007). Leader-member exchange and citizenship behaviors: A meta-analysis. *Journal of Applied Psychology*, *92*(1), 269–277.

International Agency for Research on Cancer (2019). *List of classifications by cancer sites with sufficient or limited evidence in humans.* IARC Monographs. Retrieved from https://monographs.iarc.fr/wp-content/uploads/2019/07/Classifications_by_cancer_site.pdf

International Management Group (2016, September 22). Dangers of ignoring risk management in M&A. Retrieved from https://imgcorp.co.uk/dangers-ignoring-risk-management-mergers-acquisitions/

Issawi, C. (1978). The 1973 oil crisis and after. *Journal of Post Keynesian Economics*, *1*(2), 3–26.

Jacobs, C. D., Oliver, D., & Heracleous, L. (2013). Diagnosing organizational identity beliefs by eliciting complex, multimodal metaphors. *Journal of Applied Behavioral Science*, *49*(4), 485–507.

Jain, A. (2016). Learning by hiring and change to organizational knowledge: Countering obsolescence as organizations age. *Strategic Management Journal (John Wiley & Sons, Inc.)*, *37*(8), 1667–1687.

Jansen, A. S. P., Nguyen, X. V., Karpitskiy, V., Mettenleiter, T. C., & Loewy, A. D. (1995). Central command neurons of the sympathetic nervous system – Basis of the fight-or-flight response. *Science*, *270*, 644–646.

Jansen, J. J. P., Vera, D., & Crossan, M. (2009). Strategic leadership for exploration and exploitation: The moderating role of environmental dynamism. *Leadership Quarterly*, *20*(1), 5–18.

Jensen, M. C. (1986). Agency costs of free cash flow, corporate finance, and takeovers. *American Economic Review*, *76*(2), 323.

Jetten, J., Duck, J., Terry, D. J., & O'Brien, A. (2002). Being attuned to intergroup differences in mergers: The role of aligned leaders for low-status groups. *Personality and Social Psychology Bulletin*, *28*(9), 1194–1201.

Jetten, J., & Hutchison, P. (2011). When groups have a lot to lose: Historical continuity enhances resistance to a merger. *European Journal of Social Psychology*, *41*(3), 335–343.

Jetten, J., O'Brien, A., & Trindall, N. (2002). Changing identity: Predicting adjustment to organizational restructure as a function of subgroup and superordinate identification. *British Journal of Social Psychology*, *41*(2), 281–298.

Jin, J. L., Zhou, K. Z., & Wang, Y. (2016). Exploitation and exploration in international joint ventures: Moderating effects of partner control imbalance and product similarity. *Journal of International Marketing*, *24*(4), 20–38.

John, G., Weiss, A. M., & Dutta, S. (1999). Marketing in technology-intensive markets: Toward a conceptual framework. *Journal of Marketing*, *63*(4), 78–91.

Jonason, P. K., & Krause, L. (2013). The emotional deficits associated with the Dark Triad traits: Cognitive empathy, affective empathy, and alexithymia. *Personality and Individual Differences*, *55*(5), 532–537.

Joslin, F., Waters, L., & Dudgeon, P. (2010). Perceived acceptance and work standards as predictors of work attitudes and behavior and employee psychological distress following an internal business merger. *Journal of Managerial Psychology*, *25*(1), 22–43.

Judge, T. A. (1993). Does affective disposition moderate the relationship between job satisfaction and voluntary turnover? *Journal of Applied Psychology*, *78*(3), 395–401.

Judge, T. A., & Bono, J. E (2000). Five-factor model of personality and transformational leadership. *Journal of Applied Psychology*, *85*(5), 751–765.

Judge, T. A., & Bono, J. E. (2001). A rose by any other name: Are self-esteem, generalized self-efficacy, neuroticism, and locus of control indicators of a common construct? In B. W. Roberts & R. Hogan (Eds.), *Decade of behavior. Personality psychology in the workplace* (pp. 93–118). Washington, DC: American Psychological Association.

Judge, T. A., Colbert, A. E., & Ilies, R. (2004). Intelligence and leadership: A quantitative review and test of theoretical propositions. *Journal of Applied Psychology*, *89*(3), 542–552.

Judge, T. A., Erez, A., Bono, J. E., & Thoresen, C. J. (2002). Discriminant and incremental validity of four personality traits: Are measures of self-esteem, neuroticism, locus of control, and generalized self-efficacy indicators of a common core construct? *Journal of Personality and Social Psychology*, *83*, 693–710.

Judge, T. A., Ilies, R., Bono, J. E., & Gerhardt, M. W. (2002). Personality and leadership: A qualitative and quantitative review. *Journal of Applied Psychology*, *87*(4), 765–780.

Judge, T. A., & LePine, J. A. (2007). The bright and dark sides of personality: Implications for personnel selection in individual and team contexts. In J. Langan-Fox, C. Cooper, & R. Klimoski (Eds.), *Research companion to the dysfunctional workplace: Management challenges and symptoms* (pp. 332–355). Cheltenham, UK: Edward Elgar Publishing.

Judge, T. A., & Piccolo, R. F. (2004). Transformational and transactional leadership: A meta-analytic test of their relative validity. *Journal of Applied Psychology*, *89*(5), 755–768.

Judge, T. A., Piccolo, R. F., & Kosalka, T. (2009). The bright and dark sides of leader traits: A review and theoretical extension of the leader trait paradigm. *Leadership Quarterly*, *20*(6), 855–875.

Judge, T. A., Thoresen, C. J., Pucik, V., & Welbourne, T. M. (1999). Managerial coping with organizational change: A dispositional perspective. *Journal of Applied Psychology*, *84*, 107–122.

Jung, J., & Dobbin, F. (2012). Finance and institutional investors. In K. K. Cetina & A. Preda (Eds.), *The Oxford handbook of the sociology of finance* (pp. 52–74). Oxford, UK: Oxford University Press.

Junni, P. (2011). Knowledge transfer in acquisitions: Fear of exploitation and contamination. *Scandinavian Journal of Management*, *27*(3), 307–321.

Junni, P., & Sarala, R. M. (2014). The role of leadership in mergers and acquisitions: A review of recent empirical studies. In Sydney Finkelstein & Cary L. Cooper (Ed.), *Advances in mergers and acquisitions* (pp. 181–200). Bingley, UK: Emerald Group Publishing Limited.

Junni, P., & Teerikangas, S. (2019, April 26). Mergers and acquisitions. *Oxford Research Encyclopedia of Business and Management*. Oxford University Press. Retrieved from https://oxfordre.com/business/view/10.1093/acrefore/9780190224851.001.0001/acrefore-9780190224851-e-15

Kamau, C. (2009). Strategising impression management in corporations: Cultural knowledge as capital. In D. Harorimana (Ed.), *Cultural implications of knowledge sharing, management and transfer: Identifying competitive advantage*. New York, NY: Information Science Reference, IGI Global, Chapter 4.

Kamau, C. (2013). What does being initiated severely into a group do? The role of rewards. *International Journal of Psychology, 8*(3), 399–406.

Kamau, C., & Oancea, C. (2020a). 15-point taxonomy of classifying acquisitions. In C. Oancea and C. Kamau (Eds.), *Organizational psychology of mergers and acquisitions*. Abingdon: Routledge.

Kamau, C., & Oancea, C. (2020b). Employee Emotireon Assessment Toolkit (EEAT). In C. Oancea and C. Kamau (Eds.), *Organizational psychology of mergers and acquisitions*. Abingdon: Routledge.

Kaplan, A. D. H. (1955). The current merger movement analyzed. *Harvard Business Review, 33*(3), 91–98.

Kaplan, S., & Weisbach, M. (1992). The success of acquisitions: Evidence from divestitures. *The Journal of Finance, 47*(1), 107–138.

Kavanagh, M. H., & Ashkanasy, N. M. (2006). The impact of leadership and change management strategy on organizational culture and individual acceptance of change during a merger. *British Journal of Management, 17*, S81–S103.

Keller, T., & Weibler, J. (2015). What it takes and costs to be an ambidextrous manager: Linking leadership and cognitive strain to balancing exploration and exploitation. *Journal of Leadership & Organizational Studies, 22*(1), 54–71.

Kelly, K. (2001, December 14). United defence industries is set to make debut in IPO market. *The Wall Street Journal.* Retrieved from www.wsj.com/articles/SB1008284423863543720

Keltner, D., & Haidt, J. (1999). Social functions of emotions at four levels of analysis. *Cognition & Emotion, 13*(5), 505–521.

Kernis, M. H., & Sun, C. R. (1994). Narcissism and reactions to interpersonal feedback. *Journal of Research in Personality, 28*, 4–13.

Kickert, W. (2012). How the UK government responded to the fiscal crisis: An outsider's view. *Public Money & Management, 32*(3), 169–176.

Kiessling, T., Harvey, M., & Moeller, M. (2012). Supply-chain corporate venturing through acquisition: Key management team retention. *Journal of World Business, 47*(1), 81–92.

Kim, B. R., Liss, A., Rao, M., Singer, Z., & Compton, R. J. (2012). Social deviance activates the brain's error-monitoring system. *Cognitive, Affective, & Behavioral Neuroscience, 12*(1), 65–73.

Kim, T., & Rhee, M. (2009). Exploration and exploitation: Internal variety and environmental dynamism. *Strategic Organization, 7*(1), 11–41.

King, M. W. L. (1912). The Canadian combines investigation act. *The ANNALS of the American Academy of Political and Social Science, 42*(1), 149–155.

Klendauer, R., & Deller, J. (2009). Organizational justice and managerial commitment in corporate mergers. *Journal of Managerial Psychology, 24*(1), 29–45.

Klucharev, V., Hytonen, K., Rijpkema, M., Smidts, A., & Fernandez, G. (2009). Reinforcement learning signal predicts social conformity. *Neuron, 61*(1), 140–151.

Koch, J. L., & Steers, R. M. (1976). *Job attachment, satisfaction and turnover among public employees.* Technical Report No. 6, Office of Naval Research, University of Oregon.

Kollewe, J. (2019). *Just Eat £9bn merger plan sends shares soaring.* Retrieved from www.theguardian.com/business/2019/jul/29/just-eat-merger-takeawaycom

Kotter, J. P. (1996). *Leading change.* Boston: Harvard Business School Press.

Kouzes, J. M., & Posner, B. Z. (2003). *Credibility: How leaders gain and lose it, why people demand it.* San Francisco, CA: John Wiley & Sons, Inc.

Kovacic, W. E., & Shapiro, C. (2000). Antitrust policy: A century of economic and legal thinking. *Journal of Economic Perspectives, 14*(1), 43–60.

Kovoor-Misra, S., & Smith, M. A. (2008). In the aftermath of an acquisition: Triggers and effects on perceived organizational identity. *The Journal of Applied Behavioral Science, 44*(4), 422–444.

Kovoor-Misra, S., & Smith, M. A. (2011). Artifacts, identification and support for change after an acquisition. *Leadership & Organization Development Journal, 32*(6), 584–604.

Koza, M. P., & Lewin, A. Y. (1998). The Co-evolution of strategic alliances. *Organization Science, 9*(3), 255–264.

Kramer, R. (1991). Intergroup relations and organizational dilemmas. The role of categorization processes. In B. Staw & L. Cummings (Eds.), *Research in organizational behavior* (Vol. 13, pp. 191–228). Greenwich, CT: JAI Press.

Krug, J. A., & Nigh, D. (2001). Executive perceptions in Foreign and domestic acquisitions: An analysis of foreign ownership and its effect on executive fate. *Journal of World Business, 36*(1), 85.

Kuhnert, K. W., & Lewis, P. (1987). Transactional and transformational leadership: A constructive/developmental analysis. *The Academy of Management Review, 12*(4), 648–657.

Kumar, V., & Sharma, P. (2019). *An insight into mergers and acquisitions.* Singapore: Palgrave Macmillan.

Kurman, J. (2001). Self-enhancement: Is it restricted to individualistic cultures? *Personality and Social Psychology Bulletin, 27*(12), 1705–1716.

Lambrecht, B. M. (2004). The timing and terms of mergers motivated by economies of scale. *Journal of Financial Economics, 72*(1), 41–62.

Lamoreaux, N. R. (1985). *The great merger movement in American business, 1985–1904.* Cambridge, UK: Cambridge University Press.

Langley, A., Golden-Biddle, K., Reay, T., Denis, J., Hébert, Y., Lamothe, L., & Gervais, J. (2012). Identity struggles in merging organizations: Renegotiating the sameness – difference dialectic. *Journal of Applied Behavioral Science, 48*(2), 135–167.

Latack, J. C. (1986). Coping with job stress: Measures and future directions for scale development. *Journal of Applied Psychology, 71,* 377–385.

Lavie, D., Kang, J., & Rosenkopf, L. (2011). Balance within and across domains: The performance implications of exploration and exploitation in alliances. *Organization Science, 22*(6), 1517–1538.

Lavie, D., & Rosenkopf, L. (2006). Balancing exploration and exploitation in alliance formation. *Academy of Management Journal, 49*(4), 797–818.

Lavie, D., Stettner, U., & Tushman, M. L. (2010). Exploration and exploitation within and across organizations. *The Academy of Management Annals, 4*(1), 109–155.

Lawlor, J. (2013). Employee perspectives on the post-integration stage of a micro-merger. *Personnel Review, 42*(6), 704–723.

Lazarus, R. S., Kanner, A. D., & Folkman, S. (1980). Emotions: A cognitive-phenomenological analysis. In R. Plutchik & H. Kellerman (Eds.), *Emotion: Theory, research, and experience: Vol. I. Theories of emotion* (pp. 189–217). New York, NY: Academic Press.

Lazer, D., & Friedman, A. (2007). The network structure of exploration and exploitation. *Administrative Science Quarterly, 52*(4), 667–694.

Le Mens, G., Hannan, M. T., & Pólos, L. (2015). Age-related structural inertia: A distance-based approach. *Organization Science, 26*(3), 756–773.

Leary, M. R., & Kowalski, R. M. (1990). Impression management: A literature review and two-component model. *Psychological Bulletin, 107*(1), 34–47.

Lebedev, S., Peng, M. W., Xie, E., & Stevens, C. E. (2015). Mergers and acquisitions in and out of emerging economies. *Journal of World Business, 50*(4), 651–662.

Lee, D., Kim, K., Kim, T. G., Kwon, S., & Cho, B. (2013). How and when organizational integration efforts matter in South Korea: A psychological process perspective on the post-merger integration. *International Journal of Human Resource Management, 24*(5), 944–965.

Lee, W. B., & Cooperman, E. S. (1989). Conglomerates in the 1980: A performance appraisal. *The Journal of the Financial Management Association, 18*(1), 45–54.

Lei, L., Liang, Y. X., & Krieger, G. R. (2004). Stress in expatriates. *Clinics in Occupational and Environmental Medicine, 4*, 221–229.

Leigh, T. W., & Summers, J. O. (2002). An initial evaluation of industrial buyers' impressions of salespersons' nonverbal cues. *Journal of Personal Selling & Sales Management, 22*(1), 41–53.

LePine, J. A., Colquitt, J. A., & Erez, A. (2000). Adaptability to changing task contexts: Effects of general cognitive ability, conscientiousness, and openness to experience. *Personnel Psychology, 53*, 563–593.

Levinson, H. (1976). *Psychological man*. Oxford: Levinson Inst.

Lewin, A. Y., Long, C. P., & Carroll, T. N. (1999). The coevolution of new organizational forms. *Organization Science, 10*(5), 535–550.

Lewis-Mikhael, A.-M., Bueno-Cavanillas, A., Ofir Giron, T., Olmedo-Requena, R., Delgado-Rodríguez, M., & Jiménez-Moleón, J. J. (2016). Occupational exposure to pesticides and prostate cancer: A systematic review and meta-analysis. *Occupational and Environmental Medicine, 73*(2), 134–144.

Li, J. J. (2008). How to retain local senior managers in international joint ventures: The effects of alliance relationship characteristics. *Journal of Business Research, 61*(9), 986–994.

Liddicoat, A. J. (2017). Interpretation and critical reflection in intercultural language learning: Consequences of a critical perspective for the teaching and learning of pragmatics. In M. Dasli & A. R. Diaz (Eds.), *The critical turn in language and intercultural communication pedagogy* (pp. 22–39). New York and London: Routledge.

Liden, R. C., & Graen, G. (1980). Generalizability of the vertical dyad linkage model of leadership. *Academy of Management Journal, 23*, 451–465.

Liden, R. C., Sparrowe, R. T., & Wayne, S. J. (1997). Leader-member exchange theory: The past and potential for the future. In G. R. Ferris (Ed.), *Research in personnel and human resources management* (pp. 47–119). Greenwich, CT: JAI.

Lin, L.-H. (2014). Exploration and exploitation in mergers and acquisitions: An empirical study of the electronics industry in Taiwan. *International Journal of Organizational Analysis, 22*(1), 30–47.

Linde, B., & Schalk, R. (2008). Influence of pre-merger employment relations and individual characteristics on the psychological contract. *South African Journal of Psychology, 38*(2), 305–320.

Lindquist, K. A., Satpute, A. B., Wager, T. D., Weber, J., & Feldman Barrett, L. (2016). The brain basis of positive and negative affect: Evidence from a meta-analysis of the human neuroimaging literature. *Cerebral Cortex, 26*, 1910–1922.

Lipponen, J., Olkkonen, M., & Moilanen, M. (2004). Perceived procedural justice and employee responses to an organizational merger. *European Journal of Work and Organizational Psychology, 13*(3), 391–413.

Lipsett, M., & Campleman, S. (1999). Occupational exposure to diesel exhaust and lung cancer: A meta-analysis. *American Journal of Public Health*, *89*(7), 1009–1017.

Livermore, S. (1935). The success of industrial mergers. *Quarterly Journal of Economics*, *50*(1), 68–96.

Lo, M.-C., Ramayah, T., Min, H. W., & Songan, P. (2010). The relationship between leadership styles and organizational commitment in Malaysia: Role of leader-member exchange. *Asia Pacific Business Review*, *16*(1/2), 79–103.

Lord, R. G., & Brown, D. J. (2004). *Leadership processes and follower self-identity*. Mahwah, NJ: Lawrence Erlbaum.

Lord, R. G., & Hall, R. J. (2005). Identity, deep structure and the development of leadership skill. *The Leadership Quarterly*, *16*(4), 591–615.

Lovallo, D., & Kahneman, D. (2003). Delusions of success. How optimism undermines executives' decisions. *Harvard Business Review*, *81*(7), 56–63, 117.

Lowe, K. B., Kroeck, K. G., & Sivasubramaniam, N. (1996). Effectiveness correlates of transformation and transactional leadership: A metaanalytic review of the MLQ literature. *Leadership Quarterly*, *7*, 385–425.

Lubatkin, M., Schweiger, D., & Weber, Y. (1999). Top management turnover in related M & A's: An additional test of the theory of relative standing. *Journal of Management*, *25*(1), 55–73.

Luhtanen, R., & Crocker, J. (1992). A collective self-esteem scale: Self-Evaluation of one's social identity. *Personality and Social Psychology Bulletin*, *18*(3), 302–318.

Lundbäck, M., & Hörte, S. (2005). Decision-making in conditions of constant change – a case within the automotive industry. *Management Decision*, *43*(2), 220–235.

Luo, B., Zheng, S., Ji, H., & Liang, L. (2018). Ambidextrous leadership and TMT-member ambidextrous behavior: The role of TMT behavioral integration and TMT risk propensity. *The International Journal of Human Resource Management*, *29*(2), 338–359.

Lupina-Wegener, A. A. (2013). Human resource integration in subsidiary mergers and acquisitions: Evidence from Poland. *Journal of Organizational Change Management*, *26*(2), 286–304.

Lupina-Wegener, A. A., Schneider, S. C., & van Dick, R. (2011). Different experiences of socio-cultural integration: A European merger in Mexico. *Journal of Organizational Change Management*, *24*(1), 65–89.

Lusyana, D., & Sherif, M. (2016). Do mergers create value for high-tech firms? The hounds of doctcom bubble. *The Journal of High Technology Management Research*, *27*(22), 196–213.

MacKenzie, S. B., Podsakoff, P. M., & Rich, G. A. (2001). Transformational and transactional leadership and salesperson performance. *Journal of the Academy of Marketing Science*, *29*(2), 115–134.

Mael, F. A., & Ashforth, B. E. (1995). Loyal from day one: Biodata, organizational identification, and turnover among newcomers. *Personnel Psychology*, *48*(2), 309–333.

Mael, F. A., Waldman, D. A., & Mulqueen, C. (2001). From scientific careers to organizational leadership: Predictors of the desire to enter management on the part of technical personnel. *Journal of Vocational Behavior*, *59*, 132–148.

Maguire, S., & Phillips, N. (2008). 'Citibankers' at Citigroup: A study of the loss of institutional trust after a merger. *Journal of Management Studies*, *45*(2), 372–401.

Mahony, D. M., & Klaas, B. S. (2008). The role of compensatory and retributive justice in determining damages in employment disputes. *Journal of Management, 34*(2), 218–243.

Mäkikangas, A., Feldt, T., & Kinnunen, U. (2007). Warr's scale of job-related affective well-being: A longitudinal examination of its structure and relationships with work characteristics, *Work & Stress, 21*(3), 197–219.

Makri, E., & Hantzi, A. (2012). Merger pattern, pre-merger organizational status, and the mediating role of individual-level variables in predicting post-merger turnover intentions. *Interdisciplinary Journal of Contemporary Research in Business, 4*(4), 165–190.

Makri, E., & Ntalianis, F. (2015). Post M&A ill-health: Main, moderating and mediating effects of job stressors and perceived organizational support. *Employee Relations, 37*(2), 176–191.

Makri, M., Hitt, M. A., & Lane, P. J. (2010). Complementary technologies, knowledge relatedness, and invention outcomes in high technology mergers and acquisitions. *Strategic Management Journal, 31*(6), 602–628.

Maksimovic, V., & Phillips, G. (2001). The market for corporate assets: Who engages in mergers and asset sales and are there efficiency gains? *The Journal of Finance, 56*, 2019–2065.

Mănescu, C. B., & Nuño, G. (2015). *Quantitative effects of the shale oil revolution.* Working Paper Series, European Central Bank, 1855.

Mann, T. (2017, January 19). GE Earnings: What to Watch; Shipment targets, update on merger with Baker Hughes will be focus when General Electric reports its earnings. *Wall Street Journal* (Online). Retrieved from https://www.wsj.com/articles/ge-earnings-what-to-watch-1484845602

Manne, H. G. (1965). Mergers and the market for corporate control. *Journal of Political Economy, 73*(2), 110.

March, J. G. (1991). Exploration and exploitation in organizational learning. *Organization Science, 2*(1), 71–87.

March, J. G. (1996). Continuity and change in theories of organizational action. *Administrative Science Quarterly, 41*(2), 278–287.

March, J. G. (2001). The pursuit of intelligence in organizations. In T. K. Lant & Z. Shapira (Eds.), *Organizational cognition: Computation and interpretation* (pp. 61–72). Mahwah, NJ: Lawrence Erlbaum Associates Publishers.

March, J. G. (2006). Rationality, foolishness, and adaptive intelligence. *Strategic Management Journal (John Wiley & Sons, Inc.), 27*(3), 201–214.

Marinova, S. V., Peng, C., Lorinkova, N., Van Dyne, L., & Chiaburu, D. (2015). Change-oriented behavior: A meta-analysis of individual and job design predictors. *Journal of Vocational Behavior, 88*, 104–120.

Marmenout, K. (2010). Employee sensemaking in mergers: How deal characteristics shape employee attitudes. *Journal of Applied Behavioral Science, 46*(3), 329–359.

Marshall, J. N., Pike, A., Pollard, J. S., Tomaney, J., Dawley, S., & Gray, J. (2012). Placing the run on northern rock. *Journal of Economic Geography, 12*(1), 157–181.

Martin, F., & Griffiths, H. (2014). Relating to the 'Other': Transformative, intercultural learning in post-colonial contexts. *Compare: A Journal of Comparative & International Education, 44*(6), 938–959.

Martinko, M. J., Harvey, P., & Douglas, S. C. (2007). The role, function, and contribution of attribution theory to leadership: A review. *Leadership Quarterly, 18*(6), 561–585.

Martynova, M., & Renneboog, L. (2008). A century of corporate takeovers: What have we learned and where do we stand? *Journal of Banking & Finance, 32,* 2148–2177.

Mason, R. H., & Goudzwaard, M. B. (1976). Performance of conglomerate firms: A portfolio approach. *The Journal of Finance, 31*(1), 39–48.

M&A Statistics Database (n.d. a). *Institute for mergers and acquisitions.* Retrieved from https://imaa-institute.org/m-and-a-by-industries/

M&A Statistics Database (n.d. b). *Institute for mergers and acquisitions.* Retrieved on January 25, 2016, from https://imaa-institute.org/resources/statistics-mergers-acquisitions/

Mathieu, J. E., & Zajac, D. M. (1990). A review and meta-analysis of the antecedents, correlates, and consequences of organizational commitment. *Psychological Bulletin, 108*(2), 171–194.

Matsumoto, D., Yoo, S. H., Hirayama, S., & Petrova, G. (2005). Development and validation of a measure of display rule knowledge: The display rule assessment inventory. *Emotion, 5,* 23–40.

Matsusaka, J. G. (1993). Takeover motives during the conglomerate merger wave. *RAND Journal of Economics (RAND Journal of Economics), 24*(3), 357–379.

Mattioli, D., Linebaugh, K., & Lublin, J. S. (2016, October 27). General electric in talks to buy baker hughes; Deal would be biggest in GE's history, extend its bet on the battered oil industry. *Wall Street Journal.* Retrieved from http://ezproxy.lib.bbk.ac.uk/docview/1832939101?accountid=8629

Mayer, D., Nishii, L., Schneider, B., & Goldstein, H. (2007). The precursors and products of justice climates: Group leader antecedents and employee attitudinal consequences. *Personnel Psychology, 60,* 929–963.

Mayfield, C., Perdue, G., & Wooten, K. (2008). Investment management and personality type. *Financial Services Review, 17*(3), 219–236.

McCrae, R. R., & Costa, Jr. P. T. (1994). The stability of personality: Observations and evaluations. *Current Directions in Psychological Science, 3*(6), 173–175.

McElroy, J. C., Morrow, P. C., & Rude, S. N. (2001). Turnover and organizational performance: A comparative analysis of the effects of voluntary, involuntary, and reduction-in-force turnover. *Journal of Applied Psychology, 86*(6), 1294–1299.

McEntire, M. H., & Bentley, J. C. (1996). When rivals become partners: Acculturation in a newly-merged organization. *International Journal of Organizational Analysis (1993–2002), 4*(2), 135.

McGarty, C. (1999). *Categorization in social psychology.* London, UK: Sage Publications.

McHugo, G. J., Lanzetta, J. T., Sullivan, D. G., Masters, R. D., & Englis, B. G. (1985). Emotional reactions to a political leader's expressive displays. *Journal of Personality and Social Psychology, 49,* 1512–1523.

Medisauskaite, A., & Kamau, C. (2019a). Does occupational distress raise the risk of alcohol use, binge eating, ill health and sleep problems among medical doctors? A UK cross-sectional study. *BMJ Open, 9,* e027362.

Medisauskaite, A., & Kamau, C. (2019b). Reducing burnout and anxiety among doctors: Randomized controlled trial. *Psychiatry Research, 474,* 383–390.

Mehlhorn, K., Newell, B. R., Todd, P. M., Lee, M. D., Morgan, K., Braithwaite, V. A., Hausmann, D., Fiedler, K., & Gonzalez, C. (2015, April 6). Unpacking the exploration – exploitation tradeoff: A synthesis of human and animal literatures. *Decision.* Advance online publication.

Meindl, J. R. (1990). On leadership: An alternative to the conventional wisdom. *Research in Organizational Behavior, 12,* 159.

Melnik, A., & Pollatschek, M. A. (1973). Debt capacity, diversification and conglomerate mergers. *Journal of Finance, 28*(5), 1263–1273.

Mercer, G. (2019, February 3). BF Goodrich warned about rubber health risks. *The Record.* Retrieved from www.therecord.com/news-story/9157594-bf-goodrich-warned-about-rubber-health-risks/

Meyer, C. B. (2006). Destructive dynamics of middle management intervention in postmerger processes. *Journal of Applied Behavioral Science, 42*(4), 397–419.

Meyer, D. (2019, March 14). Bayer has now lost over 44% of its value since its Monsanto merger. *Fortune.* Retrieved from https://fortune.com/2019/05/14/bayer-stock-monsanto-verdict/

Meyer, J. P., & Allen, N. J. (1991). A three-component conceptualization of organizational commitment. *Human Resource Management Review, 1*(1), 61.

Meyer, J. P., Stanley, D. J., Herscovitch, L., & Topolnytsky, L. (2002). Affective, continuance, and normative commitment to the organization: A meta-analysis of antecedents, correlates, and consequences. *Journal of Vocational Behavior, 61*(1), 20–52.

Michel, A., & Shaked, I. (1972). Does business diversification affect performance? *Financial Management, 13*(4), 18–25.

Michel, A., & Shaked, I. (1984). Does business diversification affect performance? *Financial Management,* 18–25.

Michela, J. L., & Vena, J. (2012). A dependence-regulation account of psychological distancing in response to major organizational change. *Journal of Change Management, 12*(1), 77–94.

Microsoft (2016, May 18). *Microsoft selling feature phone business to FIH Mobile Ltd. and HMD Global, Oy.* [Press release]. Retrieved from https://news.microsoft.com/2016/05/18/microsoft-selling-feature-phone-business-to-fih-mobile-ltd-and-hmd-global-oy/

Millwar, L., & Kyriakidou, O. (2004). Linking pre- and post-merger identities through the concept of career. *The Career Development International, 9*(1), 12–27.

Minbaeva, D. B., & Muratbekova-Touron, M. (2011). Experience of Canadian and Chinese acquisitions in Kazakhstan. *International Journal of Human Resource Management, 22*(14), 2946–2964.

Miner, J. B. (2005). *Organizational behavior 1.* Armonk, NY: M.E. Sharpe.

Mirc, N. (2012). Connecting the micro- and macro-level: Proposition of a research design to study post-acquisition synergies through a social network approach. *Scandinavian Journal of Management, 28*(2), 121–135.

Mohammed, S. (2008). 2007: A story of two halves. In Booz & Co (Ed.), *International mergers and acquisitions. Creating value in an increasingly complex corporate environment.* Birmingham, UK: Financier Worldwide.

Molodovsky, N. (1968). Corporate mergers and antitrust policy. *Financial Analysts Journal, 24*(2), 23–33.

Monin, P., Noorderhaven, N., Vaara, E., & Kroon, D. (2013). Giving sense to and making sense of justice in postmerger integration. *Academy of Management Journal, 56*(1), 256–284.

Morf, C. C., & Rhodewait, F. (2001). Unraveling the paradoxes of narcissism: A dynamic self-regulatory processing model. *Psychological Inquiry, 12,* 177–196.

Motley Fool Transcribers (2019, November 7). *Baker hughes, a GE company (BHGE) Q3 2019 earnings call transcript.* The Motley Fool. Retrieved from https://www. fool.com/earnings/call-transcripts/2019/11/07/baker-hughes-a-ge-company-bhge-q3-2019-earnings-ca.aspx

Mudambi, R., & Swift, T. (2011). Proactive R&D management and firm growth: A punctuated equilibrium model. *Research Policy, 40*(3), 429–440.

Muehlfeld, K., Sahib, P. R., & Van Witteloostuijn, A. (2012). A contextual theory of organizational learning from failures and successes: A study of acquisition completion in the global newspaper industry, 1981–2008. *Strategic Management Journal, 33*(8), 938–964.

Mumford, M. D., Zaccaro, S. J., Harding, F. D., Jacobs, T. O., & Fleishman, E. A. (2000). Leadership skills for a changing world: Solving complex social problems. *The Leadership Quarterly, 11*(1), 11–35.

Murphy, F. C., Nimmo-Smith, I., & Lawrence, A. D. (2003). Functional neuroanatomy of emotions: A meta-analysis. *Cognitive, Affective & Behavioral Neuroscience, 3*(3), 207–233. doi:10.3758/CABN.3.3.207

Murray, S. L., Derrick, J. L., Leder, S., & Holmes, J. G. (2008). Balancing connectedness and self-protection goals in close relationships: A levels-of-processing perspective on risk regulation. *Journal of Personality and Social Psychology, 94*(3), 429–459.

Murray, S. L., Holmes, J. G., & Collins, N. L. (2006). Optimizing assurance: The risk regulation system in relationships. *Psychological Bulletin, 132*(5), 641–666.

Nadolska, A., & Barkema, H. G. (2014). Good learners: How top management teams affect the success and frequency of acquisitions. *Strategic Management Journal, 35*(10), 1483–1507.

Nahrgang, J. D., Morgeson, F. P., & Ilies, R. (2009). The development of leader-member exchanges: Exploring how personality and performance influence leader and member relationships over time. *Organizational Behavior and Human Decision Processes, 108*, 256–266.

Nemanich, L. A., & Keller, R. T. (2007). Transformational leadership in an acquisition: A field study of employees. *The Leadership Quarterly, 18*(1), 49–68.

Nemanich, L. A., & Vera, D. (2009). Transformational leadership and ambidexterity in the context of an acquisition. *Leadership Quarterly, 20*(1), 19–33.

New York Stock Exchange (2018). *Alcoa Corporation NYSE Historical prices.* Retrieved from https://uk.finance.yahoo.com/quote/AA/history?period1 = 1527807600& period2 = 1535670000&interval=1d&filter=history&frequency=1d

Newell, A. (1990). *Unified theories of cognition.* Cambridge, MA: Harvard University Press.

Newton, L. (1988). Charting shark-infested waters: Ethical dimensions of the hostile takeover. *Journal of Business Ethics, 7*(1/2), 81–87.

Nikandrou, I., & Papalexandris, N. (2007). The impact of M&A experience on strategic HRM practices and organisational effectiveness: Evidence from Greek firms. *Human Resource Management Journal, 17*(2), 155–177.

Nikolaou, I., Vakola, M., & Bourantas, D. (2011). The role of silence on employees' attitudes "the day after" a merger. *Personnel Review, 40*(6), 723–741.

Niphadkar, C. (2017). The new age transformational leader: Richard Branson. *International Journal of Scientific & Engineering Research, 8*(6), 542–547.

Northouse, P. G. (1997). *Leadership: Theory and practice.* Thousand Oaks, CA: Sage.

Oancea, C., & Kamau, C. (2015). CEO overconfidence in mergers and acquisitions: A revision of the conceptual framework. In D. Tipuric, I. Vrdoljak & M. Darabos

(Eds.), *Dynamics of organizational change: Beyond identity and reputation*. Harlow, UK: Pearson Education.

Oancea, C., & Neundlinger, K. (2017). *Negotiation of social standing in merged organizations: A perspective on intergroup dialectics and collective acting*. Paper presented at the 8th International Symposium on Process Organization Studies.

O'Brien, A. P. (1988). Factory size, economies of scale and the great merger wave of 1898–1902. *Journal of Economic History, 48*(3), 639–649.

Office of Response and Restoration (2013, March 27). *Alcoa aluminum factories settle $19.4 million for pollution of St. Lawrence river watershed, most will fund restoration of tribal culture, recreational fishing, and habitat*. Retrieved from https://response.restoration.noaa.gov/about/media/alcoa-aluminum-factories-settle-194-million-pollution-st-lawrence-river-watershed-most-w

O'Reilly III, C. A., & Tushman, M. L. (2013). Organizational ambidexterity: Past, present, and future. *Academy of Management Perspectives, 27*(4), 324–338.

Organ, D. W., & Ryan, K. (1995). A meta-analytic review of attitudinal and dispositional predictors of organizational citizenship behavior. *Personnel Psychology, 48*(4), 775–802.

Panchal, S., & Cartwright, S. (2001). Group differences in post-merger stress. *Journal of Managerial Psychology, 16*(5/6), 424.

Papadakis, V. M. (2005). The role of broader context and the communication program in merger and acquisition implementation success. *Management Decision, 43*(2), 236–255.

Pasztor, A. (1997, August 27). Carlyle beats general dynamics in bidding for united defense. *The Wall Street Journal*. Retrieved from www.wsj.com/articles/SB872599088507278500

Patel, D. (2011). Occupational travel. *Occupational Medicine, 61*(1), 6–18.

Patel, V. L., & Groen, G. J. (1991). The general and specific nature of medical expertise: A critical look. In K. A. Ericsson & J. Smith (Eds.), *Toward a general theory of expertise: Prospects and limits* (pp. 93–125). New York, NY: Cambridge University Press.

Paulhus, D. L., & Williams, K. M. (2002). The Dark Triad of personality: Narcissism, Machiavellianism, and psychopathy. *Journal of Research in Personality, 36*(6), 556.

Peck, E., Towell, D., & Gulliver, P. (2001). The meanings of 'culture' in health and social care: A case study of the combined Trust in Somerset. *Journal of Interprofessional Care, 15*(4), 319–327.

Peel, M. J. (1995). The impact of corporate restructuring: Mergers, divestments and MBOs. *Long Range Planning, 28*(2), 92–101.

Peltokorpi, V. (2006). Japanese organizational behaviour in Nordic subsidiaries: A Nordic expatriate perspective. *Employee Relations, 28*(2), 103–118.

Pennebaker, J. W. (Ed.). (1995). *Emotion, disclosure, & health*. Washington, DC: American Psychological Association.

Pettigrew, T. F. (1979). Foreword. In G. W. Allport (Ed.), *The nature of prejudice*. Reading, MA: Addison-Wesley.

Phelps, C. C. (2010). A longitudinal study of the influence of alliance network structure and composition on firm exploratory innovation. *Academy of Management Journal, 53*(4), 890–913.

Phene, A., Tallman, S., & Almeida, P. (2012). When do acquisitions facilitate technological exploration and exploitation? *Journal of Management, 38*(3), 753–783.

Piekkari, R., Vaara, E., Tienari, J., & Säntti, R. (2005). Integration or disintegration? Human resource implications of a common corporate language decision in a cross-border merger. *The International Journal of Human Resource Management, 16*(3), 330–344.

Platt, E., & Crooks, E. (2018a, June 26). GE break up intensifies with large-scale spinoffs. *Financial Times.* Retrieved from ft.com/content/69d5f832-7928-11e8-bc55-50daf11b720d

Platt, E., & Crooks, E. (2018b, June 27). GE takes stride towards break-up by spinning off two of largest units. *Financial Times.* Retrieved from http://ezproxy.lib.bbk.ac.uk/docview/2077266671?accountid=8629

Porrini, P. (2004). Can a previous alliance between an acquirer and a target affect acquisition performance? *Journal of Management, 30*(4), 545–562.

Porter, L. W., Steers, R. M., Mowday, R. T., & Boulian, P. V. (1974). Organizational commitment, job satisfaction, and turnover among psychiatric technicians. *Journal of Applied Psychology, 59*(5), 603–609.

Posner, J., Russell, J. A., & Peterson, B. S. (2005). The circumplex model of affect: An integrative approach to affective neuroscience, cognitive development, and psychopathology. *Development and Psychopathology, 17*(3), 715–734.

Povtak, T. (2012, April 12). *Appeals court: Pfizer liable for asbestos claims against Quigley corp.* Retrieved from www.asbestos.com/news/2012/04/12/pfizer-liable-for-quigley-asbestos/

Povtak, T. (2013, July 16). *Asbestos mining in Russia still fuels the economy in some cities.* Retrieved from www.asbestos.com/news/2013/07/16/asbestos-mining-russia-fuels-economy/

Prabhu, J. C., Chandy, R. K., & Ellis, M. E. (2005). The impact of acquisitions on innovation: Poison pill, placebo, or tonic? *Journal of Marketing, 69*(1), 114–130.

Pratto, F., Sidanius, J., Stallworth, L. M., & Malle, B. F. (1994). Social dominance orientation: A personality variable predicting social and political attitudes. *Journal of Personality and Social Psychology, 67*(4), 741–763.

Press Association (2015, September 8). *Paddy power and Betfair merger agreed.* Retrieved from www.theguardian.com/business/2015/sep/08/paddy-power-and-betfair-merger-agreed

Quah, P., & Young, S. (2005). Post-acquisition management: A phases approach for crossborder M&As. *European Management Journal, 23*(1), 65–75.

Rachman, S. (2010). Betrayal: A psychological analysis. *Behaviour Research and Therapy, 48*(4), 304–311.

Rafferty, A. E., & Restubog, S. D. (2010). The impact of change process and context on change reactions and turnover during a merger. *Journal of Management, 36*(5), 1309–1338.

Randall, J., & Procter, S. (2013). When institutional logics collide: Reinforcing dominance in a merged government department. *Journal of Change Management, 13*(2), 143–158.

Ravenscraft, D., & Scherer, F. (1987). *Mergers, sell-offs, and economic efficiency.* Washington, DC: Brookings Institution Press.

Ray, S. L., & McGee, D. (2006). Psychiatric nurses' perspectives of spirituality and spiritual needs during an amalgamation. *Journal of Psychiatric and Mental Health Nursing, 13*(3), 330–336.

Resick, C. J., Whitman, D. S., Weingarden, S. M., & Hiller, N. J. (2009). The bright-side and the dark-side of CEO personality: Examining core self-evaluations, narcissism, transformational leadership, and strategic influence. *The Journal of Applied Psychology, 94*(6), 1365–1381.

Reuters (2015, December 9). *Dow Chemical and DuPont in talks for $120bn merger.* Retrievedfromwww.theguardian.com/business/2015/dec/09/dow-chemical-dupont-chemical-giant-merger

Richardson, J., & McKenna, S. (2006). Exploring relationships with home and host countries: A study of self-directed expatriates. *Cross Cultural Management, 13*(1), 6–22.

Richmond, K. A. (2001). *Ethical reasoning, machiavellian behavior, and gender: The impact on accounting students' ethical decision making.* Doctoral dissertation, Virginia Polytechnic Institute and State University, Blacksburg, United States. Retrieved from https://vtechworks.lib.vt.edu/bitstream/handle/10919/27235/richmond.pdf.prn.pdf?sequence=1&isAllowed=y

Richmond, V. P., McCroskey, C. J., & Johnson, A. D. (2003). Development of the Nonverbal Immediacy Scale (NIS): Measures of self- and other-perceived nonverbal immediacy. *Communication Quarterly, 51*, 504–517.

Rivas, T. (2018, November 13). General electric stock rises on baker hughes news. Is it a "Fire Sale"? *Barron's.* Retrieved from https://www.barrons.com/articles/general-electric-stock-rises-on-baker-hughes-news-is-it-a-fire-sale-1542126212

Roll, R. (1986). The hubris hypothesis of corporate takeovers. *The Journal of Business, 59*(2), 197–216.

Röller, L. H., Stennek, J., & Verboven, F. (2006). Efficiency gains from mergers. In F. Ilzkovitz & R. Meiklejohn (Eds.), *European merger control: Do we need an efficiency defence?* (pp. 84–201). Cornwall, UK: Edward Elgar Publishing.

Rosenfeld, P., Giacalone, R. A., & Riordan, C. A. (1995). *Impression management in organizations: Theory, measurement, practice.* London: Routledge.

Rosenthal, S. A., & Pittinsky, T. L. (2006). Narcissistic leadership. *The Leadership Quarterly, 17*(6), 617–633.

Rothaermel, F. T. (2001). Incumbent's Advantage through exploiting complementary assets via interfirm cooperation. *Strategic Management Journal (John Wiley & Sons, Inc.), 22*(6/7), 687.

Rothaermel, F. T., & Deeds, D. L. (2004). Exploration and exploitation alliances in biotechnology: A system of new product development. *Strategic Management Journal (John Wiley & Sons, Inc.), 25*(3), 201–221.

Roundy, P. T. (2010). Gaining legitimacy by telling stories: The power of narratives in legitimizing mergers and acquisitions. *Journal of Organizational Culture, Communication and Conflict, 14*(1), 89–105.

Rousseau, D. (1998). The "Problem" of the psychological contract considered. *Journal of Organizational Behavior, 19*, 665–671. Retrieved from www.jstor.org/stable/3100282

Rowold, J. (2005). *Multifactor leadership questionnaire.* Redwood City, CA: Mind Garden.

Rowold, J., & Laukamp, L. (2009). Charismatic leadership and objective performance indicators. *Applied Psychology: An International Review, 58*(4), 602–621.

Rubenstein, A. L., Eberly, M. B., Lee, T. W., & Mitchell, T. R. (2017). Surveying the forest: A meta-analysis, moderator investigation, and future-oriented discussion of the antecedents of voluntary employee turnover. *Personnel Psychology, 71*, 23–65.

Russell, J.A. (1980). A circumplex model of affect. *Journal of Personality and Social Psychology, 39*(6), 1161–1178.

Russell, J. A. (1991). Culture and the categorization of emotions. *Psychological Bulletin, 110*(3), 426–450.

Russell, J. A. (2003). Core affect and the psychological construction of emotion. *Psychological Review, 110*(1), 145–172.

Russell, J. A., & Barrett, L. F. (1999). Core affect, prototypical emotional episodes, and other things called emotion: Dissecting the elephant. *Journal of Personality and Social Psychology, 76*(5), 805–819.

Sabidussi, A., Lokshin, B., & Duysters, G. (2018). Complementarity in alliance portfolios and firm innovation. *Industry & Innovation, 25*(7), 633–654.

Sachs, J. (1982). Stabilization policies in the world economy: Scope and skepticism. *American Economic Review, 72*(2), 56–61.

Saemundsson, R. J., & Candi, M. (2014). Antecedents of innovation strategies in new technology-based firms: Interactions between the environment and founder team composition. *Journal of Product Innovation Management, 31*(5), 939–955.

Sarala, R. M. (2010). The impact of cultural differences and acculturation factors on post-acquisition conflict. *Scandinavian Journal of Management, 26*(1), 38–56.

Schawbel, D. (2014, September 23). Richard Branson's three most important leadership principles. *Forbes.* Retrieved from forbes.com/sites/danschawbel/2014/09/23/richard-branson-his-3-most-important-leadership-principles/#44b9433d5098

Schoenberg, R. (2006). Measuring the performance of corporate acquisitions: An empirical comparison of alternative metrics. *British Journal of Management, 17*(4), 361–370.

Schweiger, D. M., & Denisi, A. S. (1991). Communication with employees following a merger: A longitudinal field experiment. *Academy of Management Journal, 34*(1), 110–135.

Schweiger, D. M., Ivancevich, J. M., & Power, F. R. (1987). Executive actions for managing human resources before and after acquisition. *Academy of Management Executive (08963789), 1*(2), 127–138.

Schweizer, L., & Patzelt, H. (2012). Employee commitment in the post-acquisition integration process: The effect of integration speed and leadership. *Scandinavian Journal of Management, 28*(4), 298–310.

Searle, R. H., & Ball, K. S. (2004). The development of trust and distrust in a merger. *Journal of Managerial Psychology, 19*(7), 708–721.

Segerstrom, S. C., & Miller, G. E. (2004). Psychological stress and the human immune system: A meta-analytic study of 30 years of inquiry. *Psychological Bulletin, 130*(4), 601–630.

Selye, H. (1936). A syndrome produced by diverse nocuous agents. *Nature, 138,* 32.

Shackman, A. J., Salomons, T. V., Slagter, H. A., Fox, A. S., Winter, J. J., & Davidson, R. J. (2011). The integration of negative affect, pain and cognitive control in the cingulate cortex. *Nature Reviews Neuroscience, 12,* 154–167.

Shamir, B., House, R. J., & Arthur, M. B. (1993). The motivational effects of charismatic leadership: A self-concept based theory. *Organization Science, 4*(4), 577–594.

Shearer, C. S., Hames, D. S., & Runge, J. B. (2001). How CEOs influence organizational culture following acquisitions. *Leadership & Organization Development Journal, 22*(3), 105–113.

Sherman, S. J., Hamilton, D. L., & Lewis, A. C. (1999). Perceived entitativity and the social identity value of group memberships. In D. Abrams & M. A. Hogg (Eds.), *Social identity and social cognition* (pp. 80–110). Malden: Blackwell Publishing.

Shimei, Y., & Yaodong, Z. (2013). Impact of psychological contract violation on interpersonal trust during mergers and acquisitions. *Social Behavior & Personality: An International Journal, 41*(3), 487–495.

Sidanius, J., & Pratto, F. (1999). *Social dominance: An intergroup theory of social hierarchy and oppression.* New York, NY: Cambridge University Press.

Sidhu, J. S., Commandeur, H. R., & Volberda, H. W. (2007). The multifaceted nature of exploration and exploitation: Value of supply, demand, and spatial search for innovation. *Organization Science, 18*(1), 20–38.

Siegel, P. H. (2000). Using peer mentors during periods of uncertainty. *Leadership & Organization Development Journal, 21*(5), 243–253.

Singh, S. (2012). Investor irrationality and self-defeating behaviour: Insights from behavioral finance. *Journal of Global Business Management, 8*(1), 116–122.

Sitkin, S. B., & Pablo, A. (2004). Leadership and the M&A process. In A. L. Pablo & M. Javidan (Eds.), *Mergers and acquisitions: Creating integrative knowledge* (pp. 181–191). Malden, MA: Blackwell Publishing Ltd.

Sitkin, S. B., & Pablo, A. (2005). The neglected importance of leadership in mergers and acquisitions. In G. K. Stahl & M. E. Mendenhall (Eds.), *Mergers and acquisitions: Managing culture and human resources* (pp. 412–422). Stanford, CA: Stanford University Press.

Smith, C. A., & Ellsworth, P. C. (1985). Patterns of cognitive appraisal in emotion. *Journal of Personality and Social Psychology, 48*(4), 813–838.

Smith, E. R. (1996). What do connectionism and social psychology offer each other? *Journal of Personality and Social Psychology, 70*(5), 893–912.

Smith, E. R., & DeCoster, J. (1998). Knowledge acquisition, accessibility, and use in person perception and stereotyping: Simulation with a recurrent connectionist network. *Journal of Personality and Social Psychology, 74*(1), 21–35.

Smith, E. R., & DeCoster, J. (2000). Dual-process models in social and cognitive psychology: Conceptual integration and links to underlying memory systems. *Personality and Social Psychology Review, 4*(2), 108–131.

Smith, P., da Cunha, J. V., Giangreco, A., Vasilaki, A., & Carugati, A. (2013). The threat of dis-identification for HR practices: An ethnographic study of a merger. *European Management Journal, 31*(3), 308–321.

Solís-Molina, M., Hernández-Espallardo, M., & Rodríguez-Orejuela, A. (2018). Performance implications of organizational ambidexterity versus specialization in exploitation or exploration: The role of absorptive capacity. *Journal of Business Research, 91*, 181–194.

Solomon, S., Greenberg, J., & Pyszczynski, T. (1991). A terror management theory of social behavior: The psychological functions of self-esteem and cultural worldviews. *Advances in Experimental Social Psychology, 24*(C), 93–159.

Sørensen, J. B. (2002). The strength of corporate culture and the reliability of firm performance. *Administrative Science Quarterly, 47*(1), 70–91.

Spencer, J. (2018, January 29). GE Discount weighs on baker hughes. *Wall Street Journal.* Retrieved from http://ezproxy.lib.bbk.ac.uk/docview/1991890746?accountid=8629

Spicer, D. P. (2011). Changing culture: A case study of a merger using cognitive mapping. *Journal of Change Management, 11*(2), 245–264.

Spong, A., & Kamau, C. (2012). Cross-cultural impression management: A cultural knowledge audit model. *Journal of International Education in Business, 5*(1), 22–36.

Srivastava, R. K., Shervani, T. A., & Fahey, L. (1988). Market-based assets and share-holder value: A framework for analysis. *Journal of Marketing, 62*, 2–18.

Stahl, G. K., Chua, C. H., & Pablo, A. L. (2012). Does national context affect target firm employees' trust in acquisitions? *Management International Review (MIR), 52*(3), 395–423.

Stanbury, W. T. (1976). Penalties and remedies under the Combines Investigation Act 1889–1976. *Osgoode Hall Law Journal, 14*(3), 571–631.

Steers, R. M. (1975). Problems in the measurement of organizational effectiveness. *Administrative Science Quarterly, 20*(4), 546–568.

Steers, R. M. (1977). Antecedents and outcomes of organizational commitment. *Administrative Science Quarterly, 22*(1), 46–56.

Stewart-Brown, S. (1998). Emotional wellbeing and its relation to health. *BMJ, 317*(7173), 1608–1609.

Stiebale, J., & Reize, F. (2011). The impact of FDI through mergers and acquisitions on innovation in target firms. *International Journal of Industrial Organization, 29*(2), 155–167.

Stigler, G. J. (1950). Monopoly and oligopoly by merger. *American Economic Review, 40*(2), 23–34.

Stiglitz, J. E., Orszag, J. M., & Orszag, P. R. (2002). The impact of asbestos liabilities on workers in bankrupt firms. *American Insurance Association.* Retrieved from https://www.instituteforlegalreform.com/hooks/1/get_ilr_doc.php?fn=StiglitzReport.pdf

Stogdill, R. M. (1948). Personal factors associated with leadership: A survey of the literature. *Journal of Psychology, 25*, 35–71.

Stovel, K., & Savage, M. (2006). Mergers and mobility: Organizational growth and the origins of career migration at lloyds bank. *American Journal of Sociology, 111*(4).

Strand, T. (2019). *Quigley company history of asbestos use.* Retrieved from www.mesothelioma.com/asbestos-exposure/companies/quigley-company/

Styhre, A., Börjesson, S., & Wickenberg, J. (2006). Managed by the other: Cultural anxieties in two Anglo-Americanized Swedish firms. *International Journal of Human Resource Management, 17*(7), 1293–1306.

Sutton, S. K., & Davidson, R. J. (1997). Prefrontal brain asymmetry: A biological substrate of the behavioral approach and the behavioral inhibition systems. *Psychological Science, 8*, 204–210.

Tajfel, H. (1970). Experiments in intergroup discrimination. *Scientific American, 223*(5), 96–102.

Tajfel, H., Billig, M. G., Bundy, R. P., & Flament, C. (1971). Social categorization and intergroup behaviour. *European Journal of Social Psychology, 1*(2), 149–178.

Tajfel, H., & Turner, J. C. (1979). An integrative theory of intergroup conflict. In W. G. Austin, & S. Worchel (Eds.). *The social psychology of intergroup relations* (pp. 33–47). Monterey, CA: Brooks/Cole.

Teece, D. J., Pisano, G., & Shuen, A. (1997). Dynamic capabilities and strategic management. *Strategic Management Journal, 18*, 509–533.

Teerikangas, S. (2012). Dynamics of acquired firm pre-acquisition employee reactions. *Journal of Management, 38*(2), 599–639.

Templer, K. J. (2012). Five-Factor model of personality and job satisfaction: The importance of agreeableness in a tight and collectivistic Asian society. *Applied Psychology: An International Review, 61*(1), 114–129.

Teram, E. (2010). Organizational change within morally ambiguous contexts: A case study of conflicting postmerger discourses. *Journal of Applied Behavioral Science, 46*(1), 38–54.

Terry, D. J., & Callan, V. J. (1998). In-group bias in response to an organizational merger. *Group Dynamics: Theory, Research, and Practice, 2*(2), 67–81.

Terry, D. J., Callan, V. J., & Sartori, G. (1996). Employee adjustment to an organizational merger: Stress, coping and intergroup differences. *Stress Medicine, 12*(2), 105–122.

Terry, D. J., Carey, C. J., & Callan, V. J. (2001). Employee adjustment to an organizational merger: An intergroup perspective. *Personality and Social Psychology Bulletin, 27*(3), 267–280.

Tett, R. P., & Meyer, J. P. (1993). Job satisfaction, organizational commitment, turnover intention, and turnover: Path analyses based on meta-analytic findings. *Personnel Psychology, 46*(2), 259–293.

TheStreet (2016, November 11). *General electric and baker hughes 'Disruptive' partnership deal looks good.* Retrieved from www.thestreet.com/markets/mergers-and-acquisitions/general-electric-and-baker-hughes-disruptive-partnership-deal-looks-good-13890134

Thomson Reuters (2015). *Mergers and acquisitions review, full year 2014.* Retrieved January 30, 2016, from http://dmi.thomsonreuters.com/Content/Files/4Q2014_Global_MandA_Financial_Advisory_Review.pdf

Tienari, J., Søderberg, A., Holgersson, C., & Vaara, E. (2005). Gender and national identity constructions in the cross-border merger context. *Gender, Work & Organization, 12*(3), 217–241.

Tierney, P., Farmer, S. M., & Graen, G. B. (1999). An examination of leadership and employee creativity: The relevance of traits and relationships. *Personnel Psychology, 52*(3), 591–620.

Top Class Actions (2018, July 23). *Reynolds metals faces woman's lung cancer asbestos lawsuit.* Retrieved from https://topclassactions.com/lawsuit-settlements/lawsuit-news/850671-reynolds-metals-faces-womans-lung-cancer-asbestos-lawsuit/

Treanor, J. (2015, March 25). *Kraft and Heinz to merge after $40bn deal with 3G.* Retrieved from www.theguardian.com/business/2015/mar/25/kraft-40bn-offer-3g-capital

Triandis, H. C., & Gelfand, M. (1998). Converging measurement of horizontal and vertical individualism and collectivism. *Journal of Personality and Social Psychology, 74*, 118–128.

TUPE Regulations (2006). *The transfer of undertakings (Protection of Employment) regulations 2006.* Retrieved from www.legislation.gov.uk/uksi/2006/246/contents/made

Turner, J. C., Hogg, M. A., Oakes, P. J., Reicher, S. D., & Wetherell, M. S. (1987). *Rediscovering the social group: A self-categorization theory.* Cambridge, MA: Basil Blackwell.

Tushman, M. L., & O'Reilly, III C. A. (1996). Ambidextrous organizations: Managing evolutionary and revlutionary change. *California Management Review, 38*(4), 8–30.

Tushman, M. L., & O'Reilly, C. A. (1997). Ambidextrous organizations: Managing evolutionary and revolutionary change. *Quality Control and Applied Statistics, 42*, 215–218.

Tyler, T. R. (1999). Why people cooperate with organizations: An identity-based perspective. In R. I. Sutton & B. M. Staw (Eds.), *Research in organizational behavior* (Vol. 21, pp. 201–246).

Uddin, M., & Boateng, A. (2014). *Cross-border mergers and acquisitions: UK dimensions*. New York, NY: Routledge.

Uhlenbruck, K., & De Castro, J. O. (2000). Foreign acquisitions in central and eastern Europe: Outcomes of privatization in transitional economies. *Academy of Management Journal, 43*(3), 381–402.

Ullmann, S. H., Goldman, N., & Massey, D. S. (2011). Healthier before they migrate, less healthy when they return? The health of returned migrants in Mexico. *Social Science and Medicine, 73*(3), 421–428.

Ullrich, J., Wieseke, J., & Van Dick, R. (2005). Continuity and change in mergers and acquisitions: A social identity case study of a German industrial merger. *Journal of Management Studies, 42*(8), 1549–1569.

Unite Union (2019, March 28). *Pilots and cabin crew launch court action against airlines in toxic air dispute*. Retrieved from https://unitetheunion.org/news-events/news/2019/march/pilots-and-cabin-crew-launch-court-action-against-airlines-in-toxic-air-dispute/

United Defense Industries (2004, April 26). *Carlyle group sells 4.5 million united defence shares*. [Press release]. Retrieved from www.businesswire.com/news/home/20040426006067/en/Carlyle-Group-Sells-4.5-Million-United-Defense

United States Federal Trade Commission (1984). *Federal trade commission decisions. Findings, opinions and orders*. Washington, DC: US Government Printing Office.

US Department of Justice (2000, May 3). *Justice department requires significant in Alcoa/Reynolds Aluminium merger*. Retrieved from www.justice.gov/archive/atr/public/press_releases/2000/4666.htm

Väänänen, A., Ahola, K., Koskinen, A., Pahkin, K., & Kouvonen, A. (2011). Organisational merger and psychiatric morbidity: A prospective study in a changing work organization. *Journal of Epidemiology and Community Health, 65*(8), 682–687.

Väänänen, A., Pahkin, K., Kalimo, R., & Buunk, B. P. (2004). Maintenance of subjective health during a merger: The role of experienced change and pre-merger social support at work in white- and blue-collar workers. *Social Science & Medicine, 58*(10), 1903.

Vaara, E. (2000). Constructions of cultural differences in post-merger change processes: A sensemaking perspective on Finnish-Swedish cases. *M@N@Gement, 3*(3), 81–110.

Vaara, E. (2001). Role-bound actors in corporate combinations: A socio-political perspective on post-merger change processes. *Scandinavian Journal of Management, 17*, 481–509.

Vaara, E. (2002). On the discursive construction of success/failure in narratives of post-merger integration. *Organization Studies, 23*(2), 211–248.

Vaara, E., Junni, P., Sarala, R. M., Ehrnrooth, M., & Koveshnikov, A. (2014). Attributional tendencies in cultural explanations of M&A performance. *Strategic Management Journal, 35*(9), 1302–1317.

Vaara, E., Sarala, R., Stahl, G. K., & Björkman, I. (2012). The impact of organizational and national cultural differences on social conflict and knowledge transfer in international acquisitions. *Journal of Management Studies, 49*(1), 1–27.

Vaara, E., & Tienari, J. (2011). On the narrative construction of multinational corporations: An antenarrative analysis of legitimation and resistance in a cross-border merger. *Organization Science, 22*(2), 370–390.

Vaara, E., Tienari, J., & Laurila, J. (2006). Pulp and paper fiction: On the discursive legitimation of global industrial restructuring. *Organization Studies, 27*(6), 789–810.

Vaara, E., Tienari, J., Piekkari, R., & Säntti, R. (2005). Language and the circuits of power in a merging multinational corporation. *Journal of Management Studies, 42*(3), 595–623.

Vaara, E., Tienari, J., & Säntti, R. (2003). The international match: Metaphors as vehicles of social identity-building in cross-border mergers. *Human Relations, 56*(4), 419–451.

Valliere, D., & Peterson, R. (2004). Inflating the bubble: Examining dot-com investor behaviour. *Venture Capital, 6*(1), 1–22.

van der Schalk, J., Fischer, A., Doosje, B., Wigboldus, D., Hawk, S., Rotteveel, M., & Hess, U. (2011). Convergent and divergent responses to emotional displays of ingroup and outgroup. *Emotion, 11*(2), 286–298.

van Dick, R., Wagner, U., & Lemmer, G. (2004). Research note: The winds of change – Multiple identifications in the case of organizational mergers. *European Journal of Work & Organizational Psychology, 13*(2), 121–138.

van Dijk, R., & van Dick, R. (2009). Navigating organizational change: Change leaders, employee resistance and work-based identities. *Journal of Change Management, 9*(2), 143–163.

van Knippenberg, D., van Knippenberg, B., Monden, L., & de Lima, F. (2002). Organizational identification after a merger: A social identity perspective. *The British Journal of Social Psychology, 41*(Pt 2), 233–252.

van Leeuwen, E., van Knippenberg, D., & Ellemers, N. (2003). Continuing and changing group identities: The effects of merging on social identification and ingroup bias. *Personality and Social Psychology Bulletin, 29*(6), 679–690.

Van Maele-Fabry, G., & Willems, J. L. (2003). Occupation related pesticide exposure and cancer of the prostate: A meta-analysis. *Occupational and Environmental Medicine, 60*(9), 634–642.

van Oudenhoven, J. P., & de Boer, T. (1995). Complementarity and similarity of partners in international mergers. *Basic & Applied Social Psychology, 17*(3), 343–356.

van Vuuren, M., Beelen, P., & de Jong, M. T. (2010). Speaking of dominance, status difference, and identification: Making sense of a merger. *Journal of Occupational and Organizational Psychology, 83*(3), 627–643.

Vancea, M. (2013). Mergers and acquisition waves from the European Union perspective. *Annals of the University of Oradea, Economic Science Series, 22*(2), 272–283.

Vasilaki, A. (2011). The relationship between transformational leadership and post-acquisition performance. *International Studies of Management & Organization, 41*(3), 42–58.

Vaughan, G. M., Tajfel, H., & Williams, J. (1981). Bias in reward allocation in an intergroup and an interpersonal context. *Social Psychology Quarterly, 44*(1), 37–42.

Vilela, B. B., González, J. A. V., Ferrín, P. F., & del Río Araújo, M. L. (2007). Impression management tactics and affective context: Influence on sales performance appraisal. *European Journal of Marketing, 41*(5–6), 624–639.

Voss, G. B., Sirdeshmukh, D., & Voss, Z. G. (2008). The effects of slack resources and environmental threat on product exploration and exploitation. *Academy of Management Journal, 51*(1), 147–164.

Vul, E., Harris, C., Winkielman, P., & Pashler, H. (2009). Puzzlingly high correlations in fMRI studies of emotion, personality, and social cognition. *Perspectives on Psychological Science, 4*, 274–290.

Waldman, D. A., Bass, B. M., & Yammarino, F. J. (1988). *Adding to leader-follower transactions: The augmenting effect of charismatic leadership.* ONR Technical Report No. 3, Binghampton University, Center for Leadership Studies, Binghamptom, NY.

Walsh, J. P. (1988). Top management turnover following mergers and acquisitions. *Strategic Management Journal, 9*(2), 173–183.

Walsh, J. P. (1989). Doing a deal: Merger and acquisition: Negotiations and their impact upon target company top management turnover. *Strategic Management Journal (John Wiley & Sons, Inc.), 10*(4), 307–322.

Walsh, J. P., & Kosnik, R. D. (1993). Corporate raiders and their disciplinary role in the market for corporate control. *Academy of Management Journal, 36*(4), 671–700.

Walumbwa, F. O., Morrison, E. W., & Christensen, A. L. (2012). Ethical leadership and group in-role performance: The mediating roles of group conscientiousness and group voice. *The Leadership Quarterly, 23*(5), 953–964.

Walumbwa, F. O., & Schaubroeck, J. (2009). Leader personality traits and employee voice behavior: Mediating roles of ethical leadership and work group psychological safety. *Journal of Applied Psychology, 94*(5), 1275–1286.

Wang, Z. (2007). Technological innovation and market turbulence: The dot-com experience. *Review of Economic Dynamics, 10*(1), 78–105.

Ward, A. (2017, July 3). Baker Hughes looks to GE's edge in big data. *Financial Times.* Retrieved from https://www.ft.com/content/134c1d8a-6000-11e7-8814-0ac7eb84e5f1

Warr, P., Bindl, U. K., Parker, S. K., & Inceoglu, I. (2013). Four-quadrant investigation of job-related affects and behaviours. *European Journal of Work and Organizational Psychology, 23*(3), 342–363.

Waterson, J. (2019, February 8). *Satirical news website the Daily Mash sold for £1.2m.* www.theguardian.com/media/2019/feb/08/the-daily-mash-sold-to-digitalbox-satirical-news

Watson, D., & Tellegen, A. (1985). Toward a consensual structure of mood. *Psychological Bulletin, 98,* 219–235.

Watson, D., Wiese, D., Vaidya, J., & Tellegen, A. (1999). The two general activation systems of affect: Structural findings, evolutionary considerations, and psychobiological evidence. *Journal of Personality and Social Psychology, 76*(5), 820–838.

Wayne, S. J., & Liden, R. C. (1995). Effects of impression management on performance ratings: A longitudinal study. *Academy of Management Journal, 38*(1), 232–260.

Weber, R. A., & Camerer, C. F. (2003). Cultural conflict and merger failure: An experimental approach. *Management Science, 49*(4), 400–415.

Weber, Y. (1996). Corporate cultural fit and performance in mergers and acquisitions. *Human Relations, 49*(9), 1181–1203.

Westphal, J. D., & Stern, I. (2007). Flattery will get you everywhere (especially if you are a male Caucasian): How ingratiation, boardroom behaviour, and demographic minority status affect additional board appointments at U.S. companies. *Academy of Management Journal, 50*(2), 267–288.

Weyant, C. (2019). *Roundup verdicts: See every jury decision at a glance.* Retrieved from www.consumersafety.org/news/roundup-verdicts/

Wicker, A. W., & Kauma, C. E. (1974). Effects of a merger of a small and a large organization on members' behaviors and experiences. *Journal of Applied Psychology*, *59*(1), 24–30.

Wickramasinghe, V., & Karunaratne, C. (2009). People management in mergers and acquisitions in Sri Lanka: Employee perceptions. *International Journal of Human Resource Management*, *20*(3), 694–715.

Williams, L. J., & Anderson, S. E. (1991). Job satisfaction and organizational commitment as predictors of organizational citizenship and in-role behaviors. *Journal of Management*, *17*(3), 601–617.

Williams, S. D. (2004). Personality, attitude, and leader influences on divergent thinking and creativity in organizations. *European Journal of Innovation Management*, *7*(3), 187–204.

Wilson, J. (2003). *Globalization and the limits of national merger control laws*. Hague, Netherlands: Kluwer Law International.

Wind, J., & Mahajan, V. (1997). Issues and opportunities in new product development: An introduction to the special issue. *Journal of Marketing Research (JMR)*, *34*(1), 1–12.

Wittmann, C., Hunt, S., & Arnett, D. (2009). Explaining alliance success: Competences, resources, relational factors, and resource-advantage theory. *Industrial Marketing Management*, *38*(7), 743–756.

Wood, Z. (2019, April 25). Sainsbury's-Asda merger blocked by competition watchdog. *The Guardian*. Retrieved from www.theguardian.com/business/2019/apr/25/sainsburys-asda-merger-blocked-by-competition-watchdog

Xia, T., & Dimov, D. (2019). Alliances and survival of new biopharmaceutical ventures in the wake of the global financial crisis. *Journal of Small Business Management*, *57*(2), 362–385.

Yang, H., Lin, Z. (John), & Peng, M. W. (2011). Behind acquisitions of alliance partners: Exploratory learning and network embeddedness. *Academy of Management Journal*, *54*(5), 1069–1080.

Yoo, S. H., Matsumoto, D., & LeRoux, J. A. (2006). The influence of emotion recognition and emotion regulation on intercultural adjustment. *International Journal of Intercultural Relations*, *30*(3), 345–363.

Zaccaro, S. J., & Klimoski, R. J. (2001). *The nature of organizational leadership: Understanding the performance imperatives confronting today's leaders*. San Francisco, CA: Jossey-Bass.

Zehir, C., Müceldili, B., Altindağ, E., Şehitoğlu, Y., & Zehir, S. (2014). Charismatic leadership and organizational citizenship behavior: The mediating role of ethical climate. *Social Behavior & Personality: An International Journal*, *42*(8), 1365–1375.

Zhang, L., Rana, I., Shaffer, R. M., Taioli, E., & Sheppard, L. (2019). Exposure to glyphosate-based herbicides and risk for non-Hodgkin lymphoma: A meta-analysis and supporting evidence. *Mutation Research*, *781*, 186–206.

Zhou, J., Shin, S. J., & Cannella, A. J. (2008). Employee self-perceived creativity after mergers and acquisitions: Interactive effects of threat-opportunity perception, access to resources, and support for creativity. *Journal of Applied Behavioral Science*, *44*(4), 397–421.

Zhu, Y., & McKenna, B. (2012). Legitimating a Chinese takeover of an Australian iconic firm: Revisiting models of media discourse of legitimacy. *Discourse & Society: An*

International Journal for the Study of Discourse and Communication in Their Social, Political and Cultural Contexts, 23(5), 525–552.

Zimmerman, B. J. (2013). From cognitive modeling to self-regulation: A social cognitive career path. *Educational Psychologist, 48*(3), 135–147.

Zoega, G. (2019). Greece and the western financial crisis. *Atlantic Economic Journal, 47,* 113–126.

Zollo, M. (2009). Superstitious learning with rare strategic decisions: Theory and evidence from corporate acquisitions. *Organization Science, 20*(5), 894–908.

Zollo, M., & Reuer, J. J. (2010). Experience spillovers across corporate development activities. *Organization Science, 21*(6), 1195–1212.

Index

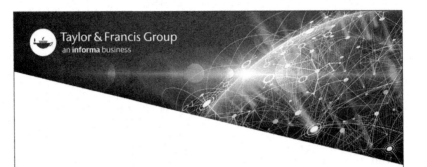

Printed in the United States
by Baker & Taylor Publisher Services